REA

**DO NOT REMOVE
CARDS FROM POCKET**

AMERICAN JAILS

AMERICAN JAILS
Public Policy Issues

Edited by

Joel A. Thompson
Appalachian State University

and

G. Larry Mays
New Mexico State University

Nelson-Hall Publishers
Chicago

The editors gratefully acknowledge the National Institute of Corrections for financial support for this project. Special thanks to William Frazier of the NIC Jail Center. However, only the authors are responsible for the ideas advocated herein.

Library of Congress Cataloging-in-Publication Data

American jails : public policy issues / edited by Joel A. Thompson and G. Larry
    Mays : in conjunction with the Policy Studies Organization Advisory Board.
        p. cm.
    Includes bibliographical references and indexes.
    ISBN 0-8304-1251-4—. 0-8304-1262-x (pbk.)
        1. Prisons—Government policy—United States. 2. Prison administration—
United States. 3. Prisoners—Health and hygiene—United States. 4. Criminal
justice. Administration of—United States. I. Thompson, Joel A. II. Mays, G.
Larry. III. Policy Studies Organization. Advisory Board.
HV9469.A774 1990
365'.973—dc20   90-13486
                                                                                      CIP

Manufactured in the United States of America.

10   9   8   7   6   5   4   3   2   1

TM The paper used in this book meets the minimum requirements of American National Standard for Information Sciences—Permanence of Paper for Printed Library Materials, ANSI Z39.48–1984.

Contents

SECTION TWO
Health and Safety in the American Jail   59

SECTION THREE
Crowding and Management Issues Facing the American Jail   129

SECTION FOUR

Unfinished and Emerging Issues Confronting the 195
American Jail

Introduction

KENNETH E. KERLE,
AMERICAN JAIL ASSOCIATION

People familiar with the American jail scene realize that jails rank at the bottom of the criminal justice hierarchy in influence. Courts, prosecuting attorneys, police, and even probation and parole officials exert more political clout than jail administrators. Jail population figures have nearly doubled in a decade, and now more than 300,000 ADP (average daily population) are found in the 3,338 jails in the 3,000 plus counties and cities that operate these institutions of incarceration. During 1987, there were more than 17 million admissions and releases from county and city jails. These local government agencies serve as the dumping grounds for the arrested criminal, the chronic drunk, the DWI (driving while intoxicated), the mentally ill, the homeless, and juveniles ranging from the runaway to the amoral killer.

The general public and the media ignore jails unless there are escapes, fires, suicides, riots, or titillating tales of corruption or wrongdoing by the staff or elected sheriff. Money to build a new institution almost certainly will grab the news-reading public's attention. Even if voters approve new jail construction, there is no guarantee that the building will be properly sited, constructed, or staffed; in some instances county governing bodies deliberately avoid staffing a new institution with sufficient personnel to operate it. Staffing can devour from 70 percent to 80 percent of a jail budget, but in the long run an attempt to save taxpayers' dollars can prove to be "penny wise and pound foolish."

When Dick Ford and I surveyed over 2,600 jails in 1982, we confirmed what a lot of jail administrators and sheriffs already knew: many jails nationally were in a mess and most of the impetus toward dramatic change was instigated by the courts. In fact, 529 jails (19.9 percent) responded that they were parties to pending lawsuits, and 285 (10.7 percent) replied that they were currently under court order (Kerle and Ford, 1982: 43, 51).

The jail survey covered areas such as legal, administrative, physical description of the jail, staffing, inmate population, programs and services provided inmates, and the foremost problems identified by participants. In the last category, the jail administrator was asked to "list the five most serious problems in your jail in order of their importance to your situation." Listed in descending order of count were: (1) personnel, (2) modernization, (3) overcrowding, (4) recreation, and (5) funding (Kerle and Ford, 1982: 225).

People unfamiliar with jails usually ask why recreation is considered by jail administrators to be one of the top five most serious problems. The answer is to be found in the reasons enumerated as to why jails were under court order. The reasons were:

1.	Crowded conditions	209	Jails
2.	Recreation	206	
3.	Structure (modernization)	181	
4.	Medical	164	
5.	Visitation	158	
6.	Fire hazards	111	
7.	Other	104	
9.	Staffing	102	
10.	Food	102	
11.	Health area	94	
12.	Personal hygiene	93	
13.	Mentally ill	47	
14.	Suicides	26	

Things have not changed much as the decade of the 1980s draws to a close. Guynes (1988) noted that jail managers rank staff shortages as the second most serious problem confronting them; crowding was first. At the 16th annual conference of the Washington State Jail Association (May 31–June 3, 1988), I distributed a questionnaire. People were asked to identify the three biggest problems facing jails in Washington. The answers were pretty much the same as those given in 1982: inadequate number of staff (14), overcrowding (10), and budget (5).

The American Jail Association

One organization working toward jail improvement is the American Jail Association (AJA), born in June 1981 as a result of the merger of the National Jail Association and the National Jail Managers Association. This merger was facilitated by the director of the Jail Center of the Nation Institute of Corrections (NIC), who indicated that training and grant problems would be much easier to deal with if NIC could interact with one national organization representing jails.

When the American Jail Association began, it was a mixture of jail staff of all ranks, jail administrators, sheriffs, county governing officials, attorneys, judges, academics, engineers, private citizens, and a number of people who represented companies in the private sector. Initially, the membership of the AJA was about three hundred; within three years the number had grown to nine hundred, and just recently (1989) the membership passed the four thousand mark.

The American Jail Association is one of the sixty-plus affiliates of the American Correctional Association. Its permanent headquarters was established in 1986, and *American Jails* magazine was first published in the spring of 1987. Since then, AJA has developed a monthly training bulletin (*Jail Operations Bulletin* or *JOB*), secured a federal grant to administer drug treatment programs and provide training, and produced a number of training tapes in cooperation with Instructional Video, Inc. It is a good start, but much remains to be done.

Jails and Academe

During the late 1970s, I began a jail odyssey that through 1989 has taken me into over 660 jails in forty-eight states and in seven of the ten Canadian provinces. I do not include early visits to prisons in Europe and Asia in this count because I had the idea then that prisons were more important and that jails simply were not worth the bother to investigate. I was still on a college faculty when I started to visit foreign countries, but the opportunity to work in a jail presented itself, and I resigned my teaching position.

The 1979 meeting of the Academy of Criminal Justice Sciences was my first academic criminal justice conference, and I was surprised to find that only one faculty person (Jay Moynahan of Eastern Washington University) had prepared a paper on jails. The next year at the ACJS meeting in Oklahoma City, I prevailed upon the organization's executive board to pass a resolution encouraging more interest and support from academics in local corrections, and over the past several years I have noted an increase in the number of jail panels at these conferences. Yet, much remains to be done.

Both Dick Ford, Executive Director of the American Jail Association, and I have taught college-level criminal justice courses over the years, and we are acutely aware of the lack of interest in jails among professors of criminal justice. A text I used in the fall 1988 semester in a course entitled "Introduction to American Corrections" made the following comment: "Among the institutions and programs of the corrections enterprise, the jail is the one most neglected by scholars and officials and least known to the public" (Clear and Cole, 1986: 195).

I examined a compendium of the criminal justice curricula of 900-plus universities and colleges in the United States and found that only fifteen offered a specific course on jails. A telephone call to one of the fifteen schools revealed that the jail course had not been taught in ten years and that, at the time it was taught, an instructor from the Federal Bureau of Prisons used the training books of the bureau's jail operation correspondence course.

Academics need to be more cognizant of jails and their daily operations through more involvement, and I encourage them to consider participating in the annual AJA training conference. Additionally, the AJA needs to make a concerted effort to encourage jail administrators to work on raising the academic qualifications for jail staff recruitment of internships for criminal justice majors, and jail administrators should make an effort to extend the welcome mat to faculty in their communities. To bridge the communications gap between jail personnel and academics, there should be a way to get people in contact with each other. Conferences and training programs are good places to start. The American Jail Association participated, at the 1989 ACJS conference in Washington, D.C., in an effort to stimulate more interest among criminal justice faculty on jail issues and problems, and I am pleased to note that several of the writers in this book presented papers on jail topics at that conference.

Ray Brown, Director of the National Institute of Corrections during the Reagan Administration, left a fine legacy to corrections when he appointed a Council on Curriculum Development to produce a model curriculum for the higher education of correctional officers. This gesture should set the climate for education standards in the 1990s for American jails and prisons. Professors and practitioners have a wonderful opportunity to work together to produce a model that can contribute in a significant way to the professionalization of jail staff.

Public Policy Issues

A number of people contributed to this book and the four sections dealing with the policy environment of the jail, health and safety issues, jail crowding and management issues, and what are called "emerging issues." Actually, all of the writers deal with critical issues, some of which have plagued jails for years.

The editors set the tone in the introductory chapter by stating that American jails have been and still are in a state of crisis. Their overall critique of the jail crisis is appropriate and their concluding recommendations are eminently sensible: if the states had met their obligations years ago by enforcement of mandatory jail standards (including proper staffing), insistence on proper training for jail officers, and financial support to replace fire-trap jails, much of the litigation discussed by Dean Champion in his chapter might have been avoided.

Yet, even with the best of efforts, some of the problems that afflict jails are not of their own making. Several of the writers mention reasonable alternative punishments as substitutes for jail time. Michael Welch in his chapter cites another contributor, John Klofas, for his suggestion of a cybernetic (i.e., the science dealing with the comparative study of human control systems—the brain and nervous system—and complex electronic systems) approach to jail use through improved planning. This is accomplished by expanding communication between key decision-makers, such as judges, prosecutors, and police officials. The real problem is, How do you make this happen in the real world of politics? In a sense, the root of the jail malaise is what James Lawrence and Van Zwisohn called *"Politics, Politics, Politics"* in their chapter on AIDS in jails.

In 1977, forty national groups banded together in a National Jail Coalition with three objectives: to get the mentally ill, public inebriates, and juveniles out of American jails. This coalition was comprised of some heavy-hitters like the American Bar Association, the National Sheriffs' Association, the National Association of

County Officials, the American Civil Liberties Union, the American Correctional Association, and the American Association on Public Health. The three goals were not accomplished. Thirty-nine states have decriminalized public drunkenness and the Juvenile Justice and Delinquency Prevention Act has been on the books since 1974. Progress has been made, but nowhere near what one might expect.

The fact that this book contains four chapters—two on mental health services, one on suicide, and another on juveniles in jails—indicates the extent to which problems still exist. The National Jail Coalition collapsed when federal funding ceased. The common drunk remains a headache for jails despite the decriminalization of public drunkenness. Many jurisdictions have given up diverting the mentally ill from jails; they treat them within the institutions and do an acceptable job of it. The chapter by Jerrell and Komisaruk describes how this treatment can be provided in a cost effective, efficient, and humane manner.

Why is the jail world like it is? Jackson, in his chapter, discusses briefly the correctional philosophies of deterrence, incapacitation, rehabilitation, and just deserts. He maintains that the deterrence and incapacitation ideologies are unlikely to be rejected by the public in the foreseeable future, and the just deserts model is making inroads in several states through determinate and guideline sentencing. Despite the fact that there are differences in jail use as a sanction, the present public mood seems to be punishment oriented. As long as this is true, jails are destined to be crowded.

The chapter by Wayne Welsh and his colleagues indicates that policymakers should be more sensitive to the complexity of public opinion—and, in fact, the public holds attitudes that are less punitive and more diverse than commonly acknowledged. I could not agree more. The suggestion that policymakers should more aggressively use media and public information to present correctional problems and solutions is on the mark. Part of the problem in smaller facilities is that often the staff does not have a background in journalism or public relations. Nevertheless, media contact should be undertaken more often by sheriffs and jail administrators. The needs assessment recommendation is a good suggestion and has been a part of the PONI program (planning of a new institution) by the Jail Center at the National Institute of Corrections for a number of years.

Zupan and Menke provide a very important chapter. There is no doubt that the new podular/direct supervision facilities are, as they note, "safer and provide a more positive incarcerative and work environment for inmates and staff than do traditional jails."

They correctly stress the need for better managerial skills among officers; more attention must be paid to the recruitment, selection, and retention of appropriate personnel.

This is the nub of the problem, for as Mays and Thompson point out, all too often salaries for jail employees are lower than salaries for sheriffs' deputies. It is important to note that the National Sheriffs' Association has passed a resolution in favor of pay parity for jail staff and deputies. Once pay parity is established, young people can think seriously about corrections at the local level as a career with a future.

Complementing the chapter by Zupan and Menke is the one by Poole and Pogrebin. They discuss better personnel utilization in jails and challenge the traditional hierarchical model for organizing staff and call for the flattening of the management hierarchy. This is certainly the *sine qua non* of the direct supervision jail concept, for without it the operation will not function properly. The line officer must assert much more leadership and management in the podular/direct supervision model than in the traditional linear jail, where middle level supervisors make many of the decisions.

Cox and Osterhoff provide a realistic examination of the public-private partnership approach. I concur with their conclusion that, historically, the private sector has "produced both significant advances and flagrant abuses in corrections." It is doubtful that any significant number of county or city governments are going to turn over their jails to private sector management. The suggestion that private sector involvement be viewed as a continuum for private-public cooperation makes good sense. Cooperation is a basic principle of good management, and if it can be accomplished, the taxpayers benefit. Like everything else in an organization, its operations have to be audited and scrutinized by an outside agency. This is an endemic problem that haunts a number of jails in states that provide no mandatory, enforceable jail inspections.

I hope that the research attention of the authors in this volume (both academics and practitioners) and the efforts of organizations like the Academy of Criminal Justice Sciences and the American Jail Association will keep jails from continuing to be neglected. The problems of jails must be kept at the forefront of criminal justice efforts and solutions sought with great diligence.

SECTION ONE

THE POLICY ENVIRONMENT OF THE AMERICAN JAIL

Jails are complex institutions. They are called on to do a number of things, some of which are appropriate (housing dangerous pretrial detainees, short-term sentenced inmates, work releasees, and those awaiting transport to state or federal corrections systems) and some of which are not appropriate (serving as a drunk tank, short-term mental ward, truant hall, and holding facility for people who cannot be placed anywhere else). Part of the reason that jails are so used and misused is that they are almost totally dependent on other institutions within their environment and have very little control over their own destiny. As a result jails must look for support and resources from others while continuing to serve as a "dumping ground for . . . society's problems" (Moynahan and Stewart, 1980: 104).

In chapter 1 Mays and Thompson discuss the political and organizational environment of the jail. Jails depend on other actors for resources: the public, the local government, and the sheriff. The public knows very little about jails and, in most cases, cares very little about them. Within the local power structure jails must compete for scarce resources with schools, hospitals, parks,

1

and other more popular facilities. Finally, within the sheriff's department jails must compete with more politically salient programs—patrol, crime prevention, and drug interdiction. The end result is a tradition of underfunding that has allowed jails to deteriorate into a crisis condition.

In chapter 2 Patrick Jackson attempts to clarify the purpose and meaning of jail confinement. Utilizing a unique longitudinal data set, he investigates the purposes of confinement in three California jurisdictions. His findings suggest that most pretrial inmates are charged with nonserious offenses, have relatively nonserious prior records, and come from marginal socioeconomic backgrounds. In addition, many eventually have their original charges dropped. Among those convicted, relatively few spend additional time in jail, and even fewer are sentenced to prison. Jackson concludes that pretrial detention for purposes of ensuring appearance at trial is overused and is likely to contribute to the problem of jail crowding.

In the final chapter in this section John Klofas complements Jackson's research by focusing on jail use across local jurisdictions in Illinois over a ten-year period. Among his findings: jail use is more complex than prison use, jail growth is not monolithic but varied and dependent on the proportion of inmates serving sentences, crowding is not simply a function of available space but related to use patterns, and use patterns remain relatively stable over time. From these findings he concludes that some local jurisdictions have established more effective use patterns than others and calls for more policy-relevant research on the causes of jail crowding.

Collectively these three articles provide a broad policy framework for examining jails and set out the policy environment within which jails operate. Both must be understood to bring about changes in our troubled jails.

CHAPTER 1

The Political and Organizational Context of American Jails

G. LARRY MAYS AND JOEL A. THOMPSON

People working in criminal justice and members of the general public hold a variety of opinions about jails, and almost without exception these opinions are negative. The jail has been characterized as the "ultimate ghetto" (Goldfarb, 1975), the "cloacal region" of the criminal justice system (Mattick, 1974), and an instrument for managing the underclass or rabble of society (Irwin, 1985). Whatever their problems, jails are a necessary component of the criminal justice system.

It is accurate to say that American jails are in a crisis (Advisory Commission on Intergovernmental Relations [ACIR], 1984; Allinson, 1982; Thompson and Mays, 1988b). However, even a cursory reading of jail literature indicates that recently there has been an increasing sense of crisis, heightened by inmate litigation and court intervention.

This chapter looks at the jail's unique role within the American criminal justice system's sociopolitical context. It examines the factors and institutions that influence jail decision making and the ways, in turn, jails influence other criminal justice agencies.

Understanding the Sociopolitical Context of Jails

To be understood more fully, jails and their environments can be thought of as comprising three concentric circles. The innermost circle represents the jail and the actors directly involved in its day-to-day operations. The middle ring is comprised of those actors and institutions having close and continuing, although not daily, interaction with jail inmates and personnel. The outermost circle includes those individuals and groups that may affect both the jail and its immediate environment but usually in indirect or unintentional ways. Each of these arenas will be explored, and examples will be given of boundary-spanning activities.

The Operational Jail Environment

Inmates. In some ways the operational environment is a very small world indeed; the main occupants are inmates, and, while estimates vary somewhat, about 265,000 people are in U.S. jails on any given day (Bureau of Justice Statistics [BJS], 1987). Furthermore, there were around 16.6 million admissions and releases from July 1, 1984, to June 30, 1985 (Bureau of Justice Statistics, 1987). Those passing through (and some residing in) jails include individuals with drug and/or alcohol dependencies, the mentally ill (Guy et al., 1985; Kalinich et al., 1988; Steadman and Ribner, 1980), adults and juveniles, men and women, pretrial detainees, and convicted misdemeanants and felons. Although much attention has focused on those individuals incarcerated in jails (e.g., Irwin, 1985; Jackson, 1988), the operating environment includes the keepers as well as the kept (see Crouch, 1980, for similar observations on prisons).

Law Enforcement Officials. Operationally, jails are a local government function. The Bureau of Justice Statistics (1983c: 78) defines these institutions as facilities designed "to hold persons awaiting trial or those sentenced to confinement for less than one year." There are 3,493 of these institutions, or almost one per county nationwide. While administrative arrangements vary from state to state, more than 70 percent of all jails function under law enforcement agency auspices (Kerle and Ford, 1982; McGee, 1975).

Custodial Personnel. Line correctional officers (uniformed guards) and support or programming personnel constitute the final group in the jail's operational environment. Often great cleavages exist between these two types of employees, based on differences in education, background, and orientation. Custodial officers tend to give the greatest emphasis to the jail's security function. These employees may be career-line correctional officers (see Pogrebin and Poole, 1988), or they may be uniformed sheriff's deputies with varying jail duty assignment lengths. Support or programming personnel more often are college educated and are involved in delivering educational, recreational, and health (dental, medical, and mental) services. These individuals frequently focus on the jail's treatment or rehabilitative activities.

Many dilemmas are associated with jail officers. In fact, in a survey conducted for the National Sheriffs' Association, Kerle and Ford (1982) found that personnel concerns were the most frequently mentioned problems. These problems, however, while easily identified, are not easily solved. In simplest terms, jail line officers are too few in number, untrained or poorly trained, and vastly undercompensated (see, e.g., National Advisory Commission, 1973: 276). Local jail officers often find themselves in one of two positions: either they are sheriff's deputies assigned jail duty for disciplinary reasons or awaiting transfer to road patrol, or they are permanent correctional officers with little chance for advancement or job enhancement. In a sense they are as much locked in as the inmates.

Agencies in the Jail's Immediate Environment

Jails and their problems do not exist in isolation. They are part of a local network of agencies including funding bodies (such as boards of county commissioners) and criminal justice agencies (such as district attorneys, courts, grand juries, police departments, and corrections departments).

Law Enforcement Agencies and Prosecutors. Police departments and sheriffs' departments are the primary jail referral sources. In most instances persons are booked into jail immediately after arrest and allowed to make bail or held awaiting bail. Law enforcement policies, such as drunk driver crackdowns, can have immediate and significant impacts on jail populations and thus on jail conditions (see National Institute of Justice, 1984).

Once cases are referred by the police, screening and processing policies by the district come into play. Some district attorney's offices employ extensive preprosecution or pretrial diversion programs not only to keep minor offenders out of jail but out of the formal prosecutorial system. Conversely, some prosecuting attorneys advocate strict bail policies including, occasionally, preventive detention. Such policies may be followed for public safety purposes or to gain a tactical advantage in plea bargaining (Eisenstein and Jacob, 1977; Walker, 1985; Weinreb, 1977).

Courts. In responding to actions by the police and prosecutors, judges become the jail's actual gatekeepers (see Juszkiewicz, 1988). Judges' actions can have direct and immediate impacts on jail populations. For example, less restrictive bail policies—expanded use of release on recognizance (ROR), percentage bail deposits, or other alternatives to the traditional money bail system—will speed up the processing of most jail inmates and reduce the time they must wait prior to release. By the same token case processing rapidity, especially for those inmates unable to afford bail, substantially can reduce pretrial detainee populations. It is important to note, however, that even if the jail could reduce the pretrial detainee population to zero, in most instances the available space would be filled by sentenced misdemeanants or felons (Allinson, 1982: 24).

Grand juries in most states play a relatively unique role in regard to county jails. In several states grand juries are mandated constitutionally or statutorily to inspect jails and certain other institutions regularly and to issue a report regarding the conditions and deficiencies. These visits vary in frequency and duration, but it is not unusual for grand juries to report that jail conditions are deficient only to find that little can or will be done to remedy the deficiencies; or that the sheriff is doing a surprisingly good job despite a meager budget and small staff. While the grand jury potentially has the power to bring about constructive change—and, some would add, an equal potential for mischief—the results of most grand jury visits and reports on jail conditions seem to be an acknowledgment of deficiencies by those in the jail operational environment and a tendency to ignore the problems by all others in the jail's immediate environment.

Correctional Agencies. Although corrections departments mainly are state agencies (most of which are in the jail's extended environment), prison policies and capacities are intimately linked with jail operations. First, almost all state prisoners have spent some time, often on several occasions, in local jails. Thus jails are conduits for prisoners entering the state correctional system (Rottman and Kimberly, 1975). Second, when prisons fill to capacity, sentenced felons "back up" awaiting transportation to prison, making jails *de facto* extensions of the state corrections network (Allinson, 1982). The ironic feature of the crowding crisis is that prisons in more than 35 states are under federal court orders for confinement conditions; the response has been to hold back sentenced inmates in local jails where the confinement conditions typically are worse than in the prisons under court order (Taft, 1979: 27).

Somewhat related to state corrections departments are agencies responsible for implementation of jail standards and, where applicable, jail inspection and enforcement procedures. In some instances the state corrections department is the agency for all three functions: development/implementation, inspection, and enforcement. However, there are a variety of structural arrangements (see Thompson and Mays, 1988a). In terms of standards, jails fit into one of four categories:

- states that have mandatory standards applicable to all jails
- states that have standards that can be voluntarily adopted if county or jail administrators choose to do so
- states that have developed jail standards but for political or other reasons have not implemented them
- six states that do not have jail standards[1]

Aside from merely having standards, there is also the inspection issue; for jail standards to be effective there must be a meaningful inspection system. The agency responsible for conducting jail inspections varies from state to state, and the interval between inspections ranges from every three or six months to annually/regularly or never.[2]

Not only do states have varying patterns of jail standards but at least four distinct enforcement systems:

- enforcement by a court
- enforcement by the corrections department
- enforcement by some other state agency, or
- enforcement by voluntary compliance.[3]

All of these categories are self-explanatory except that of "other state agency." In two states agencies other than those associated with the criminal justice system have responsibility for ensuring compliance with jail standards. In North Carolina the jail standards agency is located within the Division of Facilities Services of the Department of Human Resources. In Wisconsin enforcement authority rests with the Department of Health and Human Services.

Inmate Advocacy and Jail Reform Groups. It often has been said that inmates form a small and ineffective political constituency. Their welfare may be of concern to them and their families but typically will not be an issue for many public policymakers. There are some exceptions, however. Local religious or civil rights groups might lobby for jail and prison inmates' rights. At the national level organizations like the American Civil Liberties Union's National Prison Project, the National Moratorium on Prison Construction, and the National Coalition for Jail Reform have entered the jail improvement fight and in some instances have expanded rights and protections, especially through litigation on inmates' behalf. These organizations can be persistent advocates for changes in jail conditions and operating practices. Their presence and effectiveness, however, vary greatly from one jurisdiction to the next, and in many localities there is no one advocating jail reform.

The Extended Jail Environment

Other state and federal agencies also influence jail operations. These agencies are in the jail's extended environment because they are separated from the operational arena geographically, because they lack daily contact (what might be termed *intimacy*), or both.

Executive agencies include investigative organizations such as the state police or Federal Bureau of Investigation, which are called on to investigate suicides, homicides, or abuses of force occurring in jails (also included may be fire-related deaths and those resulting from riots and other disturbances). State executive agencies such as the corrections department and the mental health department may be responsible for subsidizing local jail operations, especially in the treatment programs area (see especially Kalinich et al., 1988). These agencies also may provide funding through subsidies for inmates retained locally rather than being sent to state institutions, payments for work release participants, or increased per diem rates for state inmates sentenced but not yet transported to state facilities (ACIR, 1984).

Legislatures can have a multitude of effects on local jails. First, in some states jail standards have been instigated by legislators and given "teeth" by being enacted into law instead of remaining administrative regulations. Second, legislatures can affect the financial picture of jails by setting reimbursement rates for state prisoners retained in local jails. More important, legislative bodies normally are required to approve increases in local tax rates and/ or the issuance of bonds to provide for renovation or new jail construction. The costs related to jail capital improvements are not small items. The Bureau of Justice Statistics (1988e: 123–24) has estimated, for example, that each new jail bed space costs $43,000 to construct and $9,360 per year to operate. The difficulty comes when local problems—jail crowding or deteriorating facilities— cannot be solved by local bodies because they lack authority and instead require direct state aid (Council of State Governments, 1977).

Additionally, one of the most dramatic legislative impacts on jails is in the area of sentencing. The ACIR (1984: 168) has said that "the sentencing policies of state governments have had a profound, though often indirect and sometimes ill-conceived effect of the nation's jails." Jails have been affected by sentencing policies in at least three ways. First, an emphasis on alternatives to incarceration may substantially reduce the jails' short-term, but especially the long-term population. Second, because of sentencing law changes—notably the move from indeterminate to determinate sentencing—prison populations have grown to maximum capacities, and some states treat jails as repositories for prison population overflow (see especially Allinson, 1982; Taft, 1979). Third, some states now allow short jail sentences combined with traditional probation ("shock probation") in lieu of sentences to already crowded prisons (ACIR, 1984: 168; Blackmore, 1978: 51). Finally, legislatures can positively influence jails by removing statutory impediments to policy changes. For example, many state statutes prohibit some or all types of "interlocal cooperative arrangements" (ACIR, 1984: 171). When legislatures remove the prohibitions these agreements can allow for cooperative arrangements such as regional jails or joint organizations to provide certain types of space (e.g., for females or juveniles), certain types of services, or to meet mandates of specific state policy changes (such as those relating to DWI [driving while intoxicated], mandatory sentencing, and so forth).

Judicial involvement in jails, characteristic of the extended environment, is typified by state and federal appellate court reviews of prison conditions and prisoners' rights. Of federal appeals, the Advisory Commission on Intergovernmental Relations (1984: 171) has said:

> No recent initiative in local or state corrections can equal the impact of federal judicial intervention. The results of that intervention—

both in terms of actual judicial decrees and litigious actions—have been impressive. Thus, one of every five cases filed in federal courts today is on behalf of prisoners; civil rights petitions filed by state prisoners in federal courts increased from 218 in 1966 to 16,741 in 1981; between ten and 13 percent of all jails are under court order; between 16 and 22 percent have been involved in court actions; and between 17 and 20 percent are now party to a pending lawsuit.

However impressive the involvement might be (see, e.g., Thomas et al. 1985, 1986) Frug (1978) maintains that when federal courts order changes in budget allocations they are usurping legislative and executive powers. Thus, "judicial intervention has an effect not only on the conditions in the institutions but also on the basic allocation of power in American government" (Frug, 1978: 733). These imbalances occur not only among the government's three branches (separation of powers) but also between the federal and state levels of government (federalism).

Public Attitudes Toward Jails. For the most part, the general public holds one of two attitudes toward jails: indifference or strongly negative views. Those that are indifferent have little or no contact with jails or jail inmates. Clearly it is a case of out of sight, out of mind (see Moynahan and Stewart, 1980: 79; Thompson, 1986: 210). Because most people have no contact with the jail, there is seldom pressure on the sheriff or administrator to increase jail expenditures. Since most members of the public are not clamoring for jail improvements, sheriffs tend to put their budgets into those items that have the greatest public visibility—notably uniformed patrol and crime prevention (Goldfarb, 1975: 15–16).

People who hold negative views either believe that jails are bad but "criminals" should be punished, or they personally have experienced the jail's stark reality (see, e.g., Irwin, 1985). Emerging, however, is a class of "new" inmates who are sensitive to, and critical of, jail conditions: those incarcerated for drunk driving (National Institute of Justice, 1984). These new jail inmates, swept up in police crackdowns on DWI, more frequently are middle-class whites than "traditional" jail inmates; their real impact may be to bring jail conditions to the attention of a segment of society not traditionally associated with jail reform—the middle class (see Thompson, 1986: 217–18).

The News Media. At times the news media will focus on the plight of jails (see, e.g., Guadayol, 1985; Morris, 1986; "State Prison Overcrowding Filters Down," 1987). News coverage, however, must be examined in light of several constraints. First, through no particular fault of the media, very complex issues tend to be presented in simplistic terms. Thus unless there is an ongoing investigation and a series of reports or articles, jail news appears as a single newspaper item or as one- or two-minute spots on local television stations. This means that if there are any jail news stories they will, of necessity, be local and usually "sensational."

The second constraint involves media access to jails. In some instances reporters have been prevented from entering jails to observe inmates' confinement conditions. Ostensibly the reasons are for "institutional security," "inmate privacy," or "prevention of disruption." If reporters *are* permitted to enter jails they may be restricted to the same areas available to the general public (see *Houchins v. KQED*, 438 U.S. 1 (1978)). Because of cases such as *Houchins*, jail administrators and the news media may be pitted against each other as adversaries. What jail administrators overlook, however, is that news coverage can be used to the jail's advantage (see, e.g., Taft, 1982). Thus for jails and their problems not to remain out of sight and out of mind, responsible news coverage of jail deficiencies should be welcomed.

Boundary-Spanning Issues

Now that the jail and its environments have been described, it is appropriate to examine a variety of specific policy areas to illustrate how jails interact with these environments. To illustrate the concept of boundary-spanning issues, this section will focus on five policy areas: (1) local politics and limits on funding, (2) changes in law enforcement policies, (3) jail standards and inspections, (4) state corrections department policies, and (5) jail reform litigation.

Local Politics and Funding

Jails clearly are local institutions and very much part of the local political milieu (Thompson, 1986); and, while local political control is not a negative feature in and of itself, it causes jails to face a "double whammy": political conservatism and fiscal restraint (Clear and Cole, 1986). In most of the more than three thousand counties in the United States, sheriffs have operational responsibility for the jail, often under constitutional mandate (Mays and Thompson, 1988). However, it should be noted that sheriffs often are not master of their own fates. They are politically accountable to the county's voters, and jail issues normally have a low degree of salience with voters.

Beyond political accountability to local voters, sheriffs also face *political* and *financial* accountability to local funding bodies such as county commissions (Pogrebin, 1982a, 1982b; Ricci, 1986). These funding bodies are responsible for allocating sheriffs' departments operating budgets, of which the jail represents a small proportion. Moynahan and Stewart (1980: 79) note in regard to retention of local control that "some cities and counties fight to retain this dubious honor, while the harried administrators of these jails would eagerly shed their frustrating responsibilities of management and control." There are, however, at least three alternatives to local control: state-run jails, cooperative (regional) arrangements, and state subsidy programs.

State-Run Jails. Currently six states—Alaska, Connecticut, Delaware, Hawaii, Rhode Island, and Vermont—have assumed full operational responsibility for jails. This sort of centralized authority, responsibility, and service delivery has been advocated by some for more than a decade (see, e.g., Goldfarb, 1975: 419 ff.; Newman and Price, 1977: 508–9).

Ideally, state-run jails would offer at least four advantages (Moynahan and Stewart, 1980: 101). First, there would be greater operational efficiency; states could more equitably distribute personnel and inmate populations to different institutions as needed. Second, states can develop, implement, and adhere to statewide standards in a more consistent way than is now possible. Third, by achieving economies of scale jails would be less costly when operated by states. Finally, state operation would minimize local political interference.

Although the objectives of state-run jails seem desirable, there has been no apparent rush by states to assume responsibility for local jails. Several reasons have been suggested for this lack of initiative in consolidating jail operations, one of which is political opposition by counties. Additionally, because the federal government is handing funding responsibilities to the states for many programs ("new federalism"), states often are not in a position to assume total jail operational and financial responsibility (see Frug, 1978; McCoy, 1982; Pogrebin and Neugarten, 1982). Finally, the six states that have centralized jail operations have some features in common that distinguish them from the other forty-four states: "(1) the states are small in area or population, or both; (2) county government has been abolished, or is weak, or the state government is dominant in state-local financing and spending responsibility; and (3) assumption took place in the context of a more comprehensive reform of correctional activities within the state" (ACIR, 1984: 170). This means that state-run jails is one option to the ongoing American jail crisis, but this approach is not likely to be selected by many states.

Cooperative Arrangements among Local Governments. Since state-run jails seem unlikely for most states, another alternative is the development of "interlocal cooperative arrangements" (ACIR, 1984). These interlocal (regional or multicounty) arrangements seem desirable for two basic reasons: the one hundred largest jails in the country are operating with inmate populations at least 5 percent over capacity, while about 65 percent of our nation's jails house twenty-one or fewer inmates each day and are sufficiently under capacity to be inefficient to operate (see Bureau of Justice Statistics, 1983c, 1986a; Mays and Thompson, 1988; National Institute of Justice, 1985).

Local governments can approach interlocal cooperative arrangements in several different ways. First, if one jurisdiction already has an adequate jail it may be possible for neighboring cities and counties to contract on a per diem basis for housing prisoners. Second, a group of local governments may decide that no existing facility is adequate and that a new regional jail or "detention center" is needed. In such cases, financing and site selection become critical concerns. Also, local governments may decide to specialize and choose different populations to house: juveniles, females, the mentally defective, pretrial detainees, and/or convicted felons awaiting transportation to prison.

Although there is no accurate count of the number of interlocal cooperative arrangements now in existence, the ACIR (1984: 171) says that such agreements "appear to be in wide use for providing jail services." These arrangements are not without their problems, however, and at least three considerations limit or prohibit their use: transportation problems, especially of pretrial detainees who often must be moved back and forth from jail to court; multijurisdictional funding problems, i.e., who pays, how much, and when; and turf disputes among the local governments attempting to solidify interjurisdictional arrangements (McGee, 1975: 11). A final prohibitive factor relating to local jails is that in some states local governments need, and do not have, legislative authorization to enter into an interlocal cooperative arrangement (ACIR, 1984: 171).

State Subsidies. A third way to reach beyond the limits of local politics and financial constraints is through use of state subsidies to local jails (Council of State Governments, 1977). State subsidies assist local governments in developing community corrections programs and other alternatives to incarceration (Blackmore, 1978). Some subsidy programs have been aimed at capital improvements ordered by courts or to assist local jails in complying with state standards. Additionally, almost 60 percent of the states provide technical assistance to local governments having jail problems, and about 50 percent provide some jail personnel training (ACIR, 1984: 170).

The Advisory Commission on Intergovernmental Relations has been encouraged by the trend in state subsidies and notes: "The number of states providing subsidy programs for local jails increased from twelve programs in nine states in 1976 to twenty-four programs in seventeen states in 1982" (ACIR, 1984: 170). Such cooperative ventures may be one of the most promising strategies to the local political and financial stranglehold on jails.

Changes in Law Enforcement Policies

A number of state and local law enforcement strategies affecting local jails could be discussed, but perhaps no policy change better demonstrates the dilemma facing local jails than that of increased arrests for DWI. The National Institute of Justice (1984) noted in a research bulletin: "Since 1981, more than thirty states have enacted legislation directed at drunk driving control, most often by prescribing more severe sanctions such as mandatory confinement."

The results of such policy changes have been fairly predictable: arrest and incarceration rates have increased. To mitigate the effects of incarceration for drunk drivers—many of whom are middle class, have families and jobs—some judges have started imposing weekend sentences (May, 1978). However, the problems associated with incarcerating this new group of inmates, especially on weekends, are manifold.

First, many of these inmates are not "criminals" in the traditional sense of the word and generally should not be housed with convicted felons or violent offenders. Jails often have weekend population increases from 10 percent to 20 percent anyway (BJS, 1983c); thus, adding an extra group of drunk drivers or motor vehicle offenders creates logistical problems (May, 1978).

Second, to avoid displacing full-time inmates (some of whom

may be serving sentences of one year or more) with weekend detainees, some states are using other buildings as jail annexes or "satellite jails" (Healey, 1987; National Institute of Justice, 1984; Thompson, 1986). These annexes may be facilities specially constructed to accommodate jail population overflows, or they may be renovated schools, hospitals, or warehouses.

Finally, it should be understood that changes in enforcement patterns—for example, issuing citations in lieu of arrest—can have an impact on jail populations and conditions. Typically the more crowded the jails, the more rapid the deterioration of these facilities.

Jail Standards and Inspections

Jail standards have been hailed as potentially the most effective way to correct the many deficiencies of jails and to bring them to a constitutionally acceptable level (see, e.g., ACIR, 1984: 169; Sweeney, 1982). Standards for jails have been articulated by several groups including the American Correctional Association (1981) and the National Advisory Commission on Criminal Justice Standards and Goals (1973).

Even though these standards have been widely circulated and copied in whole or in part by several states, jail conditions in many jurisdictions remain deplorable. There are at least three reasons why standards have not made an overwhelming difference in jail conditions, and these reasons say something about the jail and its environment(s) (Weimer and Reixach, 1982: 240, 242).

First, many times the adoption or implementation of jail standards requires major capital expenditures. These costs go beyond the normal budgetary parameters of virtually all counties and require either a bond approval referendum or provision of additional state tax dollars, each of which is difficult to obtain. As Pogrebin (1982a: 74) notes: "jails are rarely a popular public priority." This is especially the case when they are competing with more popular programs—schools, highways, hospitals, and recreation facilities—for scarce tax dollars.

Second, standards advocate a more rational, efficient allocation of jail space and resources. Small jails inherently suffer from problems of economies of scale (Mays and Thompson, 1988). This means that, while certain basic services always must be provided, small jails have high costs per unit in delivering these services. Moreover, most treatment programs associated with progressive jail administration (medical and suicide screening, educational services, and recreational programs) often are conspicuously absent in small jails. The implication of most jail standards, then, is that small, inefficient jails should be consolidated into "regional detention centers" large enough to provide a full range of needed services and adequate staffing levels (see Goldfarb, 1975: 419; Weimer and Reixach, 1982: 242).

The third reason for the lack of discernible impact of jail standards is that agencies developing standards often lack enforcement authority (see, e.g., Sweeney, 1982: 30 ff.). Whether the group is a national organization or a state jail board, lack of legislative authority to conduct inspections and enforce compliance (at times by ordering jails to be closed) makes for a fairly toothless tiger (see Thompson and Mays, 1988a).

State Corrections Department Policies

Corrections department policies easily demonstrate how the jail is tied to both the immediate and extended environments. Corrections policies are related to jails and jail inmates by determining who and how many are incarcerated and how soon.

The *who* question addresses the types of inmates put in prison, and this concern can be illustrated in different ways. First, changes in state criminal codes, especially in sentencing and pretrial detention policies, may create excess local space in which to "store" state prisoner overflows (Allinson, 1982: 24). This means that state corrections officials may see jails as suitable holding facilities for "incoming" inmates. Additionally, several states are advocating expanded use of community corrections (Blackmore, 1978), and some of these programs may call for expanded jail use in conjunction with traditional probation, public service programs, or weekend incarceration (May, 1978). Community corrections programs define a group of inmates as not really suitable for prison but who need something more than straight probation.

Although some types of subsidies have been discussed, states can include jail subsidies in their correctional policies to deal with the question of who should go to prison. Thus, with or without a community corrections act, states can provide subsidies (over and above normal per diem rates) for localities willing to retain prisoners locally (an approach similar to California's probation subsidy program). To ensure a proper level of care states could make the subsidy rates high enough to be attractive (but less than the cost to house people in prison) and require fines for jails holding inmates under substandard conditions. The corrections department also could subsidize professional services, such as medical care, to make these programs work (Weimer and Reixach, 1982: 242–43).

Prison capacity will determine how many inmates can be taken into the state corrections apparatus at any one time and, conversely, how many state prisoners must be retained in local jails. A good illustration of this is Texas (Alpert et al., 1984), which, as a result of ongoing prison litigation, is under federal court order to stop admissions to Department of Corrections facilities when prison populations reach 95 percent of rated capacity. When this happens, prison inmates must be released or no new admissions can be received from county jails (see, e.g., "Houston Sheriff Threatens . . . ," 1987; "Texas Jails Packed . . . ," 1987).

In answering *how many,* state prisons will have to be expanded in capacity, alternatives to incarceration will have to be developed, or local jails will continue to be viewed as overflow space for an increasing number of state prisoners. If the third option is chosen, local jails will be untenable and unmanageable (see, e.g., Carney, 1982).

It should be obvious that the who, how many, and how soon questions are all related. If state prisons have the room, they can absorb sentenced felons from county jails fairly quickly. If they must await the release of inmates on parole or through good-time accumulation, increasing numbers of state prisoners could back up for a year or more in county jails (Allinson, 1982; Taft, 1979). The delay, variety of inmates, and large amounts of idle time create an especially volatile mixture, one that is increasingly drawing the courts' attention.

Jail Reform Litigation

A great deal of scholarly attention has been paid to the prison litigation issue (see, e.g., Fair, 1982; Fairchild, 1984; Mays and Taggart, 1985; McCoy, 1982; Yarbrough, 1984, 1985), but much less to jail litigation (Mays and Bernat, 1988). Two important points need to be made: first, prison condition lawsuits may or may not be applicable to jails (see, e.g., *Bell v. Wolfish,* 441 U.S. 520 (1979)); second, states retain some immunity from lawsuits and the collection of damages that local governments may not enjoy (McCoy, 1982). This means that where confinement conditions are constitutionally deficient, local jails have a high potential for being litigation targets.

In a study conducted for the National Sheriffs' Association (NSA), Kerle and Ford (1982: 43–49) found that 423 (15.9 percent) of their respondents had been under court order. Furthermore, 285 jails (10.7 percent) currently were under court order, with the five most common reasons being (in descending order): (1) crowded conditions, (2) lack of recreational facilities or programs, (3) poor conditions of the jail structure itself, (4) lack of medical care or personnel, and (5) inadequate (or absent) visitation privileges. These findings are supported by the latest National Jail Census (Bureau of Justice Statistics, 1983b), which indicates that inspected jails (n = 2,414) most frequently are under court order to limit populations (8.2 percent) and to improve general confinement conditions (10.4 percent). For noninspected jails (n = 724), 15.3 percent were under court order to limit populations and 15.2 percent were under court order to improve general confinement conditions (see Thompson and Mays, 1988b).

The final NSA study question concerning litigation dealt with pending litigation (Kerle and Ford, 1982: 51–55). When asked "Is [your] jail a party to a pending lawsuit?" 529 respondents (19.9 percent) said yes. From this number, 374 were facing federal lawsuits, 144 were anticipating state suits, and the remainder gave no indication of the type of suit pending.

In summarizing the litigation issue, Kerle and Ford (1982: 56) note that the odds are high that many jails will be involved in litigation if they are not already, and they blame both county governments and states. Of county governments they say: ". . . too many county governing bodies in this country, whether out of budgetary constraints, stubbornness, or ignorance, refuse to bite the bullet to help sheriffs and jail administrators overcome these problems by providing them with sufficient funds to remedy these unsafe and unconstitutional jails" (Kerle and Ford, 1982: 56). In assessing the responsibilities of states they add: "Governors and legislatures have sat idly by in many instances and have turned thumbs down on a set of workable jail standards against which jail operations could be measured" (Kerle and Ford, 1982: 56).

The upshot of this neglect and indifference over many years is a growing number of lawsuits by aggrieved inmates (Mays and Bernat, 1988). The increase in litigation by inmates attests to the fact that jails, left to their own devices, will not become better institutions. Typically, although not always, there is too much organizational inertia for those associated with the jail to affect much change; they simply cannot pull themselves up by their own bootstraps.

Summary

American jails are in a state of crisis (ACIR, 1984: 167; Thompson and Mays, 1988b) and always have been because by their nature they are crisis-oriented institutions. Some jail problems have been identified and discussed. Nevertheless, it is important to make two points in closing a discussion of the sociopolitical context of American jails. First, jails did not get into their current situations overnight. This means that their problems will not be solved quickly or inexpensively. Second, jails are complex social and political institutions. Thus while we may long for simple solutions we should be skeptical of those who offer them. Individuals and groups committed to jail reform should be prepared to stay for the long haul and to rejoice in even small victories.

NOTES

1. States with *mandatory standards* are Arkansas, Florida, Illinois, Indiana, Iowa, Kentucky, Maine, Maryland, Massachusetts, Michigan, Minnesota, Nebraska, New Jersey, New York, North Carolina, North Dakota, Ohio, Oklahoma, Oregon, Pennsylvania, South Carolina, Texas, Virginia, Washington, and Wisconsin. States with *voluntary standards* are California, Georgia, Idaho, Kansas, Tennessee, and Utah. States with *developed but not implemented standards* are Arizona, Colorado, Missouri, Montana, New Mexico, South Dakota, and Wyoming. States with *no standards* are Alabama, Louisiana, Mississippi, Nevada, New Hampshire, and West Virginia.

2. Inspecting agencies and intervals:

AL - No inspections
AK - State-operated jails
AZ - No inspections
AR - Jail board; annually/regularly
CA - Jail board; regularly (every 24 months)
CO - No inspections
CT - State-operated jails
DE - State-operated jails
FL - Dept. of Corrections; every three to six months

GA - Dept. of Corrections; no mandated inspections
HI - State-operated jails
ID - Other agency; annually/regularly
IL - Dept. of Corrections; every three to six months
IN - Dept. of Corrections; annually/regularly
IA - Dept. of Corrections; annually/regularly
KS - Dept. of Corrections; every three to six months
KY - Dept. of Corrections; every three to six months
LA - Jail board; no inspections
ME - Dept. of Corrections; annually/regularly
MD - No inspections
MA - Dept. of Corrections; every three to six months
MI - Dept. of Corrections; annually/regularly
MN - Dept of Corrections; annually/regularly
MS - No inspections
MO - No inspections
MT - No inspections
NE - Jail board; annually/regularly
NV - No inspections
NH - No inspections
NJ - Dept. of Corrections; annually/regularly
NM - No inspections
NY - Jail board; every three or six months
NC - Other agency; every three or six months
ND - Attorney general; annually/regularly
OH - Dept. of Corrections; annually/regularly
OK - Other agency; every three or six months
OR - Dept. of Corrections; annually/regularly
PA - Dept. of Corrections; every three or six months
RI - State-operated jails
SC - Dept. of Corrections; annually/regularly
SD - No inspections
TN - Dept. of Corrections; annually/regularly
TX - Dept. of Corrections; annually/regularly
UT - Other agency; annually/regularly
VT - State-operated jails
VA - Jail board; every three or six months
WA - Jail board; annually/regularly
WV - No inspections
WI - Dept. of Corrections; annually/regularly
WY - No inspections

3. States with *standards enforced by courts* include Arkansas, Indiana, Massachusetts, Minnesota, Nebraska, Oklahoma, and Oregon. States with *enforcement by the department of corrections or another law enforcement agency* include Florida, Illinois (attorney general), Iowa, Kentucky, Maine, Maryland, Mississippi, New Jersey, New York, North Dakota (at-

torney general), Ohio, Pennsylvania, South Carolina, Texas, Virginia, and Washington. States with *voluntary compliance* include California, Georgia, Idaho, Kansas, Tennessee, and Utah. States with *no enforcement mechanism* include Alabama, Arizona, Colorado, Missouri, Montana, Nevada, New Hampshire, New Mexico, South Dakota, West Virginia, and Wyoming.

CHAPTER 2

Competing Ideologies of Jail Confinement

PATRICK G. JACKSON

Contemporary research and reform strategies on jails must appreciate the numerous constraints that this unique form of social organization places on achieving the varied purposes—related to pretrial detention and sentencing—proposed for them. One of the most distinctive features of jails is the movement of massive numbers of pretrial and sentenced inmates through them each year. The perennial problem of jail crowding, which recently has worsened in many jurisdictions, amplifies the underlying impediments that jails present to the realization of the various goals claimed by most correctional agencies.

This chapter will clarify the purpose and meaning of jails and jail confinement in the administration of justice and the imposi-

This research was supported by grant 81-IJ-CX-0068 from the National Institute of Justice through the National Council on Crime and Delinquency, San Francisco, California. Opinions expressed here do not necessarily represent those of the National Institute of Justice. I wish to thank James Austin and Barry Krisberg of NCCD, who contributed to the final report from which this chapter was in part adapted. Bill Elms provided computer support. Cindy Stearns and Bernadette Tarallo helped to collect the quantitative data. Cindy Stearns also provided helpful criticisms of the present manuscript. Responsibility for the present manuscript is mine.

tion of punishment. Most present knowledge about jails and inmates has been formulated with reference to existing data sources,
a major one being the national census of jails, a cross-sectional survey of jails and inmates conducted on a single day (Bureau of Justice Statistics [BJS], 1986b). This survey, while useful for a variety
of purposes, may not provide the data necessary to address the
multitude of long-standing questions surrounding jails. This chapter includes a brief discussion of the unique longitudinal research
design of this study and a review of traditional rationales for jail
confinement. The results of the longitudinal approach then are
presented to assess the tenability of these rationales for jail incarceration, including pretrial detention, just deserts, incapacitation,
deterrence, and rehabilitation. Where relevant, additional research also is examined. The discussion offers some suggestions for
research and social policy related to jails.

Methods

Like most jails, the three California jails in San Francisco, Yolo,
and Los Angeles counties included in the study hold pretrial defendants charged with misdemeanors or felonies as well as sentenced misdemeanant offenders. The three jails differ greatly in
size, urban/rural character, and the volume of people who pass
through them. Los Angeles Central is one of the largest jails in the
country. It primarily receives inmates who previously have been
arraigned and/or processed through one of the multitude of substa-
tions and courts located throughout the Los Angeles area. The San
Francisco main jail is a large urban facility that receives inmates
from the city and county of San Francisco. The Yolo jail, with a
much smaller inmate capacity, is a rural facility located in the city
of Woodland.

Two categories of the incoming pretrial population were
sampled in each of the jails: those newly booked and those booked
and eventually held seventy-two hours or more. This sampling procedure was necessary in San Francisco and Yolo because of the
large number of individuals who are released shortly after arrest.
These inmates were tracked from booking through disposition of
their booking charges. Sentenced inmates at each jail were
sampled as they were released from custody. The sentenced sample
excluded offenders sentenced to time served only. A variety of
quantitative information related to offense, prior record, length of
stay, and other factors was collected on over 2,100 inmates.

Jails for Pretrial Detention Purposes

Pretrial detention is a practice that assumes that custody, but not punishment, is necessary to ensure a defendant's appearance in court, to prevent possible community harm, or to ensure the integrity of the court process. Judges want defendants in court, but in two recent cases, *U.S. v. Salerno*, 107 S. Ct. 2095 (1987) and *Schall v. Martin*, 104 S. Ct. 2403 (1984), the U.S. Supreme Court found it constitutional for pretrial detention to be used to prevent pretrial crime among defendants defined as dangerous. *Salerno* dealt with the constitutionality of the Federal Bail Reform Act of 1984 concerning preventive detention among adults and *Schall* with the question of juvenile preventive detention. In both cases pretrial detention was defined as a regulatory, not a penal, action.

As suggested by these decisions, of all the jail's functions, pretrial detention probably has been the most significant and controversial. There is a continuing national debate over the conditions under which it is appropriate or desirable to detain accused criminal defendants, who constitute over half of daily jail populations (BJS, 1986b). The underlying issue is the appropriate balance between the liberty interests of untried defendants and the societal concern with protection from potential harm by released defendants.

In the not-so-distant past, numerous efforts were made to improve the ability of indigent defendants to secure release from jail. Early bail reform efforts, for example, led to development of appearance-based criteria for pretrial release and to the growth of release on recognizance and citation release programs. At the federal level the early bail reform movement culminated in passage of the federal Bail Reform Act of 1966 (BRA 1966),[1] which made a presumption in favor of release (Goldkamp, 1985).

Subsequent to this act, increased attention centered on crimes committed by pretrial releasees (Thomas, 1976). A 1970 law permitting pretrial preventive detention was passed in the District of Columbia.[2] This D.C. law cited defendant dangerousness as one criterion to be used in setting release conditions or in denying release altogether. The statute was used very little because of questions surrounding the constitutionality of preventive detention as well as the availability of alternative means for detaining defendants, such as high money bail (Bases and MacDonald, 1972). Moreover, the U.S. Supreme Court declined to hear constitutional challenges to the D.C. law.

Since passage of the D.C. law, there have been calls for more stringent pretrial release criteria on grounds that a small group of dangerous criminals are being unwisely released and committing crimes against the public (President's Task Force on Victims of Crime, 1982). Several organizations also have offered support for preventive detention, including the National Association of Pretrial Services Agencies (1978) and the American Bar Association (1981). Also, over half the states and the District of Columbia have developed rules or passed laws that permit defendant dangerousness to be considered in setting release conditions or in denying release altogether. Many of these are not used, however.

A clear indicator of change in the balance between individual and societal interests in the area of pretrial detention has been passage of the federal Bail Reform Act of 1984 (BRA 1984), which permits the pretrial detention of defendants in federal courts on grounds that they may pose a public danger. Moreover, the U.S. Supreme Court in *U.S. v. Salerno* (1987) heard a case challenging the constitutionality of the act after having earlier decided in favor of preventive detention in *Schall v. Martin* (1984). In upholding the new federal law, the Court found that (1) there is a legitimate state interest in protecting the public from the potential crimes of pretrial defendants, (2) pretrial detention is a regulatory and not a penal device, and (3) prediction of future behavior is permissible (and possible) in this context as it is elsewhere in the criminal justice process.

In examining the debate over pretrial detention in the jail context, this chapter examines the reasons for detention and the characteristics of pretrial detainees in three local jails, along with discussion of the extent to which pretrial detention is used in lieu of a more formal punitive sanction. This is important because longitudinal and cross-sectional designs provide different ways of viewing the characteristics of pretrial detainees. This information is relevant to the debate over the "dangerousness" of pretrial detainees as measured by prior criminal history, current charge(s), and the disposition of charges that were the basis of their confinement. In addition to these data there is a brief review of the preventive detention experience in the federal system, as well as research on how much pretrial crime would be reduced in other state jurisdictions if defendants were detained for dangerousness.

Study Findings. Data previously presented on pretrial inmates (Jackson, 1988) indicate that most are arrested for relatively minor offenses. For example, between 72 percent and 78 percent of the San Francisco and Yolo jail bookings, but only 58 percent of

L.A. Central's, were for offenses not involving major personal or property crime but for violations of public order, drunk driving, court process, traffic violations, and others. Fully 45 percent of Yolo's pretrial population was intoxicated at booking, compared to 16 percent at San Francisco and 17 percent at L.A. Central. Differences in offense types across the sites decline when comparing inmates held seventy-two hours or longer. Less than 8 percent of Yolo's and San Francisco's intake were charged with violent offenses compared to almost 17 percent in Central, reflecting the latter's use as a postarraignment facility. These findings contrast with the results of the National Jail Census (BJS, 1983a), which found that fully 78 percent of pretrial inmates were charged with more serious personal or property offenses.

Inmates' prior records vary greatly across the jails, although complete data are not available at Central. Over half of Yolo's and over 80 percent of San Francisco's inmates have no prior history of a misdemeanor conviction; between 15 percent and 18 percent have a prior felony conviction. In these two jails, between 5 percent and 8 percent had experienced a prior prison term; 2 percent to 5 percent had a prior California Youth Authority (youthful offender) stay; and less than 5 percent (0.4 percent in San Francisco) had an escape history. Fewer than 17 percent of Central's incoming pretrial inmates had a history of prison or CYA, while 3 percent had an escape history.

Inmate personal characteristics reveal a disadvantaged status. Minorities are overrepresented in the jails relative to each county's population; the average inmate has less than a high school education; between 17 percent and 25 percent are married; and the average age ranges from twenty-five to twenty-nine. Over half of the Yolo and Central inmates are unemployed; those employed primarily have blue-collar or laborer occupations.

Finally, the offense dispositions of the pretrial inmates, which also bear on the underlying reason for their detention, reveal substantial variability across the jails. Only 20 percent of Yolo's and 29 percent of Central's inmates had their charges dropped or dismissed, while about two-thirds of the charges against inmates in San Francisco similarly were dropped. There were few or no prison sentences at Yolo (none), San Francisco (1.5 percent), or Central (5.4 percent). No more than 21 percent (at Central) of the inmates received additional jail time subsequent to conviction; 12.8 percent of San Francisco inmates received additional time, followed by 11.3 percent of the Yolo inmates.

The characteristics of defendants booked into jail shed some light on the appropriate uses of pretrial detention. Unlike inmate characteristics revealed by the census approach, most defendants admitted to pretrial detention are charged with misdemeanor offenses and do not have extensive criminal histories. Inmates are of low socioeconomic standing, have high levels of unemployment, low levels of education, and minimal financial resources. Many are drunk at the time of admission. The majority of these individuals will leave these high-security facilities within a few hours or a few days. Those who stay longer do so because their charges and criminal histories are more serious. However, a significant portion stay longer in pretrial custody for reasons unrelated to the seriousness of their charge (Jackson, 1988). If convicted, few will spend additional time incarcerated either in jail or in another facility. No more than 20 percent will spend additional time in jail after conviction.

Although the study shows considerable variation across the jails, the results are consistent with those of other researchers, who point out that many pretrial detainees (especially misdemeanants) are economically disadvantaged defendants accused of nondangerous, public nuisance types of behaviors and who generally do not have serious prior records. These inmates are being unnecessarily detained and processed through an expensive and inefficient pretrial system (Feeley, 1979). This is most evident in the San Francisco jail and least so at L.A. Central. From this perspective pretrial detention itself is one aspect of the process of punishment conspicuously revealed by low postconviction jail time (Feeley, 1979).

Other Studies on Defendant Dangerousness. It is not clear whether states will follow the new federal law by developing and implementing pretrial dangerousness laws, much less whether such laws would stand in the face of state legal challenges. The present concern with the preventive detention of "dangerous" defendants as represented by BRA 1984 raises the question, however, of whether jail incarceration is the most appropriate means for lowering pretrial crime levels in local jurisdictions. While information discussed previously on the prior record and current offense of pretrial jail inmates provides partial details useful in addressing this question, other research on the new federal law also is relevant.

Two studies have been conducted by federal agencies on the implementation and impact of the new federal law (General Accounting Office [GAO], 1987; BJS, 1988d).[3] An earlier study indicated that jail custody levels increased after the new law was passed (U.S. Marshal's Report, 1986). The BJS study was more comprehensive than the one conducted by the GAO, but both came to similar conclusions. First, both indicate that there has been a 5 percent increase in the overall proportion of defendants detained until trial. Second, there also has been an increase in the number of defendants detained without bail (from 1.7 percent to 18.8 percent of defendants in the BJS study) and a decrease in the percent required to post bail (44 percent before and 27 percent after the law, again in the BJS study). There has been no change in the percentage released without financial conditions. Thus, although there has been an overall increase in detention, the effect of the law has been greatest on those who would have qualified for bail release under the old law.

Only the BJS examined the change in the amount of confinement time that accompanied the new law. It showed that the average number of detention days per defendant went up 17 percent after the new law went into effect, from 20.1 days to 23.5 days. Therefore, the greater number of defendants detained after the new law are being held longer.

The final question of interest is whether the increase in jail detention and longer periods of incarceration have lowered pretrial crime rates—a major purpose of the Bail Reform Act. The BJS study is again most useful in answering this question because it covered the entire federal system, although its results are similar to the GAO study where comparable data were collected. The BJS study found that few released defendants were charged with a felony or misdemeanor, failed to appear, or experienced technical violations before or after the new law. There was an insignificant increase in minor violations of restrictions on travel and association (from 1.2 percent to 2.6 percent). Subsequent to the new law, however, it concluded: "there was no significant increase in the percent of defendants arrested for felonies or misdemeanors" (BJS, 1988d: 5). Moreover, the average number of days to those few offenses that occurred actually improved from fifty-four days before to fifty-nine days after the new law.

The research reviewed suggests that the new federal pretrial preventive detention law has resulted in (1) an increase in the number of detained defendants, (2) longer periods of pretrial confinement, and (3) jail crowding problems (U.S. Marshal's Report, 1986). However, these changes have not led to (4) a decrease in pretrial crime. Whether these changes in detention will lead to diminished pretrial crime over time is still an open question, as some reforms may take longer to show clear effects, although the amount of time necessary is unclear (see, e.g., Casper and Brereton, 1983). Given the very low level of pretrial crime, however, it seems reasonable to speculate that substantial increases in detention levels might have to occur for significant reductions in pretrial crime to result. However, it is not clear from either study whether such increases actually would lead to the detention of defendants who are responsible for existing recidivism levels.[3]

While the experience with the new federal law is of some importance in considering the appropriateness of jail for pretrial detention, it is unclear how or to what extent pretrial preventive detention would affect state and local jurisdictions. As mentioned, it is unclear whether preventive detention would stand up to challenges under state laws. It is also unclear how the implementation of pretrial detention in local jurisdictions would affect jail populations and pretrial crime levels. To explore this question, a recent study (Jackson, 1987b) reanalyzed the well-known national assessment of pretrial release procedures and pretrial crime conducted by Toborg (1978). The research examined the potential impact of 18 preventive detention policies on detention levels, jail space, and pretrial crime levels in seven jurisdictions.[4]

The results indicate that none of the 18 policies would prevent much pretrial crime. One finding is that pretrial crime, particularly serious pretrial crime, is relatively infrequent. Across the seven jurisdictions studied, for example, only three of the 2,890 defendants were convicted of a felony arrest charge that was incurred during the pretrial release period. Also, if policies were implemented that led to the detention of large numbers of defendants (such as locking up every defendant charged with a felony) and prevented the maximum possible amount of pretrial crime, the majority of pretrial crime would still occur. Moreover, in those few models and jurisdictions where reductions in pretrial crime could be expected, there would be spectacular increases in the number of detainees and in the amount of new jail space needed to house additional pretrial defendants. This implies that local jail crowding problems would be greatly aggravated by increased detention and that such detention would have little, if any, effect on the problem it is intended to solve—pretrial crime.

If we consider how preventive detention policies operate, rather than their intent, there is some evidence that use of jails for preventive detention would accomplish little crime reduction but that it could extend pretrial punishment processes to additional misdemeanants or to the felony level beyond what might exist at present. Such detention can and does occur regardless of the ultimate disposition of the offense that brought the defendant to jail. Evidence that a substantial number of preventively detained defendants are not convicted of crimes or are given sentences not involving confinement was not viewed as relevant in the Supreme Court's finding in favor of preventive detention.

All of these data suggest there is considerable local flexibility to determine how scarce pretrial jail space will be used. Such policies will determine if pretrial detention is principally used to ensure appearance at trial, prevent additional crimes from being committed, or become part of an informal sanctioning process delivered before trial. Available research suggests that use of jails for pretrial preventive detention is not likely to accomplish its primary objective—the reduction of pretrial crime—but instead may aggravate crowding problems and bring more pretrial punishment and ceremony than substance to the judicial process.

Jails for Sentencing Purposes

The other major jail use is incarceration of convicted offenders. This is a relatively recent purpose of confinement since the jail historically has served as a pretrial or presentence facility (Rothman, 1972). Unlike prison, jail sentences ordinarily last considerably less than a year. Like prison, however, the purpose of this period of incarceration is ambiguous; judges, administrators, and policymakers advocate an array of correctional goals including deterrence, incapacitation, rehabilitation, and punishment or (more recently) just deserts. In some jurisdictions jail sentences increasingly are meted out in combination with other sanctions such as probation, fines, and restitution. Brief descriptions of these correctional philosophies and their relationship to jail confinement follow.

Deterrence

Deterrence defines jail confinement as the punishment necessary to prevent crime upon the law-abiding population. The doctrine of *general deterrence* assumes that if criminals were not punished certain segments of free society would feel no compulsion to obey the law (Zimring and Hawkins, 1968) or would be demoralized (Toby, 1970). In the name of public safety judges and prosecutors routinely employ these rationales to legitimize jail use. So, too, with the notion of *specific deterrence,* in which the individual convicted and punished for a crime by jail confinement refrains from future crime because of the punishment. In classical theory the deterrent effect of punishment is greatest when it is certain and swift and the level of punishment calibrated such that the pain of punishment is greater than the benefits gained from crime.

The large numbers sanctioned by brief periods of incarceration through jail sentences could define the jail as an efficacious general and/or specific deterrent. Many offenders can be exposed to the jail's punitive aspects within a one-year period. The question, however, is whether the brevity and intensity of the incarceration are sufficient to deter most offenders from future criminal involvement, setting aside the certainty of apprehension. But to answer this question one must know the extent of jail inmates' previous contacts with the criminal justice system. If a high proportion of individuals serving sentences are repeat offenders who already have experienced juvenile and criminal courts, one might argue that subsequent jail sentences will have little impact on their criminal careers unless age, health, and other factors serve to suppress criminal activity.

Table 2.1 suggests that there is considerable diversity across the jails in terms of prior record. Between 31 percent and 41 percent of Yolo's and Central's sentenced inmates have not had a prior jail sentence, compared to nearly 81 percent of those in San Francisco.[5] Likewise, between 11 percent and 13 percent of Yolo's and Central's sentenced inmates have had a prior prison sentence compared to only 5 percent in San Francisco. Histories of prior mental health commitments and escapes are less frequent and in some cases highly variable across the jails. Indicators of personal disadvantage (marital and employment status, occupation, and ethnicity) suggest the marginal social characteristics of the sentenced population. A high proportion are single, unemployed, hold lower-class jobs, and disproportionately represent minority groups relative to the respective county populations (data not shown).

It also may be that individuals will not commit crimes because they have observed what happens to others who experience jail confinement, or general deterrence. This study does not test either deterrence rationale for sentencing. The most feasible and policy-relevant ideology to test, however, is the use of jail for specific deterrence: it may be that inmates who experience confinement will desist or reduce their criminal activity. The works of Murray and Cox (1978), Farrington (1983), and more recently Smith and Gartin (1989) suggest that the experience of arrest and

TABLE 2.1

Characteristics of Sentenced Inmates by Site

Characteristic	Yolo	San Francisco	L.A. Central
Prior jail sentences			
None	41.3	80.8	38.7
One	13.6	14.0	22.6
Two	9.2	4.4	14.2
Three	5.3	0.4	6.6
Four or more	30.6	0.4	17.9
Total prison sentences			
None	85.9	94.8	88.8
One or more	13.1	5.2	11.2
Prior CYA sentences[a]			
None	92.7	92.4	91.5
One or more	7.3	7.6	8.5
Mental health commitments			
None	92.7	99.6	97.2
One or more	7.3	0.4	2.8
Prior escapes			
None	97.6	98.0	99.1
One	2.0	1.6	0.9
Two	0.5	0.4	0.0
Marital status			
Single	47.8	73.9	65.6[b]
Married	18.1	21.1	19.7
Separated	8.3	0.7	9.8
Divorced/widowed	25.8	4.2	4.9
Employment status			
Full-time	29.8	9.4	41.4
Part-time	0.5	68.8	3.1
Unemployed	66.8	21.9	52.3
Student	2.4	—[c]	3.1
Other	0.5	—	—
Occupation[d]			
Professional, sales			
managerial, private	10.3	10.0	17.6
Clerical	4.5	7.7	2.8
Crafts, operatives,			
transport	29.7	30.0	40.9
Nonfarm labor	40.0	23.1	26.1
Farm labor	2.6	—	—
Service	5.2	19.2	10.6
Other	7.7	10.0	2.8
Average age	33.4	29.6	30.2

TABLE 2.1

Continued

Characteristic	Yolo	San Francisco	L.A. Central
Ethnicity			
Black	4.0	47.6	25.9
Hispanic	29.9	9.4	39.5
White	64.0	38.6	31.2
Other	3.0	4.3	3.4
Offense type			
Violence	6.0	13.6	7.9
Property	17.0	27.2	19.1
Public order	30.0	18.4	16.9
Court process	8.5	21.2	12.4
Traffic	9.5	1.6	8.6
Drunk driving	24.0	10.4	28.8
All other	5.0	7.6	6.4

a. Refers to the California Youth Authority, an agency with jurisdiction over youthful offenders.
b. Includes unmarried cohabitation in Los Angeles only.
c. These data were not collected separately in San Francisco.
d. Includes both employed and unemployed.

some forms of punishment may deter some individuals, particularly novice offenders. It may be that milder forms of punishment, such as arrest, will have specific deterrent effects among first-time offenders. However, more severe punishment, such as incarceration, may lead to increased criminality (e.g., Shannon, 1980, 1985).

It is an open question how severe the jail sanction is in the gradation from arrest to imprisonment. The study findings suggest that the effects of jail confinement, if any, would vary by site due to the great differences in the number of repeat offenders and time in custody, both pretrial and sentenced, across the jails. Moreover, there are differences in the means of jail punishment, particularly the conditions and length of confinement (discussed later in this chapter) that could condition the scope and intensity of deterrence.

Incapacitation

The main assumption underlying the incapacitation ideology is that individuals are prevented from committing crimes against free society while confined. Although offenders may commit crimes

TABLE 2.2

Average Length of Time Served in Days by Offense and by Site

	Yolo (N = 199)		San Francisco (N = 249)		L.A. Central (N = 266)	
	Mean	*Median*	*Mean*	*Median*	*Mean*	*Median*
Violence	123	115	86	58	68	13
Property	124	91	71	52	42	8
Public order	34	16	47	43	36	11
Court processing	75	71	20	3	8	4
Traffic	56	20	32	5	18	4
Drunk driving	86	77	31	8	18	6
Other	105	118	80	51	28	4
Total	76	44	54	30	29	7
Percent serving 90 days or more	32.5%		21.6%		9.0%	

while in jail, members of the public will not be threatened directly, and the crime rate may even go down. The argument frequently is voiced by those who wish to take offenders convicted of serious crimes out of circulation. The point is made clear by Morris (1974: 80), who says: "Virtually all criminals can have their subsequent violent crime dramatically reduced by detaining them in prison until their fiftieth birthday."

The significance of the incapacitation rationale for sentencing assumes less importance in jails compared to prisons due to the fact that inmates are incarcerated for only relatively brief time periods. While there is variation by jail in sentenced length of stay, it is in days, not years (see table 2.2). The median number of days spent in the jails studied, for example, is 44 in Yolo, 30 in San Francisco, and 7 in L.A. Central. For crimes of violence the medians are 115, 58, and 13, respectively. These relatively brief periods of confinement are also a limiting factor on the incapacitation rationale because most individuals admitted to jail are involved in episodic, not continuous, criminal activities.

The more fundamental criticism of the incapacitation ideology is the number of defendants confined in jail who would not have committed an offense if they had been released from confinement, so-called false positives. In the jail context the number of false positives is undoubtedly large. In any case, at present the ability to predict who will commit an offense in the future, particularly a serious offense, is very limited.

Rehabilitation

Another rationale for sentencing and jail confinement is rehabilitation, one purpose of which is to reduce or eliminate crime. Jail may be viewed as one aspect of treatment that will alter the underlying reasons bringing the individual to jail. This perspective embraces a pathological crime causation model and seeks to treat and correct the attitudes and behaviors of the individual offender rather than to reform society.

This ideology, which has dominated correctional philosophy for a century, has been criticized on grounds that individualized treatment is inequitable when it affects sentence lengths and parole release decisions. Moreover, the effectiveness of treatment programs has been severely questioned. For over a decade the argument that "nothing works" in the treatment of criminal offenders (Martinson, 1974; Morris, 1974; Fogel, 1975) has prevailed, although rehabilitation already shows signs of reemerging (e.g., Cullen and Gilbert, 1982; Sechrest et al., 1979).

The credibility of the rehabilitation rationale in jails is even more tenuous than incapacitation when viewed in light of the brief time available for staff to treat rapidly changing and heterogeneous inmate populations. The present data suggest that the rehabilitation rationale hangs by a thread for two reasons. First, few if any programs exist to treat or train jail inmates. Medical services were available for injury or serious illness as needed and recreation time was provided.[6] As shown in table 2.3, however, there is very little program participation or work involvement in the two jails where this information was collected.[7] The involvement that did occur was almost always some form of work needed to maintain the institutions. Thus many inmates who worked were trusties or conducted various forms of unspecified yard work, washed motor vehicles, and worked as cafeteria orderlies or, in one instance, as a shoe shiner (at Central). Only two inmates were involved in work furlough.

Second, the brief period of confinement means that the little exposure occurring is unlikely to reap any major results. The only way rehabilitation could occur would be through some continuation of the rehabilitation process after release from jail. This information suggests that for a rehabilitative or treatment program to be delivered, much less to be effective, it must be integrated closely with ongoing services. This might occur through the use of referrals as well as vocational, educational, and psychological services that are organizationally independent of the jail.

TABLE 2.3

Program and Work Participation by Site

Number Participating in Programs	San Francisco	L.A. Central
None	78.4	75.5
One	21.0	18.9
Two	0.6	2.8
Three	0.0	3.5

Just Deserts

There has been increased interest in the just deserts rationale associated with the decline of the treatment ideal and concerns over abuses of discretion. This ideology emphasizes the need for fairness and certainty in the imposition of punishment. It expresses the idea that "when a justice process is neither fair nor effective it harms both the individual and society" (Dershowitz, 1976). Jails are seen merely as places reserved for the imposition of punishment. Such a sentence, in this view, should be uniformly administered—that is, similar offenders should receive similar sentences—and punishment should be proportional to the gravity of the crime. Since the desired end is equitably applied punishment, neither individual nor general deterrence is necessarily important.

Despite indications that the ideology of rehabilitation is gradually making inroads into social science acceptance once again, and although deterrence and incapacitation ideologies are unlikely to be rejected in the foreseeable future, one author has argued that the deserts philosophy is "likely to become the winner in today's battle of ideologies" (Empey, 1978: 15). This ideology has been at the forefront of criminal justice policy and gradually has filtered down to practices of the courts in some jurisdictions. For example, major legislation in several states has enacted determinate and guideline sentencing approaches (e.g., California, Maine, Indiana, Illinois, and Oregon).

It is significant that correctional rationales seem to ignore the fact there are differences in jail use as a sanction and in the conditions of jail confinement—in short, differences in the *means* of punishment. This is especially noteworthy with respect to the just deserts rationale. As shown in table 2.2, jails do not punish uniformly for specific offenses; differences occur both within and among ju-

TABLE 2.4

Disciplinary and Injury Incidents by Site

Type of Incident	Yolo	San Francisco	L.A. Central
Record of a major disciplinary problem	1.0	3.2	2.6
Record of injury while confined	0.0	3.0	6.0
Record of disciplinary problem or injury	1.0	6.2	8.6

risdictions in relative jail and prison sentence terms. For example, San Francisco and Los Angeles show shorter periods of confinement compared to Yolo.

Moreover, there may be differences in jail confinement conditions and, hence, inequity in punishment severity. Criminal law defines punishment proportional to time sentenced to jail confinement; it uses time simply because it is highly valued (Aubert and Messinger, 1965: 30). Yet time served may be unrelated to objective confinement conditions. Greenfeld (1980) has suggested five indexes of objective confinement conditions that, taken together, are a measure of the severity of punishment.[8] The conditions of confinement (see table 2.4)—measured by disciplinary incidents, physical injuries incurred by inmates, and the physical structure of the sentenced facilities—were superior at the Yolo facility.

To the extent there are differences in sentence severity, as Greenfeld (1980) found in the Abt study of prisons (1980), one may question the argument that confinement in jail is equitable and can be known in advance. The objectives of a just deserts philosophy, while removing manifest discrimination and arbitrariness in sentencing, may leave a residual of inequity in the actual confinement conditions.

Gross disparities among the three counties in terms of who is sentenced, for what types of crimes, and the length of confinement are evidence that contradict the premise that the jail sanction serves the just deserts rationale. The likelihood that an offender will be sentenced to jail and the length of that punishment will depend not only on legal factors but on the unique sentencing policies operating within a particular county. Thus there are disparities in jail use as a sanction.

Conclusions

This chapter has examined the efficacy of a variety of rationales for jail confinement by employing a methodological approach that is sensitive to the dynamic nature of jail populations. The most controversial rationale is pretrial detention, which includes confinement to ensure a defendant's appearance at trial or to prevent dangerous defendants from committing additional crimes. The present study suggests that most pretrial inmates are charged with nonserious offenses, have relatively nonserious prior records, come from marginal socioeconomic backgrounds, and many eventually have their original charges dropped. Among those who are convicted relatively few spend additional time in jail, and even fewer are sentenced to prison. While these patterns vary across the jails the results suggest that the processing of defendants is consistent with prior work (Feeley, 1979), which indicates that detention is one aspect of the pretrial punishment process.

Research reviewed on the probable effects of pretrial defendants' preventive detention in local jails suggests that such detention would lead to significant increases in jail custody levels but would have little or no impact on pretrial crime. This parallels research findings on the new federal preventive detention law, which found that there has been no decrease in pretrial crime despite the implementation of preventive detention and the confinement of additional defendants for longer periods of time.

These inquiries suggest that pretrial detention is overused for the purpose of ensuring appearance at trial and that the proposal for preventive detention is likely to have the undesirable consequence of increasing jail populations but few or no benefits of crime reduction.

The various sentencing rationales likewise face formidable obstacles to their actualization due to some fundamental characteristics of jails: brief lengths of stay, an absence or low level of program development, wide intracounty and intercounty variation in jail use and length of sentences for similar offenses and conditions of confinement, and sentenced inmates' prior records and social characteristics. Of all the rationales, that of specific deterrence may be the most plausible, but it has not been thoroughly examined here or elsewhere and is in need of further study.

Enhancement of the just deserts objective might occur through uniform sentencing practices within and across local jurisdictions, although the differential capacity and conditions of confinement across jurisdictions may pose serious roadblocks to this, to say nothing of the resulting political issues. The urban-rural differences found here—both in length of confinement and in conditions of confinement—might be a good beginning point for dealing with this problem. Given the brief lengths of jail stays, the potential for rehabilitative strategies might be tried in the jail context, but the development of adequate programs before and after confinement might be more fruitful. Experimentation in smaller jails such as Yolo could provide a springboard for large-scale programming in larger areas such as Los Angeles and San Francisco. Incapacitation appears to be among the least tenable purposes of confinement.

It is very likely that the problems posed by local jails for the realization of competing and highly varied societal goals will persist and perhaps accelerate. The difficult problems now faced by local communities will be enhanced through a recognition of the unique character of this most obdurate form of social organization as understood through the use of the longitudinal approach.

NOTES

1. Bail Reform Act of 1986, Public Law No. 89-465, 80 Stat. 214 (1966), repealed in 1984.

2. D.C. Code, Sections 23-1321 et seq.

3. The underlying problem, of course, is that neither officials nor social scientists are able to predict accurately whether a defendant will commit a crime during the pretrial release period. See, for example, the studies by Roth and Wice (1978) and Angel et al. (1971) on the very low predictive capacity of existing models.

4. These policies included, for example, the preventive detention of defendants charged with either a felony, dangerous or violent crime, and/or who were on bail for various offenses, and/or who were on probation or parole for a prior conviction.

5. Some information on Central inmates was obtained through in-person interviews rather than official documents. In such instances the number of cases on which the percentages are based is no fewer than 106. These items include employment status, occupation, and measures of prior record.

6. Jail officials at Yolo indicate their jail is certified by the American Medical Association.

7. There is little reason to believe that the Yolo data would differ greatly.

8. When adapted to the jail they include density and occupancy of the jail; amount of inmate and staff deviant behavior; freedom of movement within the jail; access to services; and the jail's fiscal influence.

CHAPTER 3

Disaggregating Jail Use: Variety and Change in Local Corrections over a Ten-Year Period

JOHN M. KLOFAS

During the 1970s and 1980s we witnessed unparalleled increases in local jail inmate populations. Between 1978 and 1986 the nation's jail population increased by more than 73 percent, reaching a record high of 274,444 inmates. In 1987 alone there was a growth of 8 percent over the previous year, and the growth continues unabated (Bureau of Justice Statistics [BJS], 1988c).

The jail crisis and its effects are well documented. As a response to overcrowding we have embarked on the largest buildup of jail space in the nation's history (Cory and Gettinger, 1984). Programs have been developed ranging from targeting the most serious offenders (see, e.g., Greenwood, 1982) to reducing resources used by less-serious offenders through such programs as electronic monitoring (Schmidt, 1989) and home detention (Ball et al., 1988). Jail inmates now float along the Hudson River in a decommissioned naval vessel reminiscent of the British hulks of the eighteenth century. Like another early British innovation, some New York jail inmates now serve time far from their own communities. In other jurisdictions municipalities have loaned inmates money for bond and even have charged some inmates a fee for placement in uncrowded facilities (NCCD Publications, 1983). In short, the crisis in local corrections has transformed nearly all of American criminal justice.

In the face of the dramatic population increases and efforts to cope, little attention has been paid to differences across local jails. This chapter will examine the jail crisis by focusing on differences in jail use across local jurisdictions. This research will assess whether disaggregating jail use and examining data covering a ten-year period can help explain how jails have grown, what variables may influence jail growth, and what variables may explain differences across jails.

Studying Jail Use

The wave of construction and innovation in corrections has been accompanied by heightened interest in policy-relevant research. With regard to jails in particular this research has focused on the causes of, and solutions to, overcrowding (see Bolduc, 1985). Those studies make clear the need for systemwide approaches to understanding and addressing jail crowding (National Institute of Justice [NIJ], 1985). They focus attention on the roles of the police, courts, probation and parole agencies, and legislatures in contributing to and resolving overcrowding problems.

This research continues to be extremely useful in face of the correctional crisis. Much of this research, however, is best regarded as technical research (see Majchrzak, 1984) that, while action oriented, has several significant limitations. These limitations center on three issues: limited attention to basic criminal justice goals, an orientation toward jails as idiosyncratic, and a lack of concern with broader theoretical perspectives.

In the face of crisis, jail research has paid little attention to issues of criminal justice goals. Attention to broad issues such as the deterrence, incapacitation, and treatment goals of corrections is postponed in the face of more acute problems. The research primarily focuses on how to uncrowd jails, and with such a focus goals serve only to set vague policy limitations. The concern thus is with decision making and capacity as they affect crowding and not on the extent to which those decisions reflect traditional criminal justice goals.

Crowding studies incorporate criminal justice system variables, but they also tend to view jails as idiosyncratic. Crowding is caused by the unique relationships among system components and community characteristics. One implication of this view is methodological: addressing crowding requires analyses tailored to individual communities (see NIJ, 1985). Therefore, comparative analyses often have not been regarded as necessary.

Finally, the action orientation of the research has meant that jails often are not viewed in a broader theoretical context. Jails generally are examined within the criminal justice system context but only to the extent that this view is useful in diagnosing and relieving crowding. There has been little effort to examine the jail's role in the community theory context or as it relates to other social control mechanisms.

While concern with acute local corrections problems must continue, there is also much to be gained by refocusing our attention. One seemingly useful approach is to reconceptualize jail research by focusing on jail use rather than on crowding (see American Justice Institute, 1984). The goal of such an approach would be to describe and explain differences in the ways communities utilize jail space. Ultimately it would include examining questions of who goes to jail, under what circumstances, what discretionary processes control the length of time people stay in jail, and how community alternatives affect jail use. Interesting work along these lines already has begun, and substantial variation in jail use has been described for three California counties (Austin and Krisberg, 1984; Jackson, 1987a).

Such an approach can provide a useful complement to existing crowding studies. Focusing on jail use encourages comparative analysis. It calls attention to similarities and differences across communities. It also facilitates attention to traditional criminal justice goals, as differences in patterns of jail use may reflect differences in communities' attachments to goals. Finally, consideration of jail use can draw on and incorporate larger theoretical perspectives. Jail use, for example, can draw on community theory and research that attempts to explain variation in social control across communities (see, e.g., Warren, 1978).

Jail Use Typology

Attention to measurement is fundamental to research that investigates either crowding or jail use. Studies of crowding must take into account capacity measures and may consider population density, turnover, and other factors. Focusing on jail use, however, requires attention to the jail's role in the community. It has been argued that the role of local jails is more complex than that of prisons (Klofas, 1988). While incarceration rates may provide adequate measures of prison use, they do not capture the complexity of jail roles and, therefore, may not be as useful as measures of local corrections.

The complexity of jail populations is well appreciated (see Goldfarb, 1975). The jail combines those newly arrested, those awaiting trial, those in the process of trial, and some sentenced offenders; it even may contain civil and criminal violators. It is possible to argue, however, that the jail serves two general functions: processing people for the justice system and holding individuals in various stages of the judicial process. The jail processes people by booking them and initiating their progress through the judicial system. It also detains those people for varying lengths of time.

In previous research the processing function has been measured through use of rates of bookings per 10,000 county residents. The holding function has been measured using jail average daily population rates (Klofas, 1987, 1988). These measures have been correlated only modestly, indicating that either measure alone provides an inadequate description of the variation in use of jail space. A more complete picture can be obtained by simultaneously considering both the processing and holding functions of jails. To accomplish this a typology was formed based on the possible combinations of ways jail tasks could be performed. By dichotomizing the distributions of the booking rate and average daily population rate, some jails were described as *high-use* jails in that they booked and held county residents at a high rate. *Low-use* jails booked and held residents at a low rate. *Holding jails* had a high average daily population rate but a low rate of bookings. *Processing jails* booked county residents at a high rate while maintaining a low average daily population rate.[1] This typology provides a theoretically based approach to disaggregating jail use that can be used to examine the variability and change over time.

The Data

The data for this study describe jail use in Illinois for the ten-year period from 1977 through 1986. Bookings, average daily population, numbers of sentenced and unsentenced inmates, and other characteristics of the jail populations in the state's 96 county jails were made available by the Illinois Department of Corrections, which exercises some oversight of the state's local jails (Illinois Department of Corrections, 1986). The Cook County Jail, which houses approximately 5,000 inmates—a number equal to that of all other counties combined—was excluded from the analysis as an extreme outlier. Crime data were taken from the Illinois Department of Law Enforcement's annual report, which provides county-by-county crime reports used in the compilation of the Uniform Crime Reports. The offense definitions are the same as those used in the FBI reports. Population figures were taken from the Bureau of the Census and include counties' annual population estimates.

The 1986 data revealed considerable variation in the jail use measures. In the ninety-six jails, 22 percent had an average daily population rate of three or fewer per 10,000 county residents, while 6 percent of the counties had average daily population rates of over 10 per 10,000 county residents in 1986. Booking rates showed similar diversity with 100 or fewer people per 10,000 residents booked into twenty county jails while over 350 per 10,000 were booked into eleven county jails.

The correlation between the average daily population rate and the booking rate in 1986 is .49, or approximately equal to that reported in two previous studies (Klofas, 1987, 1988). This supports the idea that either measure alone is inadequate to describe the variety in jail use and suggests the appropriateness of invoking the jail use typology. It also suggests that when the typology is formed by dichotomizing the distributions, the cells will be filled unequally. Table 3.1 presents the distribution of jails across the types. As expected from previous research, as well as the zero order correlations, the most common patterns are those in which the jails are either high (n = 31) or low (n = 30) on both dimensions. Less common are the mixed types (n = 17 each). The tasks remain-

TABLE 3.1

Typology of Jail Use Patterns, 1986

		Booking Rate	
		Low	*High*
	Low	Low-Use Jails N = 30	Processing Jails N = 17
Jail Population Rate	*High*	Holding Jails N = 17	High-Use Jails N = 31

ing, then, are to examine jail use disaggregated by type, to consider how the use patterns have changed over time, and to investigate how the variability in 1986 can be explained.

Findings

Before examining the disaggregated jail use patterns it is useful to consider the jails' growth patterns when they are all combined. The growth in jail populations, which has been described nationally, is evident when the statewide mean of the jails' average daily population rate is considered. The mean average daily population rate grew from 3.33 per 10,000 in 1977 to 5.17 in 1986 (T = 6.84, sig. = .00). This parallels national findings and has meant an increase in the inmate population of nearly 75 percent. That growth, however, has not been matched by an increase in bookings. The mean booking rate has risen from 179 per 10,000 to 186, but that difference is not statistically significant (T = .59, sig. = .56).

Disaggregating jail use by type reveals a more complex picture of the changes occurring between 1977 and 1986. Figure 3.1 reveals that inmate population increases over that time period are largely due to the dramatic increases in the average daily population rates of the high-use jails and holding jails. As table 3.2 shows, the increases in the average daily population rate were significant at the .00 level for these jail use types. Nevertheless, the changes in the lower-use jails and processing jails were not significant between 1977 and 1986. The consequences of these differences are evident in figure 3.1. Based on the jail types, according to their 1986 use patterns, the gap in population rates across the types grew substantially over the ten years. Those rates were far more similar in 1977 than they were in 1986.

The disaggregated booking figures present a different impression. Figure 3.2 reveals a substantial gap between the high and low booking types, but that gap remains fairly constant over the years. As table 3.2 indicates, the only significant differences are that booking rates for low-use jails dropped marginally over the ten-year period. Increases for high-use jails do, however, approach significance. The minimal differences in booking rate changes across the types are consistent with the finding that the overall mean for the jails did not increase significantly between 1977 and 1986.

These disaggregated patterns provide useful information about how the jails in this study have grown over ten years. First, they indicate that growth has not been uniform. They also suggest that where growth has occurred it has been relatively steady over the period. This is somewhat unexpected. In 1983 there was a significant legislative change in which the Illinois Department of Corrections stopped accepting inmates who were serving sentences of less than one year. Although many jail officials saw this as a major

FIGURE 3.1

Average Daily Population Rate by Year, Disaggregated by Type

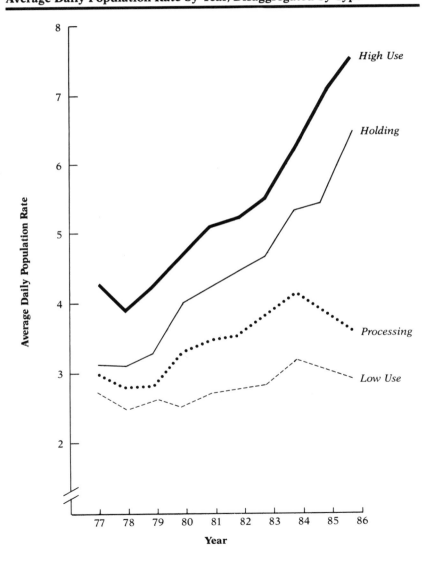

FIGURE 3.2

Booking Rate by Year, Disaggregated by Type

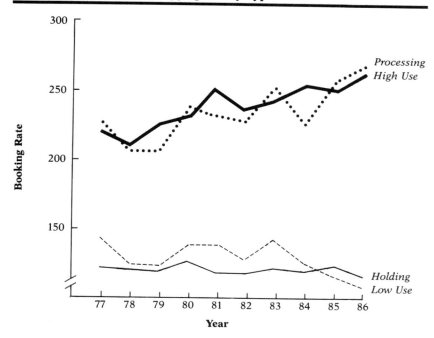

TABLE 3.2

Differences in Jail Population Rates and Booking Rates by Type

	Mean 1986	Diff. of Means (1986–77)	T	Sig. of T
Low-Use Jails				
Average daily pop. rate	2.89	.24	.89	.38
Booking rate	108.85	− 34.28	− 1.97	.05
Processing Jails				
Average daily pop. rate	3.49	.46	1.39	.18
Booking rate	262.81	33.26	1.30	.21
Holding Jails				
Average daily pop. rate	6.52	3.33	8.78	.00
Booking rate	117.55	− 6.43	− .50	.62
High-Use Jails				
Average daily pop. rate	7.57	3.29	6.03	.00
Booking rate	257.18	37.22	1.77	.08

contributor to crowding, these data make it clear that the contribution was in line with a pattern already established. Finally, it is clear that the increases in jail populations do not come from increases in bookings into the jail. It is likely, then, that they do not relate to changes in crime but rather are the result of changes in offender processing after arrest and booking.

Differences across the Jail Use Types

The data discussed indicate that in 1986 there was considerable diversity in jail space usage across the jurisdictions studied. Furthermore this diversity reflects very different growth patterns over the ten-year period. The next task is to consider variables that may be associated with both the 1986 diversity and the changes from 1977.

The variables to be investigated can be grouped into two broad categories, and in each of the categories conditions in 1986 as well as changes in the variables between 1977 and 1986 will be studied. The variables described are those external to the jail in 1986 and those regarded as internal in that they deal with jail size and the distribution of jail populations.

External variables include crime rate, county population, and jail use type in 1977. Debate over the relationship between crime rates and correctional populations continues, although most of the studies involve assessments of prisons (Abt Associates, 1980; Blumstein et al., 1980; McGuire and Sheehan, 1983). Research on the relationship between jailing and crime rates is more limited and also inconclusive. Sykes et al. (1987) used a cross-sectional design and found a small but significant relationship between jail populations and lagged violent crime rates. Irwin (1985), to the contrary, used interviews with newly admitted jail inmates and argued that jails serve no function with regard to control of serious crime. In studies utilizing the jail use typology the finding has been that crime rate is related to jail use patterns, with significant differences found between high- and low-use types.

Table 3.3 replicates the findings of these earlier studies. Analysis of variance reveals significant differences across the types with regard to crime rate. The Student–Newman Keuls procedure (SPSS, Inc., 1986) was used to identify the types that differed at the .05 level. Again the significant difference is between the low- and high-use types. The second part of table 3.3 examines the influence of changes in crime rate over the ten-year period.[2] While types differed somewhat by crime rate in 1986, there were no significant differences in the crime rate between 1977 and 1986 for any of the types.

County population figures also were included in the analysis; the justification for this relates to the use of population as a surrogate for urbanization. Considerable differences have been noted between urban and rural jails (Flynn, 1973; Handberg, 1982; Kerle, 1983; Mays and Thompson, 1988). There also have been historical arguments that many criminal justice resources are used differently between more populous and less populous areas (see Rothman, 1980: 83).

Table 3.3 indicates that there are no significant differences in the county populations across jail use types. While populations of the holding and the processing jails appear quite low compared to the low- and high-use types, these differences are not statistically significant. Likewise the change in population over a period from

TABLE 3.3

Differences in Crime Rate and Population across the Jail-Use Patterns

Part 1: Differences in 1986

Variable	Mean Low Use	Mean Processing	Mean Holding	Mean High Use	F	Sig.	Eta²
Crime Rate	1,860.77	2,272.69	2,150.05	3,526.45	7.58	.00	.20
Population	80,810	44,547	44,700	72,829	.71	.55	.02

Part 2: Change between 1977 and 1986

Variable	Diff of Means (86–77)	T	Sig. of T.
for Low-Use Jails			
Crime rate	− 135.42	.83	.41
Population	5,846.67	1.71	.09
for Processing Jails			
Crime rate	− 45.53	.31	.76
Population	529.41	.41	.69
for Holding Jails			
Crime rate	54.16	.34	.74
Population	− 549.06	− 1.11	.28
for High-Use Jails			
Crime rate	227.57	1.60	.12
Population	− 887.09	− 1.52	.14

TABLE 3.4

Pattern of Use in 1986 by Pattern of Use in 1977

	1977			
1986	Low Use	Processing	Holding	High Use
Low Use	56.6%	12.5%	31.3%	18.8%
Processing	6.7	56.2	6.3	15.6
Holding	20.0	6.3	43.6	6.3
High Use	16.7	25.0	18.8	59.3
	100%	100%	100%	100%
	(30)	(16)	(16)	(33)

Chi Square = 46.40   DF = 9   Sig. = .00
Tau = .32   Sig. = .00

1977 to 1986 is not significant for any of the jail types. Differences in population, then, are not useful in explaining the variety of jail use patterns.

The last of the external variables considered is the county's jail use pattern as it existed in 1977. The purpose of this is to examine further how the jails have changed and grown; that is, whether distribution across types has remained the same and jail population and booking rates have changed uniformly across types or whether there have been changes in the patterns. To examine this question the jail use typology was formed using the 1977 data and bisecting the distributions of average daily population and booking rates at the median as was done with the 1986 data.

Table 3.4 presents the cross tabulation of the 1977 and 1986 jail use patterns. The most prevalent tendency in the data is for the patterns in 1977 to be the same in 1986. This stability is found in 55 percent of the jails, which suggests that counties maintain their jail use patterns over time. The patterns, however, clearly are not immutable: 45 percent of the counties did, in fact, change patterns over the ten years.

Because table 3.4 is based on types formed relative to each other by different cutting points in each of the years, there are limitations to the interpretations. An alternative is to form the typology using absolute rather than relative criteria. Thus a description of the changes can be obtained by standardizing the 1986 patterns using the 1977 cutoffs. (This is the criminal justice equivalent of analyzing budgets in constant dollars.) Cross-tabulation of types using the 1977 cutoffs reveals that the number of high-use jails grew from 30 in 1977 to 54 in 1986 (chi square = 24.39, sig. = .00). For each of the types in 1977 the data reveal a substantial migration toward the high-use pattern. This is true for 30 percent of the 1977 low-use facilities, 69 percent of the processing jails, and 50 percent of the holding jails. Eighty-one percent of the high-use jails maintained their pattern over the ten years. The 1977 low-use jails also show a tendency to become holding jails in 1986; this was the case with 43 percent of the original low-use jails.

Examination of these data using two different approaches to change over time provides insight into how the jails have grown over the ten-year period. When the separate cutting points for 1977 and 1986 are used the data reveal considerable stability in patterns of use. From this it is likely that the earlier pattern will be useful in multivariate efforts to predict type in 1986. When types are standardized by 1977, there is a general escalation pattern of jail use toward the high-use types. Essentially this reflects the increases in average daily population rate over the period. The overall picture to emerge is one of considerable stability with a more or less consistent escalation in jail use. Few jails show any evidence of switching toward low-use or processing types.

Consideration of variables external to the jails in 1986 reveals some significant differences across jail use types. The second broad variable category examined relates to conditions of the jail itself or the processing of offenders. These variables include the capacity rate, percent occupied (as a measure of crowding), average length of stay in days, and the percent of the jail population sentenced.

Capacity rate provides a measure of bedspace per 10,000 county residents. Controversial hypotheses lead to different expectations of the relationship between jail use and capacity. With regard to prisons (Abt Associates, 1980) as well as jails (Cory and Gettinger, 1984) the argument has been made that capacity will drive usage, and as additional cells are built they inevitably will be filled. Research supporting this finding with regard to prison space, however, has been criticized, and the relationship appears to be much less clear (Blumstein et al., 1983).

In these jail data capacity and jail use are related, replicating a finding of a cross-sectional study using a national sample of large jail jurisdictions (Klofas, 1988). As table 3.5 reveals, capacity rate increases monotonically from the low-use jails through the processing jails and holding jails to the high-use jails. These differences, though, do not directly address the question of causality between capacity and jail use. Some insight can be gained, however, by examining the relationship between jail use and crowding, because it is there that dramatic differences are found. The most crowded jails fit the high-use patterns and are followed by the holding jails; low-use jails and processing jails are much less crowded. Taken together these differences indicate that the high-use jails and holding jails have the greatest capacity and at the same time are the most crowded. This finding implies that capacity may indeed drive use with regard to some jails but not others. It suggests that as additional jail space is made available for holding and high-use jails, it is likely to be filled.

Table 3.5 (part 1) presents information on two additional variables. The jail use types differ in 1986 on both average length of stay and on the percentage of the jail population under sentence. This provides some indication of how these jails have achieved the variety of patterns they demonstrate. The two variables show similarities in their distributions across the types. The significant differences are that holding jails are higher than other types on both percent sentenced and average length of stay.

Table 3.5 (part 2) presents information on changes in all of these variables over the ten-year period for each jail use type. These differences mirror the increases in average daily population rate discussed previously. For the low-use jails and processing jails, there are no significant differences in any of the variables over the time period. Differences appear in both the holding and high-use types. Only the difference in the percent sentenced is not significant at the .05 level for the holding jails. For the high-use jails capacity rate approaches significance, and the differences for all other variables are significant.

When the bivariate relationships are examined, the internal variables are more useful than the external variables in discriminating between the types. Among the external variables crime rate was significant but useful only in identifying the high-use jails. Previous use pattern also was related to pattern in 1986. Differences were found according to all of the internal variables, including the changes in those internal variables between 1977 and 1986. Taken together these differences address the question of jail use idiosyncrasy. The fact that internal as well as external variables differ across the types suggests that jail use productively can be understood as varied rather than idiosyncratic. The use types represent real and consistent differences in the ways jail space is used as well as real and consistent differences in the ways jails have grown and changed over ten years. While these differences are evident, the question remains as to how useful they will be in predicting use patterns.

Predicting Patterns of Jail Use

The bivariate relationships indicate that the jail use patterns differ significantly according to a number of variables as measured in 1986 as well as changes noted in several variables over time. We

TABLE 3.5

Differences in Internal Jail Variables across the Jail-Use Patterns

Part 1: Differences in 1986

Variable	Mean Low Use	Mean Processing	Mean Holding	Mean High Use	F	Sig.	Eta²
Capacity Rate	8.11	10.26	10.74	11.17	3.14	.03	.09
% Occupied	43.45	41.97	65.57	71.89	8.94	.00	.23
Average Days	10.10	6.94	21.82	10.94	21.12	.00	.41
% Sentenced	25.87	29.41	49.53	31.84	5.09	.00	.14

Part 2: Change between 1977 and 1986

Variable	Diff. of Means (1986–77)	T	Sig. of T.
for Low-Use Jails			
Capacity rate	−1.21	1.71	.09
% occupied	5.86	1.69	.10
Average days	2.17	1.76	.09
% sentenced	.37	.15	.89
for Processing Jails			
Capacity rate	.25	.59	.56
% occupied	7.26	1.46	.16
Average days	1.65	.87	.37
% sentenced	3.06	.76	.46
for Holding Jails			
Capacity rate	1.72	2.78	.01
% occupied	25.85	4.92	.00
Average days	11.44	6.30	.00
% sentenced	10.56	1.63	.12
for High-Use Jails			
Capacity rate	1.62	1.90	.06
% occupied	23.41	5.71	.00
Average days	3.19	4.93	.00
% sentenced	6.64	2.80	.01

can now turn to multivariate analysis to examine the combined effects of these variables. Because we have a categorical dependent variable and ordinal or interval level independent variables, discriminant function analysis can be used to examine how successfully the jail use patterns can be predicted. Under these circumstances the method has an interpretation very similar to multiple-regression analysis (Hair et al., 1979; Klecka, 1980). Like regression analysis, discriminant function analysis is sensitive to multicolinearity problems. Because average days in 1986 and the change in average days correlated at a level beyond .65, the difference variable was excluded from the analysis. The remainder of the internal and external variables were included. Jail use type in 1977 was entered as a dummy variable.

The results of the discriminant analysis are shown in table 3.6. Interpretation of the results of this analysis begins with the significance of the functions (part 1). The analyses produce three functions, and all are significant at the .05 level (part 2). Furthermore, examination of Wilk's Lambda, which is interpreted as an inverse measure, shows that all of the functions make substantial contributions although the first and second are by far the most powerful.

Since the functions are significant we now can examine their power at discriminating among jail use types. Part 3 of table 3.6 presents the classification results from the analysis. If jails were evenly distributed across the types we would expect proper classification of 25 percent of the jails simply due to chance; that expectation is raised to 27 percent due to the uneven distribution of jails. In fact the variables permit proper classification of 71.28 percent of the jails, which means that knowing the values of the internal and external variables permits a reduction in classification errors of more than 60 percent over chance. Part 3 of table 3.6 also reveals that the functions are relatively efficient at properly classifying the jails into each type. That efficiency is lowest for holding jails, where 25 percent of those jails are misclassified as low use.

Having examined the statistical significance of the functions and found the classification accuracy to be quite high, we can consider the relative importance of the independent variables. Part 2 of table 3.6 presents the discriminant weights for each variable. The interpretation of these weights is similar to the interpretation of beta weights in regression. In this case, because the first two functions are the most powerful we will concentrate on their coefficients. Based on their standardized weights the most important variables on function 1 are the measure of change in percent occu-

TABLE 3.6

Predicting the 1986 Jail-Use Patterns through Discriminant Analysis

Part 1: Canonical Discriminant Functions

Func	Eigen-value	Percent of Variance	Cumulative Percent	Canonical Correlation
1	1.29	51.01	51.01	.75
2	.98	39.00	90.02	.70
3	.25	9.98	100.00	.45

After Func	Wilk's Lambda		Sig. of Chi Square
0	.17		.00
1	.40		.00
2	.80		.02

Part 2: Standardized Canonical Discriminant Function Coefficients

	Func 1	Func 2	Func 3
Crime Rate 1986	.54	−.25	−.01
Holding 1977	.45	−.47	.83
Processing 1977	.09	.21	.47
High Use 1977	.58	−.08	.21
Diff. in Capacity Rate	.29	.20	.44
Diff. in % Occupied	.75	.16	.49
Diff. in % Sentenced	.04	.03	−.26
Capacity Rate 1986	.55	−.28	−.24
% Occupied 1986	.11	.03	−.85
Average Days 1986	−.07	.83	.15
% Sentenced 1986	.37	−.01	.41

Part 3: Classification Results

		Predicted Type			
Actual Type	N	1	2	3	4
Low Use	30	80.0%	10.0%	6.7%	3.3%
Processing	17	11.8	64.7	5.9	17.6
Holding	17	25.0	6.3	56.3	12.5
High Use	31	9.7	9.7	6.5	74.2

Percent of cases correctly classified: 71.28

pied between 1977 and 1986, the capacity rate in 1986, the crime rate, and the type in 1977. On function 2, average length of stay and type in 1977 are most important.

Table 3.6 provides additional information that questions the view of jail use as idiosyncratic. When the internal and external variables are taken together and significant measures of change in those variables are included, a very high proportion of the jail use types in 1986 could be predicted. As might be expected, the use pattern exhibited ten years earlier remains an important predictor variable. One surprise continues to be the role of the crime rate. While jails must deal with offenders of all seriousness levels, it is clear that the broad discretion that defines the jail population is influenced by the level of serious crime even when the other variables are included in the analysis. The role of crime is by no means clear, however, because capacity and increases in crowding also prove important predictors of jail use. When external and internal variables are considered as well as changes in those variables over time, it is clear that jail use, as measured by broad types, can be predicted with some accuracy but that it is also the result of a complex combination of variables.

Summary

Jails reflect the diversity of a criminal justice system administered primarily at the local level. Policy research has been attentive to jail differences and, through the use of individualized analysis and case study, has made important contributions to understanding and addressing problems such as jail crowding. There also are benefits to comparative methods that identify similarities as well as differences and attempt to explain them. This research has replicated and extended earlier studies of how jail space is used across local jurisdictions. Following are the principal findings of the studies.

1. Jail use can be thought of as varied rather than idiosyncratic. Patterns can be described that reveal consistent differences across the jails, and a high degree of success can be achieved in predicting those patterns from a combination of internal and external variables.
2. Jail growth has not been monolithic. When disaggregated by jail use type, the data reveal that some jurisdictions have been much more successful than others in controlling jail population growth. Furthermore, where growth has occurred

it has not been the result of increases in the jails' admissions rates. Instead it has been linked to increases in the proportion of the jail population serving sentences and to increases in inmates' length of stay.

3. Crime plays a significant but relatively modest role in explaining differences in jail use. When measured using Uniform Crime Report definitions, crime rates distinguish only between the high- and low-use jail types.

4. Crowding is not simply a function of available space but is related to jail use patterns. Holding and high-use jails are the most crowded, and these facilities also are the largest. The assertion that capacity influences jail use, therefore, seems neither universally true nor false. It is, instead, supported among high-use and holding facilities but not among the low-use or processing jails.

5. The use patterns remain relatively stable over time. They seem to represent consistent and enduring patterns of decision making throughout local criminal justice systems, and they may represent differences in community social control approaches.

Policy Implications

The crowding crisis dominates local corrections today, and the ability of jail resource management to control crowding has become a necessary measure of effectiveness. Policy with regard to jails often has come to mean the implementation of strategies to reduce crowding. The risk, of course, is that capacity considerations can drive policy in this area. This potential danger is equally present for those policies that reduce the number of inmates and those policies that expand jails to reduce crowding.

Along with the emergency response to crowding there is a need to engage in more systematic policy formulation efforts. These efforts should be data based and take into account local criminal justice goals and local social control interests. This study suggests one such approach to policy development with regard to local jails: comparative analysis involving systematic study of the costs and benefits of different patterns of jail use.

If jail resource management is an important policy consideration, this research indicates that some jurisdictions have established more effective patterns than others. There is a need, then, to recognize differences in jurisdictions' abilities to cope in the crisis climate currently engulfing local jails. Along with this is the need to augment research focused on providing immediate relief to the most crowded facilities with studies of the most successful coping efforts. This implies the development of a knowledge base built on comparative analyses. To guide policy those analyses must be directed at describing and explaining differences in jail space usage. They must investigate the specific factors enabling jurisdictions to maintain different jail use patterns, and they must facilitate discussion of whether those factors form an appropriate basis for policy to guide local corrections in other areas.

NOTES

1. For a complete description of the theoretical and empirical basis for this typology see Klofas (1988). For a revision of the typology applied to data from another state see Gido and Slater (1989).

2. The distributions of all the independent variables were examined to be certain that this approach to differences did not misrepresent the patterns over the ten-year period.

HEALTH AND SAFETY IN THE AMERICAN JAIL

Because jails are complex institutions, they have complex problems. Two of the most difficult are how to provide relatively safe housing within an inherently unsafe environment and how to provide inmates with necessary treatment programs. Jails are unsafe because they provide short-term housing for a diverse population, including some who have been judged to be a threat to themselves or society. This situation is compounded in that it has been estimated that as many as two-thirds of this population may be suffering from psychological disorders. Added to these are other health concerns: physical abuse prior to arrest or by other inmates after incarceration, the ever-present threat of suicide, and problems posed by the spread of illness and/or contagious disease. The confluence of these factors creates a real challenge for local jail administrators as they attempt to provide a safe and humane environment for inmates.

A serious question to be considered in relation to the jail environment is whether jail deaths are related to organizational and programmatic differences of local facilities or essentially a reflection of mortality in society at large. Using data from the 1978 and

1983 jail censuses, L. Thomas Winfree and John Wooldredge explore this question in chapter 4. They find no overwhelming evidence to suggest that deaths from suicides or natural causes are related to jail variables. However, they do find some evidence to suggest that the sheer volume of admissions and releases and the lack of adequate staff create greater opportunities for jail deaths. They recommend that *jailer training* be structured so as to create greater awareness of inmate needs during critical periods of incarceration, include greater emphasis on suicide prevention, and that policies be developed specifically for short-term detainees.

Mental health services are the focus of the next two selections in this section. David Kalinich and his colleagues note that, as is the case with other programs and services, jails "have little choice but to be in the business of providing mental health services to inmates manifesting such needs." This task is complicated by a number of things: imprecise legal standards, ambiguous legislative mandates, organizational inertia, staff reluctance and resistance to change, and the public's perception of the role of the local jail. Kalinich et al. recommend several changes that are necessary if jail administrators are to recognize their obligation that "inmates have a right to leave the jail in no worse physical and psychological condition than they possessed upon booking."

Mental health services present a number of policy questions: What is the nature and extent of the problem? Can these services be delivered effectively within the limitations of the jail environment? What is the most cost-effective way to deliver these services? These and other policy issues are discussed by Jeanette Jerrell and Richard Komisaruk. They relate their experiences in studying the mental health problem in Santa Clara, California, and developing programs to address the needs of the jail system.

A final health and safety issue to be addressed in this section is perhaps the most salient: Acquired Immunodeficiency Syndrome, or AIDS. The problem of AIDS poses a particularly acute challenge to corrections officials because of the significant intravenous drug use and homosexual activity occurring in confinement. Recent studies indicate that about 4 percent of the jail/ prison population is infected with AIDS, but in some locations the infection rate is much higher, reaching over 17 percent in one New York City jail. From all indications, this problem will continue to grow unless effective means are developed to identify and treat AIDS-infected inmates. In chapter 7 James Lawrence and Van Zwisohn review the development of AIDS-related programs in the state of New York and offer a number of recommendations for corrections officials. They conclude that adequate management of this problem will require "a cooperative, collegial effort among administrators, security personnel, program staff and medical care providers. An environment free of ignorance, fear and hostility is essential."

Health and safety issues always will plague jails. The questions for the future will be: How many inmates will need services? What will their problems be? How can jails best deal with health problems that would be critical even in a free society and thus are more serious in a confined environment?

CHAPTER 4

Exploring Suicides and Deaths by Natural Causes in America's Large Jails: A Panel Study of Institutional Change, 1978 and 1983

L. THOMAS WINFREE, JR. AND
JOHN D. WOOLDREDGE

Conditions of life and death in America's local jails have so dehumanized what was already a degrading experience that these facilities have been described as "the crucibles of crime" (Fishman, 1923) and, more recently, "the poorhouse of the twentieth century" (Goldfarb, 1975). Bowker (1982: 319) succinctly observes that "[i]dleness, overcrowding, deteriorating physical facilities, inadequate medical and psychiatric treatment, and the psychological stress associated with rapid changes in status all contribute to the instability and negative social climate existing in many jails."

Beginning in the late 1970s four sets of interrelated factors placed increasing pressure on America's local jails, pressure that often resulted in major organizational, policy, and management changes for individual institutions. For example, since 1981 vigorous enforcement of the nation's driving under the influence (DUI)

This research was supported in part by Purchase Order #OJP-85-M-385, National Institute of Justice, U.S. Department of Justice. Points of view or opinions stated in this paper are those of the authors and do not necessarily represent the official position of the Justice Department or its employees. The authors would like to acknowledge the editorial and general comments provided by Joel Thompson and G. Larry Mays. Any shortcomings in this chapter, however, are the sole domain of the authors.

laws and the enactment of new legislation by a number of states have resulted in increased jailing of "drunk drivers," a fact that was clearly evident in as little as three years (National Institute of Justice [NIJ], 1984). Individuals confined to jail for such offenses are, according to most jail suicide prevention profiles, high-risk suicide candidates because they have suffered both from depression and anxiety, coupled with alcohol or drug use (Kennedy, 1983, 1984; Kennedy and Homant, 1988). Moreover, mandatory confinement laws for those persons convicted of driving under the influence of drugs and alcohol have strained the existing resources of local institutions for short-term confinement (NIJ, 1984).

Second, the "alternative institutionalizing" thesis advanced by mental health experts (Price and Smith, 1985; Steadman et al., 1978, 1984) suggests that since the late 1970s the mental health decarceration movement reached fever pitch as tens of thousands of former and potential mental patients were removed from or kept out of the nation's state mental hospitals (Scull, 1981, 1984; Price and Smith, 1985; Lamb, 1984). At the same time, the percentage of the total jail population that suffered from mental illness, while always fairly high, increased dramatically (Bonovitz and Guy, 1979; Guy et al., 1985; Steadman et al., 1978; Wiehn, 1982). It also should be borne in mind that deinstitutionalized mentally ill persons not only are more prone to suicide than the general population, but their proactive health care may be worse than the average jail inmate (Guy et al., 1985; Lombardo, 1981; Steadman et al., 1984; Winfree, 1988; see too Altman, 1983; Dennis, 1980; Feldman, 1982; Glasgow, 1979; Rogers, 1984). As Belcher observed (1988: 193):

> Wandering aimlessly in the community, psychotic much of the time, and unable to manage their internal control systems [these chronically homeless, previously institutionalized mentally ill persons] found the criminal justice system was an asylum of the last resort.

It has been estimated that as many as two-thirds of all jail inmates suffer from clinically mild to severe psychological disorders (Guy et al., 1985). Steadman et al. (1984: 488) also suggest that the nation's jails, and not its prison system, have become the temporary asylum for the mentally ill. Quite possibly the influx of mentally ill individuals, individuals more prone to suicidal behavior than the average citizen incarcerated in jail, offsets any attempts by jail administrators to reduce the number of suicides by more precise inmate screening or improved health-care resources

(Steadman et al., 1984; see too Dougherty, 1984; Bowker, 1982; Hayes, 1983). Jails as total institutions are ill-equipped to deal with the special problems of the mentally ill; jail administrators rarely understand the breadth of problems associated with supervising a mentally ill clientele; and jail workers may be resistant to any changes in their work habits or their supervisors' performance expectations (Belcher, 1988; Pogrebin and Regoli, 1985; Teplin, 1983). Whatever the specific mechanisms at work, there can be little doubt that deinstitutionalization further depleted the limited resources of America's jails.

In the minds of many observers of the American jail scene, however, the most significant single force for change has come not so much from increased enforcement of DUI laws or deinstitutionalization of the mentally ill; rather it has been a product of jail crowding and an active judiciary (Kalinich and Postill, 1981; Kerle, 1983; Newman, 1978; Schmidt, 1985; Singer, 1972). The nation's courts have had little choice but to enforce the DUI laws with their mandatory jail sentences, as they were constitutionally viable pieces of legislation demanded by particularly vocal segments of an outraged populace. Furthermore, it was the Supreme Court that in *O'Connor v. Donaldson*, 422 U.S. 563 (1975) set the forces in motion to deinstitutionalize mental patients (see, too, *Wyatt v. Stickney*, 503 F. 2d 1305, 5th Cir. (1974); Stone, 1975). However, when it came to prison and jail living conditions, particularly health and safety standards, the federal courts began to show lower tolerance for the questionable practices of the past and heightened activism by the late 1970s (Bolduc, 1985; Toch, 1982; Winfree, 1987, 1988).

Indeed, judicial intervention on jail inmates' behalf is a relatively recent phenomenon. As late as 1977, American jails were relatively free of judicial interference. In 1978 the Supreme Court ruled in *Monell v. Department of Social Service*, 436 U.S. 690 (1978) that units of local government could be sued when jail inmates' and police suspects' rights were abrogated. A year later *Bell v. Wolfish*, 441 U.S. 520 (1979) was decided; as a consequence, inmates could no longer be denied adequate health care for any reason, including the fiscal shortfalls of local governments, because such denial constituted cruel and unusual punishment. By the early 1980s hundreds of jails in nearly three dozen states were under court order due to either crowding or inhuman living conditions (Anonymous, 1978; Bamonte, 1981; Bolduc, 1985; Reynolds and Tonry, 1981). In fact, Kerle and Ford (1982) reported that in 1982, over 10 percent of the jails in their survey were under court order for some condition including crowding, almost 20 percent had been under such a court order at some time in the past, and a final 20 percent faced pending lawsuits.

Despite various strategies to alleviate jail crowding, educate judges and the like, America's jail population continues to increase (Bolduc, 1985; Guynes, 1988; Hall, 1987). More people are forced into the same or fewer bed spaces and provided with more labor-intensive services—all funded by a shrinking tax base. This is the challenge facing administrators of local jails in the 1980s and beyond. It comes as no surprise, therefore, that crowding and staffing needs were the two highest ranked "most serious problems" in a recent survey of jail managers (Guynes, 1988).

These are problems for jail managers, no doubt; but what about the ultimate problem for a jail inmate, the prospect of dying in jail? In a state-level study of such highly visible jail problems as suicides and deaths by natural causes—both of which can create additional litigious and public relations problems for units of local government—it was reported that in 1983 the number of such deaths was largely unrelated to crowding and personnel ratios; they also were unrelated to other structural characteristics of the nation's jails. However, in these same states five years earlier many of these same structural variables provided considerable insights into deaths by suicide and deaths by natural causes (Winfree, 1987). While both modes of dying were ultimately described as basic demographic features of American jails, it was suggested that court-induced change may have been responsible for the diminished role of the structural variables in 1983 as compared to 1978. Unfortunately, the cross-sectional, aggregate-level analysis employed in the study was incapable of confirming these latter speculations.

It is toward the relative impact of organizational change that the present study now turns. In particular we are interested in knowing the extent to which changes in jail organizational goals, staffing patterns, initial screening and medical examinations, general health care resources, levels of crowding, average population, and turnover rate (all of which have been linked to problems of running jails by previous researchers) are related to increases or decreases in suicide and natural death probabilities in individual jails. To this end we focus on the following question: Is the increased or decreased probability of dying by one's own hand or by natural causes in jail a largely random occurrence, or is it discernibly related to recent changes in the organizational makeup of jails?

Methods

The Samples and the Data

The information necessary to answer the question posed exists within recent National Jail Census data collected and disseminated by the Bureau of Justice Statistics (BJS), through the auspices of the Inter-university Consortium for Political and Social Research. If it was as easy as simply calling forth a cross tabulation or frequency distribution from a data tape, there would be no need for this particular secondary analysis. Indeed the realities of the data sets necessitated using several logical delimiters to pare down what best can be described as a morass of data. First, only the 1978 and 1983 census data were evaluated. The instruments used in the 1970 and 1972 censuses were considerably different from those used in the most recent one, resulting in a paucity of comparable data across all four censuses. Second, the present study only addressed deaths among the adult male jail populations. (More than 90 percent of all inmates in local jails are adult males. To include the relatively small number of females or juveniles would have unnecessarily confounded the analysis.)

The 1978 and 1983 censuses of all local jails in America—or those facilities that held inmates beyond arraignment, a period which normally exceeded 48 hours, and facilities that were administered and staffed by local officials—were fairly successful. The 1978 census included information on 3,493 local jails, or in excess of 99 percent of those initially contacted. Five-and-one-half years later the Bureau of the Census, under the auspices of the BJS, reported a similar response rate, with a total of 3,358 local jails participating in the census.[1]

The final delimiter involved the size of the jails considered in the analysis. Previous researchers have observed that there is great variance in jail size, a fact that complicates jail research (Flynn, 1973; Mattick, 1974; Handberg, 1982; Klofas, 1987). To take this observation into account, the present study included all city and county jails in the United States with rated capacities of one hundred fifty to five hundred inmates in 1978. All of these jails were located in Standard Metropolitan Statistical Areas (SMSAs). Rural jails and those in the most urbanized areas of the country (e.g., New York, Los Angeles, Chicago) were excluded from the sample to enhance the study's reliability.[2] The frequency distribution of the rated capacities for all jails in the country is highly skewed toward jails in the most urbanized areas, which might have biased the regression coefficients in the analysis if these urban jails had been included in the sample. To the contrary, rural jails' rated capacities are so low that the measures of jail crowding and population turnover would have produced extremely tenuous values for these jails. For example, a rural jail might have been assigned a value of 1.10 for the degree of jail crowding, suggesting that the jail was operating at 10 percent over its rated capacity in 1978. However, the rated capacity might have been only 10 to begin with, so the value of 1.10 would have resulted from the jail being only one inmate over the rated capacity.

The figure of 150 was chosen as the lowest rated capacity for the sample because the value for the ratio variables become much more reliable around this point. The upper limit for the rated capacity was drawn at 500 to exclude jails in the most urbanized areas (the largest SMSAs) of the country. Only 1 percent of all U.S. jails have rated capacities above five hundred, yet these "mega-jails," many of which have rated capacities greater than the prison systems of some states, house more than 25 percent of the country's jail population. As a consequence, the sample consisted of 180 jails that would be classified by most objective standards as "medium-large" to "large" and urban. At the same time, these jails are neither the nation's largest nor most urban. The study's results are valid only for these types of jails.

Variable Measurements

Suicide and death by natural causes occurred in roughly 20 percent of the jails in the sample during 1978–83. Jails with more than one such death were far more uncommon (about 5 percent of the sample). The skewed distribution of the numbers of suicides and natural deaths prevented the examination of dependent variables which tapped variations in the absolute numbers of deaths. Instead, dichotomous dummy variables were constructed as the dependent variables for the analysis. Two dependent variables were constructed to examine changes in suicide probabilities between 1978 and 1983. Similarly, two dependent variables were constructed to examine changes in natural death probabilities over time.

The first suicide variable consisted of a comparison among jails with an increase in suicide probabilities over time (no suicides occurred in 1978, but they did occur in 1983) versus all other jails in the sample (suicides did or did not occur during both years examined, or suicide probabilities declined over the period). The second dependent variable involved a comparison between jails with a decrease in suicide probabilities over time versus all other jails in the sample. An examination of both variables revealed the changes in jail characteristics, which were important for increasing and decreasing suicide probabilities over time:

(1) increase in suicide probabilities:
   0 = no change or decrease in suicide probabilities
   1 = increase in suicide probabilities
(2) decrease in suicide probabilities:
   0 = no change or increase in suicide probabilities
   1 = decrease in suicide probabilities

The dependent variables used to examine natural deaths were constructed in the same fashion as those for suicides. Jails with an increase in natural death probabilities were compared with all other jails, and those with a decrease in natural death probabilities were compared with all others:

(3) increase in natural death probabilities:
   0 = no change or decrease in natural death probabilities
   1 = increase in natural death probabilities
(4) decrease in natural death probabilities:
   0 = no change or increase in natural death probabilities
   1 = decrease in natural death probabilities

The independent variables included in the analysis consisted of (1) the average jail population for the period 1978–83, (2) whether the jail changed from holding both adults and juveniles to holding adults only, (3) whether the jail changed from holding both males and females to holding males only, (4) the change in the degree of jail crowding, (5) the change in the annual population turnover rate, and (6) the change in the ratio of full-time staff to jail population.

The average jail population for the period 1978–83 was measured as an average of the daily population of the jail during 1978 and 1983:

$$(5) \text{ average jail population} = \frac{\text{average daily jail population: 1978} + \text{average daily jail population: 1983}}{2}$$

Whether jails changed from holding both adults and juveniles to adults only and whether jails changed from holding both males and females to holding males only was the basis for conducting dichotomous dummy variables:

(6) Change to an adult-only facility:
  0 = no such change
  1 = change to an adult-only facility
(7) Change to a male-only facility:
  0 = no such change
  1 = change to a male-only facility

If a jail was an adult-only facility or a male-only facility in 1978, it received a value of zero on the specific measure (i.e., no "change" occurred).

The change in the degree of jail crowding between 1978 and 1983 was measured as the difference between the degree the jail's population was under or over its rated capacity in 1983 and the degree the jail's population was under or over its rated capacity in 1978:

$$
\begin{array}{l}
\text{(8) change in} \\
\quad \text{the degree of} \\
\quad \text{jail crowding}
\end{array}
=
\frac{\text{average daily jail population: 1983}}{\text{jail's rated capacity: 1983}}
-
\frac{\text{average daily jail population: 1978}}{\text{jail's rated capacity: 1978}}
$$

The change in the annual population turnover rate between 1978 and 1983 was measured as the difference between the two annual rates:

$$
\begin{array}{l}
\text{(9) change in} \\
\quad \text{the population} \\
\quad \text{turnover rate}
\end{array}
=
\frac{\text{average daily jail population: 1978}}{\text{total releases from jail: 1978}}
-
\frac{\text{average daily jail population: 1983}}{\text{total releases from jail: 1983}}
$$

Given the construction of this variable, smaller values on each component corresponded with higher turnover rates. Negative values for the variable therefore corresponded with a decrease in annual turnover rates over time, and positive values corresponded with an increase in annual turnover rates.

The change in the full-time staff to the jail population ratio between 1978 and 1983 was measured as the difference between the two annual ratios:

(10) change in the ratio
of full-time staff to =
the jail population
$$\frac{\text{full-time staff: 1983}}{\text{average daily jail population: 1983}} - \frac{\text{full-time staff: 1978}}{\text{average daily jail population: 1978}}$$

Negative values on this variable corresponded with a decrease in the ratio over time, and positive values corresponded with an increase over time.

Other independent variables considered for inclusion in the complete model consisted of the change in the average daily jail population between 1978 and 1983, changes in the availability of doctors and nurses in the jail, changes in the existence of particu-

TABLE 4.1

Descriptive Statistics for All Variables in the Analysis

Variable	Mean	Std. Dev.	Minimum	Maximum
Dependent				
Increase in Suicide Probabilities	0.128	0.335	0.000	1.000
Decrease in Suicide Probabilities	0.172	0.379	0.000	1.000
Increase in Natural Death Probabilities	0.139	0.347	0.000	1.000
Decrease in Natural Death Probabilities	0.100	0.301	0.000	1.000
Independent				
Average Jail Population	235.497	101.191	61.500	549.000
Change to an Adult-Only Facility	0.250	0.434	0.000	1.000
Change to a Male-Only Facility	0.233	0.424	0.000	1.000
Change in the Degree of Jail Crowding	0.257	0.256	−0.329	0.994
Change in the Population Turnover Rates	0.017	0.098	−0.095	0.977
Change in the Ratio of Full-Time Staff to Inmates	−0.081	0.154	−0.660	0.428

lar medical facilities in the jail, and changes in the existence of particular medical tests. These variables were highly correlated with two of the variables included in the final analysis. Specifically, all of them were highly correlated with the average jail population for the period 1978–83, and the change in the full-time staff to the jail population ratio (r>.73). Simply put, larger jail populations and increases in the full-time staff to the jail population ratio correlated with an increase in jail populations over time, greater availability of nurses and doctors, an increase in particular medical facilities, and a greater use of particular medical tests. The second group of variables was omitted from the final analysis to avoid problems with multicollinearity. Table 4.1 presents the descriptive statistics for all of the variables included in the final analysis.

Methods of Analysis

The "change" variables tapped changes in the jails' characteristics during a five-year period. Logit regression, designed to provide regression coefficients for dichotomous dependent variables with possibly skewed marginal distributions, was the analytical method used for the study. The independent variables in a logit regression model may be continuous *only* or a *combination* of continuous and dichotomous variables. This study included a combination of both.

Results and Discussion

Table 4.2 presents the logit regression coefficients for the models predicting changes in suicide probabilities between 1978 and 1983. Part 1 of table 4.2 presents results for the model predicting whether suicide probabilities increased during the five-year period, and part 2 presents the results for the model predicting whether these probabilities decreased during this period.

The results in table 4.2, Part 1, suggest that jails that changed from holding both adults and juveniles in 1978 to holding adults only in 1983 were more likely to have experienced an increase in suicide probabilities over time compared with jails that did not change to adult-only facilities. Also, jails where the full-time staff to the jail population ratio decreased over this period were more likely to experience an increase in suicide probabilities compared with jails where the ratio remained constant or increased. The other independent variables were statistically insignificant for predicting whether suicide probabilities increased over time.

Jails that changed to holding adults only might have experienced an increase in the likelihood of suicide simply because young adults are at a higher risk of committing suicide than teenagers. By increasing the pool of higher risk individuals in jail, the chances of suicide occurring are increased simply by the laws of probability.

The finding that jails with a decrease in the full-time staff to

TABLE 4.2

Results for the Logit Models Predicting Variations in Suicide Probabilities

Part 1. Dependent Variable: Whether Suicide Probabilities Increased between 1978 and 1983

Predictors	Beta	Chi-square	Probability
Average Jail Population	0.634	0.81	.3682
Change to an Adult-Only Facility	1.092**	4.53	.0333
Change to a Male-Only Facility	0.785	2.05	.1521
Change in the Degree of Jail Crowding	0.670	0.81	.3668
Change in the Population Turnover Rate	−0.334	0.14	.7109
Change in the Ratio of Full-Time Staff to Inmates	−1.317*	2.59	.1073

Part 2. Dependent Variable: Whether Suicide Probabilities Decreased between 1978 and 1983

Predictors	Beta	Chi-square	Probability
Average Jail Population	1.036**	3.86	.0493
Change to an Adult-Only Facility	−0.383	0.60	.4385
Change to a Male-Only Facility	−1.051*	3.02	.0825
Change in the Degree of Jail Crowding	−0.690	1.21	.2712
Change in the Population Turnover Rate	−0.306	0.14	.7131
Change in the Ratio of Full-Time Staff to Inmates	1.013*	3.09	.0789

* significant at the .10 level
** significant at the .05 level

the jail population ratio over time experienced an increase in the likelihood of suicide suggests that "successful" jail suicides are a matter of opportunity. With fewer full-time staff available relative to the inmate population size, chances are greater than attempted suicides will be successful simply because fewer staff are available to prevent the opportunity from arising. The results in part 2 of table 4.2 support this idea further. Here we find that an increase in the full-time staff to the jail population ratio over time corresponded with a decline in suicide likelihood.

Table 4.2, part 2, also reveals that jails that did not change from holding both males and females to holding males only were more likely to experience a decline in suicide likelihood over time compared with jails that did change to male-only facilities. This suggests that there was a trend toward declining suicide probabilities over time in jails holding both males and females. This trend cannot be explained by differences in suicide rates between gender groups over time, because both of these rates have increased (especially for females). The source of this trend must lie elsewhere.

A separate analysis revealed that jails that held both males and females between 1978 and 1983 experienced a significantly greater decrease in the annual population turnover rate compared with jails that changed to male-only facilities. In other words, the decrease in the population turnover rate could have caused the decline in suicide probabilities over time for the male/female facilities. The zero-order correlation between the change in the population turnover rate and the decline in suicide probabilities was negative and significant at the 0.01 level. Whether jails changed to male-only facilities could have proxied the effect of changes in the population turnover rate. If so, this implies that jails that experienced reductions in their population turnover rates were more likely to have experienced reductions in suicide probabilities over time. This supports further the idea that jail suicides are shaped to some extent by the laws of probability. Given that jail suicides are most likely to occur during the first week of incarceration, a decrease in the number of inmates "passing through" a jail in a given year would decrease suicide likelihood.

Table 4.3 presents the logit regression coefficients for the models predicting changes in natural death probabilities between 1978 and 1983. Part 1 presents results for the model predicting whether natural death probabilities increased during the five-year period, and part 2 presents the results for the model predicting whether these probabilities decreased during this period.

The part 1 results suggest that no changes in the jails' characteristics were significant predictors of whether natural death probabilities increased over time. This is encouraging because it implies that nothing was changed to increase an inmate's likelihood of dying from natural causes during this period. However, some changes did occur that actually reduced the likelihood of natural deaths during this period (see table 4.3, part 2). Specifically, jails that experienced reductions in the degree of jail crowding

TABLE 4.3

Results for the Logit Models Predicting Variations in Natural Death Probabilities

Part 1. Dependent Variable: Whether Natural Death Probabilities Increased between 1978 and 1983

Predictors	Beta	Chi-square	Probability
Average Jail Population	0.140	0.05	.8309
Change to an Adult-Only Facility	0.305	0.36	.5460
Change to a Male-Only Facility	0.441	0.73	.3920
Change in the Degree of Jail Crowding	−0.635	0.79	.3728
Change in the Population Turnover Rate	0.563	0.40	.5280
Change in the Ratio of Full-Time Staff to Inmates	−0.851	1.41	.2358

Part 2. Dependent Variable: Whether Natural Death Probabilities Decreased between 1978 and 1983

Predictors	Beta	Chi-square	Probability
Average Jail Population	0.299	0.11	.7371
Change to an Adult-Only Facility	−0.410	0.43	.5122
Change to a Male-Only Facility	−1.966*	3.17	.0751
Change in the Degree of Jail Crowding	−2.695**	6.22	.0126
Change in the Population Turnover Rate	−0.310	0.12	.7324
Change in the Ratio of Full-Time Staff to Inmates	−1.171	1.44	.2301

* significant at the .10 level
** significant at the .05 level

over time were more likely to have experienced reductions in the likelihood of natural deaths compared with jails where the degree of crowding remained constant or increased. This supports the idea that jail environments may have an affect on the likelihood of natural deaths (i.e., "better" conditions of confinement may reduce this likelihood significantly).

The only other significant predictor of reductions in natural death probabilities was whether a jail changed from holding males and females to holding males only between 1978 and 1983. Jails that did not change to male-only facilities were more likely to experience a reduction in the likelihood of natural deaths compared with jails that did change. Because natural death probabilities did not change significantly for the general male and female populations during this period, the reason for this relationship must lie elsewhere. As mentioned previously, this variable was correlated with the change in the population turnover rate. The change in population turnover was also significantly correlated with the decline in natural death probabilities (p = 0.05). Therefore the change in the population turnover rate could have been the true cause of the change in the likelihood of natural deaths over time. A decrease in the annual population turnover rate could have caused a reduction in the likelihood of natural deaths simply by reducing the pool of potential "victims" in jail (similar to the explanation for suicides).

Summary

Increased and decreased probabilities of suicides or deaths by natural causes were not impacted in consistent ways by changes in personnel patterns (ratio of full-time staff to inmates), jail clientele (male only, adult only), levels of crowding, or turnover rates of the large jails included in the analysis. Overall, the analysis mitigates toward viewing death in jail as a somewhat random, demographic phenomenon, certainly a highly probabilistic occurrence.

This overarching generalization, however, does not mean that there were no significant relationships between suicide or death by natural causes and the institutional changes. It also does not free jails of moral and legal obligations to provide for inmates' medical and psychological needs. Two findings related to suicide seem particularly enlightening. First, jailhouse suicides may be a matter of opportunity: fewer full-time staff available relative to the size of the inmate population were linked to greater chances of increased suicides over time simply because fewer staff are available to prevent the opportunity from arising. Second, it was observed that where there was a decrease in the number of inmates "passing through" jails, there was a concomitant decrease in the likelihood of suicide. Collectively these findings support the conclusions of Kennedy and Homant (1988: 453), who suggest that extra awareness of inmates' needs during this critical time, awareness that is labor-intensive, may lower the suicide rate by (in our terminology) lowering the opportunity. Another suggestion flowing from the present analysis is that if the number of jail inmates who are just "passing through" (i.e., drunks sobering up, DUIs awaiting processing to court, transfers to other authorities) could be kept low, perhaps by placing them in what Kennedy and Homant described as suicide-resistant holding areas under close supervision, then there might be further reductions in the number of suicides in jails and holding areas. Irrespective of what programs are implemented or policies adopted, the fact remains that some suicides always will occur in jail, a number, owing to the special characteristics of jail inmates, that will be higher than that experienced in free world population (Kennedy and Homant, 1988; Winfree, 1988).

Jail deaths from natural causes appear to be almost entirely probabilistic in nature. Over the period examined, nothing was changed to increase an inmate's likelihood of dying from natural causes. That being said, there were changes that appeared to reduce the likelihood of such deaths: jails that experienced a decrease in crowding over time also experienced reductions in the likelihood of deaths by natural causes as compared with jails in which the level of crowding remained the same or even increased. It would appear that judicial activism is warranted on the issue of crowding: court orders establishing jail population ceilings may have saved lives and have the potential to save more in the future.

In the short term, suicides may be more amenable to changes in policy and training regimen than deaths by natural causes (see, e.g., Winfree, 1987). Enriched training programs designed to sensitize jail-bound health professionals to the unique needs and problems of troubled inmates may aid in the detection of suicide-prone individuals (Goldfarb, 1975; Stelzer, 1983; Hardy, 1984; Pfeiffer, 1984; Lamb et al., 1984; but see also Kennedy and Homant, 1988). Guards and other staff who come into daily contact with inmates may learn to recognize the danger signs of suicide proneness (Payne, 1984; Kennedy, 1983, 1985). Policy changes dictating new procedures for short-term detainees may further reduce the opportunity to commit suicide.[3] However, reducing jail crowding also may save lives by reducing deaths by natural causes.

In the long term, however, institutionally based changes and
expansion of jail resources may hold only part of the answer (see
Hayes, 1983, for more on this point). Ultimately we need to explore
the possibility that jails have become the new asylums—as they
were the old asylums—for the mentally ill and others, including
DUI suspects, prone toward acts of self-destruction (Dougherty,
1984; Bowker, 1982; Hayes, 1983). Of course if this practice is indeed contributing to the prevalence of jail suicides, then the problem moves beyond the confines of America's jails themselves and
will require more than innovative jail management and advanced
training methods to remedy them. What may be needed is a serious
reevaluation of the role of local jails in "warehousing" mentally
disordered individuals (Dougherty, 1984; Hayes, 1983; Morrisey et
al., 1984; Pogrebin and Regoli, 1985).

NOTES

1. Detailed discussions of the methodology employed during the
data collection phases of each census are available elsewhere (Bureau of
Justice Statistics, 1981b, 1983b).

2. On a more subjective level, an inmate's death in a rural Montana
jail or a small Mississippi jail due to the apparent neglect of his or her
jailers is likely to be met with a "what-else-would-you-expect" reaction.
The similar death of a jail inmate in Los Angeles or New York might pass
virtually unnoticed in cities already numbed by gang-precipitated violence and crack-house murders. A similar death in Minneapolis or St.
Louis, however, might launch a statewide investigation.

3. See Kennedy (1983, 1984) for further discussion of the theory of
transition to police authority as a cause of suicide.

CHAPTER 5

Mental Health Services for Jail Inmates: Imprecise Standards, Traditional Philosophies, and the Need for Change

DAVID KALINICH, PAUL EMBERT, AND
JEFFREY SENESE

During the past two decades local jails have been forced into providing at least minimal mental health care for an increasing number of inmates. However, when jails are managed by traditional values and a managerial philosophy that emphasizes security, even minimum mental health treatment generally will not be provided.

Failing to provide basic mental health services often will result in inmates' physical or psychological harm. Additionally, jail administrators and local governments may be subjected to civil litigation—a potential consequence that currently weighs heavily over all jail systems. This latter ramification is largely attributable to a lack of clearly articulated public, judicial, and jail policies associated with the entire mental health care issue, as well as a failure to come to grips fully with the basic reasons why jails must provide mental health services to inmates with these requirements.

There are three reasons why jails presently have little choice but to be in the business of providing mental health services to inmates manifesting such needs: (1) increasing numbers of inmates who are mentally ill but who may not be commitable to a mental hospital; (2) changes in correctional law that have increased jail inmates' standards of care while simultaneously failing to provide universally applicable or practical rules related to

79

many of these standards; and (3) a derivative need, given current standards, for mental health care for inmates who are not legally mentally ill but nonetheless require some mental health services.

The first issue, the phenomenon of an increasing number of inmates in local jails who are legally mentally ill, has been addressed by numerous writers (Bonta et al., 1983; Doughtery, 1984; Guy et al., 1985; James et al., 1980; Lamb and Grant, 1982; Runck, 1983; Whitmer, 1980). The literature also addresses those who are developmentally disabled as well as those who are mentally retarded and pseudoretarded (Briar, 1983; Halleck, 1968, 1980; Kaufman, 1973; National Coalition for Jail Reform, 1983). Many of the developmentally disabled or retarded individuals are not legally mentally ill. Moreover, the literature does not always clearly distinguish between citizens who are legally mentally ill and the extent to which they qualify for hospitalization. As a result there is some debate about the extent of the increase of mentally ill citizens who have become jail inmates (Bonovitz and Guy, 1979; Monahan and Steadman, 1983; Orr, 1978; Schuckit et al., 1977).

Nonetheless there is general agreement that the number of jail inmates with mental health problems has increased (Dunn and Steadman, 1982; Gibbs, 1982; Morgan, 1981; Morrisey et al., 1983). There is also widespread agreement that the influx of jail inmates who manifest mental health problems is largely attributable to the movement to deinstitutionalize mentally ill citizens and to treat their mental health needs within the community (Doughtery, 1984; Edwards and Coner, 1983; Kalinich et al., 1988; Petrich, 1976; Ringel and Segal, 1986; Sikka, 1975).

Another factor contributing to the increasing numbers of mentally ill persons confined in jails is the rapid growth of substance abuse, which often correlates with emotional breakdowns and mental illness (Jenkins, 1989). Yet, regardless of the reasons leading to the increased numbers of mentally ill found in county jails, a return to "warehousing" mental patients in large state mental institutions is not the answer to the problem. As noted by Steven Schnee, superintendent of San Antonio State Hospital, "It's not economically, legally, morally, ethically or clinically feasible" (Goode, 1989). Additionally, this "solution" ignores many of the problems leading to the deinstitutionalization of the mentally ill.

The movement to change the nation's mental health system to community mental health treatment can be traced to the late 1960s (Nielson, 1979; C. Warren, 1977). Changes to state mental health codes in the early 1970s literally dumped mentally ill patients en mass out of state mental health institutions. The deinstitutionalization movement has lowered state hospital populations from 558,000 in 1955 to fewer than 130,000 today (Goode, 1989). Those who fail to adjust under community mental health agency auspices often find their way into the criminal justice system (when involved in criminal behavior). One study, for example, showed that about 90 percent of new admissions to one urban jail had a psychiatric hospitalization history (Lamb and Grant, 1982). Prior to the community mental health care movement, many mentally ill jail inmates routinely were transferred from jails to state mental hospitals.

Historically, mentally ill inmate transfers from jails to state mental hospitals were a fairly routine process that all but eliminated the need for jails to be concerned with supervising mentally ill inmates. Mental health code changes, which facilitated the change from institutional to community mental health services, currently make such transfers from jails to mental institutions difficult. To effect a transfer, the codes often require an inmate be legally mentally ill. Clear objective evidence must also exist that the inmate is a real and immediate danger to himself or herself or to others; or that the inmate is unable to attend to his or her basic needs or does not understand the need for mental health treatment.[1]

This standard, when rigidly applied by judges, lawyers or doctors, effectively precludes the transfer of many inmates from jails to mental institutions. As a result, mentally ill individuals who violate the law or who historically might have been placed in state mental hospitals, are now frequently incarcerated in local jails; and, once confined, they often cannot practically be transferred to a mental facility. Both the deinstitutionalization of mentally ill citizens and the difficulty of transferring mentally ill inmates to a mental facility exacerbate jail administrators' problems.

The second issue, the revolutionary change in correctional law, has increased inmate care standards and now generally requires that inmates be provided with at least minimal, if not comprehensive, health care. In effect, current care standards represent a new set of rules imposed on jails for inmate treatment. The new rules have been developed from standards promulgated by professional organizations (like the American Correctional Association) and, especially, from case law (emanating primarily from the federal courts). Professional associations and court decisions have imposed on jails a higher duty of inmate care. As of 1984, for example, 621 jails across the country were under court order to limit populations or alter practices to improve conditions of confinement (Bureau of Justice Statistics, 1984).

In specific cases the federal courts have even seen fit to take over jail management to bring them into conformity with the new rules and standards (*Jones v. Wittenberg*, 330 F. Supp. 707, N.D. Oh. (1971)). Standards for medical care, which subsume some mental health care, are of particular relevance and concern. In some instances jails have been sued successfully after an inmate suffered harm as a result of lack of mental health (and other) care (e.g., *Ferola v. Moran*, 622 F. Supp. 814, D.C. RI (1985); *Nelson v. Collins*, 455 F. Supp. 727, D. Md. (1978)).

As a more precise illustration, jail personnel usually have a legal duty to take some efforts to prevent inmates from committing suicide while incarcerated. Generally, current standards of care require that inmates leave the jail in no worse condition (as a result of their jail experience) than when they were initially confined. It is conceivable that some inmates' conditions may even have to be improved as a result of their jail experience to meet this objective. And it is debatable whether this standard truly can be achieved given incarceration's debilitating nature.

The third issue (infrequently addressed in the literature) is the derivative standard of care, which requires that inmates who suffer from depression, drug or alcohol withdrawal, or who are suicidal, be provided with appropriate mental health services. In other words, the requirement for mental health service delivery is not limited only to those inmates who "fit" legal definitions of mental illness; rather, the requirement includes a range of related problems that seem to require the application of mental health expertise. A 1983 jail inmate survey (Bureau of Justice Statistics, 1984) showed that over 32 percent of the country's jail inmates either were alcohol or drug abusers, reported being depressed or suffered from mental problems, or had a previous mental health hospitalization record.[2]

If this figure holds today—and there is little or no evidence suggesting otherwise—the scope of the problem is frightening: about one-third of the jail inmate population requires some form of mental health care. These services must be provided in a system with a century long tradition that emphasizes security and rejects inmates' mental health care and treatment as a legitimate function.

The challenge at hand is to change jail systems from custodial institutions to correctional institutions that are funded, staffed, and managed based on current standards of care (while retaining the traditional custody function). There are, however, a number of factors that mitigate against the changes needed to provide inmates mental health services in local jails. One major intervening factor is the complexity and ambiguity of mental health care legal standards.

The Illusive Problem Defined: Legal Standards

Legal standards involving mental health care provision are among the most complex and ambiguous standards affecting jails, jail policy, and practical public policy. Like most legal standards, those relating to mental health care provision and dealing with mental illness have evolved largely from court decisions concerning a variety of separate, but related, issues: (1) criminal responsibility for an illegal act, (2) treatment of the mentally ill in mental facilities, and (3) provision of medical care (in its broad context as well as psychological and psychiatric care) to jail inmates. Additionally, the standards embrace issues of "mere negligence," error and differing medical opinions on the one hand and, on the other hand, "deliberate indifference." For example, our criminal justice, mental health, and legal systems have yet to agree on even the fundamental issue of the "insanity defense." This issue, which started with the landmark *M'Naghten* case in 1843, has seen the insanity defense subjected to extensive criticism by legal commentators, many of whom have argued that it should even be abolished (Brakel and Rock, 1971; Goldstein and Katz, 1973; Halleck, 1967; Morris, 1968, 1969; Szasz, 1963; Weintraub, 1963; Wooten, 1960).

However, while many courts have wrestled with a variety of rules involving mental illness it was not until 1960 that Morton Birnbaum, a physician-jurist, articulated the idea that someone suffering from mental illness and housed in a public mental institution had a constitutional right to treatment. Birnbaum argued that substantive due process of law does not allow a mentally ill person who has committed no crime to be deprived of liberty by indefinite mental institution confinement (Hurley, 1988).

Despite Birnbaum (and others), the courts generally failed to recognize a federal constitutional right to mental health treatment until 1971. In the *Wyatt* case a federal district court addressed the issue of mentally ill patients being constitutionally entitled to receive adequate and effective treatment and concluded that: "The purpose of involuntary hospitalization is treatment and not mere custodial care or punishment. This is the only justification, from a constitutional standpoint, that allows civil commitment to mental institutions" (*Wyatt v. Stickney*, 325 F. Supp. 781, M.D. Al. (1971)).

Subsequently, the U.S. Supreme Court ruled that inmates confined in correctional institutions had a federal constitutional right to medical treatment (*Estelle v. Gamble*, 429 U.S. 97, (1976)). In *Estelle*, the court ruled that a state must provide adequate medical care and that "deliberate indifference" to an inmate's serious medical needs violates the Eighth Amendment's proscription against cruel and unusual punishment. Although a landmark case, this decision did not present a definitive ruling that jail administrators could apply with certainty in all cases. Allegations or proof of mere negligence, error, or difference of medical opinion are not sufficient to claim a constitutional deprivation (*Daniels v. Gilbreath*, 668 F. 2d 477, 10th Cir. (1982); *Estelle v. Gamble*, 429 U.S. 97 (1976); *Johnson v. Treen*, 759 F. 2d 1236, 5th Cir. (1985); *Westlake v. Lucas*, 537 F. 2d 857, 6th Cir. (1976)). In effect, the decision opened a variety of cases to the issue of "mere negligence," as opposed to "deliberate indifference." Accordingly, it is not surprising that the federal courts have wrestled with the "deliberate indifference" standard in numerous contexts, including many cases having mental health connotations (Hurley, 1988).

Other decisions indicate that inmates' constitutional rights to medical treatment include a limited right to psychological and psychiatric care. Several federal courts have ruled, for example, that as a logical extension of this right inmates have a constitutional right to be protected from themselves (e.g., *Estate of Cartwright v. City of Concord*, 618 F. Supp. 772, N.D. Ca. (1985); *Lightbody v. Town of Hampton*, 618 F. Supp. 6 (1984); *Lyons v. Cunningham*, 583 F. Supp. 1147, S.D.N.Y. (1983); *Partridge v. Two Unknown Police Officers*, 791 F. 2d 1182, 5th Cir. (1986); *Roberts v. City of Troy*, 773 F. 2d 720, 6th Cir. (1985)).

Similarly, state courts also have recognized a legal cause for action for failure to prevent an inmate from committing suicide (*Becker v. Beaudoin*, 261 A. 2d 896, RI, (1970)). Both federal and state courts have addressed other issues associated with mental health care from a variety of perspectives. For example, one U.S. district court ruled that mentally deranged prisoners shall never be unsupervised or unescorted, the practice of chaining mentally disturbed inmates shall be stopped, and arrangements shall be made for a psychiatric care program (*Hamilton v. Landrieu*, 351 F. Supp. 549, E.D. La. (1972)). Another district court rule that if a detainee displays behavior suggestive of mental illness, such behavior shall be reported immediately to the medical staff and the inmate seen by a psychiatrist within 24 hours (*Cambell v. McGruder,* 416 F. Supp. 100, D.D.C. (1975)). In a third case, a district court ruled that a psychiatric unit is to be built in the jail and a treatment plan established (*Sykes v. Kreiger,* 451 F. Supp. 421, N.D. Oh. (1975)).

In other rulings, courts have mandated that (1) there shall be a special housing unit for detainees who require psychiatric, psychological, or other medical care (*Ahrens v. Thomas,* 434 F. Supp. 873, W.D. Mo. (1977); (2) there is no underlying distinction between the right to medical care and its psychological or psychiatric counterpart (*Bowring v. Godwin,* 551 F. 2d 44, 7th Cir. (1977)); and (3) jails may not be used to detain persons awaiting involuntary civil commitment proceedings (*Lynch v. Baxley,* 744 F. 2d 1452, 11th Cir. (1984)).

Conversely, a statutorily established policy of providing psychiatric and psychological services to pretrial detainees does not create an enforceable entitlement to such services (*Santori v. Fong,* 484 F. Supp. 1029, E.D. Pa. (1980)). Rulings such as this pose a dilemma for jail administrators and local governmental leaders who, perhaps, opt for a way around complying with more costly decisions (such as establishing psychiatric units).

More important, from this cursory overview of legal standards related to the provision of mental health care, other more basic issues become apparent: (1) how to provide adequate mental health care while avoiding liability under the "deliberate indifference" test, (2) when an inmate's right to refuse treatment legally may be overcome and the inmate involuntarily medicated, and (3) who is to be determined mentally ill or in need of mental health treatment. In effect, the nebulous standards reduce themselves to the questions of when and how much jails must treat inmates' mental health problems and under what circumstances they can do so (American Correctional Association, 1987; Fisher et al., 1987).

Finally, what this means for a jail administrator is that if an inmate needs mental health services but does not receive them and is physically or psychologically harmed as a result, the jail (in all likelihood) will be civilly sued, usually under 42 U.S.C. Section 1983. Regardless of any lack of clarity, or even practical applicability to a local situation, the jailer and local government will suffer if minimal mental health services are not provided.

From the perspective of policy and practice, mental health treatment legal standards are complex, ambiguous, and subject to debate by jurists; yet jail administrators and local political leaders must try to apply these standards or face civil litigation. From a practical standpoint, most jails confine too few inmates to justify psychiatric units (as prescribed in *Sykes*) or comply with other court rulings. Most jails serve rural areas (Mays and Thompson, 1988) and must rely on integrating community mental health agencies, if any, into the jail, as opposed to creating a complete in-house psychiatric unit. Additionally, most jail administrators are not oriented, by experience or training, even to recognize the voluminous issues related to mental health service provision to their clients.

Despite confusing and seemingly contradictory case law on inmates' rights to treatment, criteria for adequate treatment, who may refuse treatment, or even who is mentally ill, there is a clear message for sheriffs and jail administrators: if an inmate is in need of mental health services but does not receive "adequate" mental health treatment or service and the inmate suffers harm as a direct result, the sheriff or jail administrator and appropriate governmental entity probably will be sued.

The jail, its policies, procedures, personnel, and training and practices, will be subjected to court intervention to determine if "reasonable efforts" were taken to identify and treat the harmed inmate; or if, to the contrary, the jail staff neglected their duty by providing inadequate care due to "deliberate indifference" to an identifiable need. Jails managed with traditional priorities, policies, procedures, and practices most likely will be judged to have neglected their duty of care when subjected to the scrutiny of "Monday morning quarterbacking" in the courts. Sweeping changes, therefore, must taken place in most jails before current inmate care standards can be met. However, the role that tradition has molded for jails probably is viewed as the jails' legitimate role by community members, local political leaders, criminal justice policymakers, and even jail managers. The power of tradition has evoked forces that will work to negate change.

Limits of Traditional Jail Systems: Forces Preventing Change

Developing a New Philosophy

Jails must make major operational changes to deliver inmate mental health services. Standing in the way of such changes are four major impediments. First, and perhaps most crucial, is the fundamental jail management philosophy. There is some evidence that the traditional jail management philosophy is changing. The American Jail Association was organized in 1981 to upgrade the jail profession. "Podular direct-supervision" (or "new generation") jails have been built in many jurisdictions across the country, and in at least three states (Michigan, New York, and Maryland), efforts have been made to provide mental health services to jail inmates.

However, traditional jail management philosophy emphasizing custody and security, to the exclusion of other aspects of human services management, continues to dominate. Emphasizing custody and security is a philosophy of convenience for local police, courts, and government. It is a philosophy that keeps jail business costs relatively low and the jail and its managers in place, i.e., passive, unobtrusive, and powerless in effecting policies in other criminal justice system components. Yet polices in other components affect jail operations; thus traditional management philosophy and supporting policies cause jails to be passive servants of the criminal justice system and local government.

The custody and security philosophy for local jail management, therefore, is popular within local criminal justice cultures, as well as with local governments (Pinkele, 1986). We should not be surprised, then, when sheriffs or jail administrators cling to the old philosophy. The jail administrator who does not resist criminal justice system practices that overpopulate the jail, who runs the jail at a low per diem cost, and who is more concerned with serving "the system" than with providing proper inmate care, will be supported by local policymakers and political figures. In other words, the existence and continuance of the traditional jail management approach do not lie only in jail administrators' hands. In fact, jail administrators who try to implement current standards of care may meet systemwide resistance and may very well face informal sanctions from policymakers throughout the criminal justice and political systems. In effect, we are suggesting that local jail managers are constrained by local norms and traditions and are subjected directly to decisions and policies made at the local level.

Conversely, the current standards of care have been promulgated by professional organizations and, more significantly, by federal court decisions. Decisions made at this level do not have immediate impact on local jurisdictions or jails. Indeed, there is evidence of instances of deliberate indifference and both passive and active resistance to federal court decisions (Schafer, 1986).

Additionally, local decisions, expectations, and information salient in nature will be communicated readily to jail administrators through well-established communications networks, as opposed to standards and goals or case law promulgated from a distance. Local jail administrators are conditioned to be sensitive to local demands but, by virtue of their provincial nature, generally are not linked in any meaningful way to professional bodies or the federal court system. It is likely, therefore, that on the part of both jail administrators and local policymakers a significant temporal gap exists between the creation of the current standards of care— the new rules—and full comprehension of the new rules. Simply stated, many jail administrators may not yet fully comprehend current inmate care standards. In this regard, it is very likely that local governmental officials or local criminal justice system policymakers have little, if any, knowledge of the new rules for jails.

Mere knowledge of the new rules, of course, will not necessarily alter jail management philosophy and resulting policies. Jail administrators or systems that resist change may give tacit recognition to the need for providing inmates with mental health services. They may rewrite policies or procedures, issue memoranda for staff to "read and sign," or even send a correctional officer or two to an occasional seminar on suicide prevention or managing mentally ill inmates. A jail administrator may enter into this type of limited response to do enough to "get by"; that is, bring just enough change to create "window dressing," or the appearance of change, to the system to protect the status quo (Kalinich et al., 1985).

Administrators also may institute minimal changes due to the reality of resource limitations. If, indeed, local officials do not understand the standards imposed on local jails, as we have suggested, they will not be motivated to redistribute scarce resources to the jail budget. Even if they "get the message," they may supply only enough funds to allow a jail to enter into the least costly approach to change. Finally, jail administrators may be constrained from attempting to enter into substantive change due to pressures from influential criminal justice actors who hold to traditional norms regarding inmate management, for these individuals may be concerned with the effect an increased jail budget may have on their own funding.

In summary, developing a jail management philosophy and supporting policies that are congruent with current inmate care standards require a knowledge of current standards, a comprehensive understanding of the new rules, and a legitimate acceptance of current standards of care. A jail administrator's acceptance of new rules will be manifest in his or her attempts to implement the substantive changes in the jail system that will facilitate appropriate inmate care. The extent to which a jail administrator is successful in implementing the new rules depends on the administrator's leadership. Skilled and vigorous leadership is necessary to implement policies, procedures, and programs, and to acquire the resources necessary to bring a jail system into conformance with current standards of care.

Implementing Current Standards of Care

The second impediment to meaningful jail change lies in implementing a new organizational philosophy and the behavioral changes expected of jail members. The key element needed is skilled and vigorous leadership, rather than the passive survival orientation implicit in jail administrators who adopt jail security as the sole organizational philosophy.

Studying successful change in police organizations, Skolnick and Bailey (1986) argue that the chief must infuse the entire organization with a sense of purpose that supports the new programs. In addition, the chief must instill the values and programs he or she is promoting by advocating, motivating, or even manipulating departmental personnel into accepting those values.[3] The administrator acting as a change agent must garner public support as well as support from influential criminal justice community members. In essence, a change-oriented administrator must adopt a positive management philosophy toward inmate programs, reach inward to make necessary organizational changes, and then reach outward to garner support and resources. This contrasts sharply with the jail administrator who accepts security as the jail's single mission. An administrator of this ilk will play a passive role, responding to cues from his or her immediate environment and protecting the status quo.

Looking internally at implementing changes to provide inmates with programs, jail administrators must first alter overall jail policy to conform to a jail management philosophy that focuses on inmate care standards. Then administrators must create appropriate programs, rewrite procedures, and modify personnel attitudes and behaviors. Modifying the jail staff's attitudes and behaviors requires altering informal organizational norms and values, as well as formal practices. The former can be accomplished through leadership that influences and alters the social and power structure among jail personnel. Formal procedures and practices required can be implemented through formal training. New policy implementation requires the jail administrator, acting as a leader and change agent, to show a clear and unalterable dedication to the new management philosophy and policies. In addition, formal and informal reward systems may have to be altered, new staff who accept change may have to be promoted, veteran staff who "buy" into the new policies should be brought into the dominant coalition for support, transfers and shift changes may be needed to break up cliques opposed to change, and coercive force may have to be applied to those who fail to conform to new directives.

Formal comprehensive training is a more civil, if not acceptable, mode for imposing change within a jail system. Training provides a relatively direct route through which administrators can communicate the jail's changed mandate, indoctrinate staff with the new management philosophy and values, forewarn staff of policies and procedures changes, and educate staff about the changes required in their practices. Formal comprehensive training is foreign, however, to many jail systems that have functioned with security as their primary goal. Traditional jails presumably have functioned well with so-called on-the-job training, where new staff members are placed on duty for a short time with more seasoned personnel and may be required to "read and sign" memos or policy manuals. Formal training requires resources for trainers and time away from work for trainees. Typically, neither commodity is available to jail administrators, nor have they sought them with vigor. To the extent jail administrators have not attempted to include viable training as an integral part of their system, they have not been convinced of its value and similarly are not ready to justify and argue for training resources. One reason jail administrators have not been convinced of the value of training can be traced to past training, which has been inadequate. We are suggesting more sophisticated types of training than traditional jail training, most of which has been oriented toward merely changing knowledge rather than changing behavior or performance. Training intended to change knowledge requires little more than average intelligence and motivation on the student's part, and a fairly direct form of instruction, such as a simple lecture or even a memo. Conversely, changing behavior and performance requires hands-on practice, coaching, and policies and procedures consistent with the desired behavior, as well as supervisory and peer support for the proper behavior (Embert, 1969). Role play, case study, and a variety of other methods beyond lectures are needed to achieve the kinds of behavior and performance we are alluding to (Kalinich and Embert, 1987). Such behaviors are critical to the success of many inmate programs.[4]

At the core of providing inmate care is the need for programs. For jail administrators, identifying the type and scope of jail programs may be a difficult task. First, a "needs assessment" must be conducted to determine the number of inmates that have problems, as well as the variety of problems they exhibit. Based on a general problem assessment, the number and types of programs needed can be determined. Some jails may have no programs or procedures for identifying and managing inmates with medical or mental problems. Others may have programs in place that need only to be upgraded and augmented. To create and implement programs and procedures, administrators may need to increase the jail's resource base or reallocate or revitalize existing resources. Therefore, jail staff may need to utilize outside expertise to provide a needs assessment and to recommend programs and procedures to provide inmate care.

Systemic Problems

Inmates in need of mental health services are not just a jail problem but a systemwide problem (Embert, 1986); they are potential clients for local public community mental health agencies (Kalinich et al., 1988). Traditional attitudes toward jails preclude a systemic and communitywide perspective on jail problems. It is, or should be, common knowledge that sheriffs or jail administrators usually do not advertise for inmates. Inmates are placed in jails by courts, police, probation and parole offices and held there in lieu of bond pending their adjudication. Nevertheless, many of the problems that occur in jails are erroneously assumed strictly to be jail problems. For example, when jails are considered overcrowded by federal courts the sheriff typically is held responsible, ordered to reduce the jail population, and left to his or her own devices to do so. Rare is the decision or consent decree that spreads the responsibility for overcrowding to the criminal justice or local political systems. In addition, there is generally no manifest assumption that social service agencies should continue serving clients in their caseload while they are incarcerated. It is even less likely that a jail inmate will be *added* to a social service agency's caseload while incarcerated. Finally, local governments are, by their political nature, loath to reallocate resources from visible or popular public services to jail operations.

To the extent that jail administrators passively accept traditional views of the jail's role and status, they must accept full responsibility for the status quo. It is common, for example, for jail administrators to "hide" inmates during "count" to conform to a court order on jail capacity rather than allow the problem to surface so that responsibility is spread across the criminal justice system to judges, prosecutors and others who control the flow of inmates into their jails. It is also common for jail administrators and staff to presume that social service agencies will not offer any assistance because "they never have in the past." Many also fear the political consequence of battling local governmental officials for increased jail funds. This passive, dutiful posture by jail administrators may gain their approval among policymakers but merely puts off and exacerbates the problems at hand.

Jail administrators can attempt to spread responsibility for inmates with mental health problems to social service agencies and the criminal justice system. However, there are significant obstacles to "sharing the wealth," since criminal justice and community social service agencies historically have not viewed the jail as an entity that required or deserved their services. Criminal justice agencies typically see jails as institutions that serve them by storing criminal offenders and that serve the courts by bringing offenders to hearings and trials. Decisions made by local judges traditionally have been made "in the interest of justice," not in the interests or needs of the local jail or its inmates.

Jail administrators can adopt several strategies to entice social service agencies to provide services. First, they can articulate publicly the jail's problems and the extent to which they are "shared problems" (Embert, 1986; Hall, 1987). Awareness of a shared domain is the most important step in creating interorganizational relationships. Second, they can aggressively pursue cooperation from criminal justice and social service agencies for assistance. Developing professional and personal relationships with members of related organizations is also a necessary step to developing or improving interorganizational relationships (Hall, 1987). Third, they can, as a matter of record, document the extent to which other agencies enter, or fail to enter, into cooperative efforts. For example, mental health practitioners will be less likely to refuse to examine inmates or to give only cursory examinations and opinions if their name and behavior are part of an official file. Finally, they may take their case to the public through the open political forum. This step will require the ability to co-opt the media and is fraught with political risk, neither of which is in the traditional jail administrator's repertoire. These steps are by no means exhaustive. Jail administrators will develop a myriad of workable approaches to co-opt local social service agencies and criminal justice policymakers, once the need is recognized and the process begins.

In a more positive vein, spreading the responsibility for treating problem inmates can bring existing resources and expertise to jail systems. Community mental health agencies, for example, can add inmates with mental and emotional problems to their caseloads. In addition, such agencies can assist jail staff in recognizing mentally ill or suicidal inmates and provide training on interacting with them. Criminal justice policymakers can create recognizance bond programs for nonviolent but problematic inmates to remove them from the jail setting or perhaps utilize electronic technology for community placement of these individuals.

Ideally, highly structured diversion programs, supervised in conjunction with social service agencies, could be established to limit the jail's burden. Interagency expertise can further "raise consciousness" among agencies and spread responsibility for treating mentally ill inmates across the local social service network and the criminal justice system.

Physical Plant Considerations

Typically, jails are constructed for maximum inmate control with minimal supervision, which is achieved by the traditional linear/intermittent surveillance jail design. However, proper care of inmates with severe mental or emotional problems, especially suicidal inmates, requires a higher supervision level than found in a typical jail. Increasing correctional officers' ability to observe and interact with inmates is severely limited in jails designed primarily for security. This design allows inmates to be locked securely in their cells until they are transferred to court for processing or released. If security is the jail system's only concern, with this design little, if any, inmate supervision is necessary. Many of the inmates with mental or emotional problems, however, need regular supervision, and suicidal inmates need to be observed constantly.[5] Linear/intermittent surveillance facilities make frequent inmate supervision difficult and constant supervision of suicidal inmates impossible unless substantial changes are made in personnel allotments, supervision patterns, and facility modifications.

Physical plant modifications could include adding observation cells positioned near correctional officers' work areas (such as the booking/intake station), creating so-called suicide-proof cells; or adding devices, such as mirrors or TV monitors, to provide a greater range of vision throughout the jail from one vantage point. We must caution, however, that considerable research indicates that TV monitors may actually reduce supervision effectiveness because they lower viewer concentration levels.[6]

Those jurisdictions able to build new facilities can consider the popular direct supervision jail design. This design forces almost constant interaction with, and supervision of, inmates by jail staff. Current research suggests that the new-generation jails provide staff ample opportunity to observe and supervise inmates constantly. In addition, personnel satisfaction in new-generation jails appears to be much higher than in traditional jails (Zupan and Stohr-Gillmore, 1988).

In summary, jails constructed in the linear/intermittent surveillance design limit the correctional officers' routine observation of inmates. Supervision patterns will have to be altered drastically to manage inmates who have been identified as suffering from mental or emotional problems. Also, plant modifications will be needed to facilitate the officers' ability to observe inmates with regularity.

State Funding

Thus far we have focused on local government problems. An alternative to many jails' inherent systemic and physical plant problems is closer ties between state and county governments to include funding considerations. For example, Thompson (1989) has noted that North Carolina must recognize its responsibility in contributing to jail problems, strengthen its inspections program, revise its antiquated jail standards, and acknowledge that "Years of neglect at both state and local levels of government have spun a complex web of problems . . . so severe that local officials are virtually powerless to extricate themselves." Yet North Carolina is not unique in this respect. Recently, for example, Michigan has looked at increasing state funding for county jail construction. Michigan, like many states, has crowded jails; nearly all experience overcrowding at some point during a typical month. In addition, the character of jail inmates is changing; felons now represent about 40 percent of Michigan's jail population. This may be due in part to the state's overcrowded prisons, and to judges who use jails as an alternative to prison for some felons (Davis and Gaudino, 1987).

Similarly, Michigan's state standards historically have been problematic due to a lack of state and local funding to comply with state-mandated standards. Although the department of corrections published county jail standards, the state legislature has not allocated funds to the counties to ensure conformance with those standards. Additionally, county governments have been either reluctant or unable to use county funds to comply with state-mandated standards.

North Carolina and Michigan are not unique in these situations: most counties receive little state financial support for jail operations (beyond a per diem for state prisoners housed in county jails and some modest help with construction costs) (Florida Jail Assistance Bureau, 1989). In many cases the state makes the rules or knows the rules imposed by the courts, yet does not provide jail operational funds. In fact, state laws may even restrict local governments in collecting funds through laws dealing with county and local government taxation.

Summary and Conclusions

Even though the law is not clear on all issues concerning the mentally ill, the number of jail inmates generally considered as mentally ill is increasing. Further, the law is unclear on the standards of care for jail inmates who may suffer from mental or emotional problems, who are mentally retarded, or who may manifest other problems (such as alcohol or drug addiction or suicidal tendencies), all of which fall loosely under the rubric of being treatable by mental health expertise. Nonetheless, local jails may be subject to standards of care (through civil litigation) if an inmate is physically or psychologically injured due to a mental health problem while confined in a jail.

In effect, standards of care evolved from case law are not "crisp" enough to be taken directly as policy. It is the obligation of jail administrators, as it is of all public administrators, to accept the general standard of care mandates imposed on them and to alter it into "crisp" operational policies and procedures. The first step is to understand that mandates require the jail's mission to be both custody *and care* of inmates. Jails must see that inmates are not harmed as a result of their jail experience; inmates have a right to leave the jail in no worse physical and psychological condition than they were in when booked.

Changing the organization's philosophy is the first step in changing the jail into a correctional facility. Changing jail personnel practices and behaviors, however, is the real task at hand. A great deal of literature analyzes organizational change and prescribes approaches to change. We will limit our commentary to advising that change is inevitable. Ignoring forces for change will not mitigate the momentum for change but will simply place the organization at the mercy of those forces (R. Warren, 1977).

Jail changes require that sheriffs or jail administrators who wish to have some control over their destinies become change agents. As a change agent, the jail administrator must carefully plan the structural changes required and overcome resistance to change (Bennis, 1966). Resistance to change emanates from an array of personnel and organizational sources. In the former instance, organizational members may see little need for change; in the latter, the existing reward-punishment system may reinforce the status quo (Steers, 1977). The jail administrator's role as a change agent is to alter the organizational values, structure, policies, procedures, power structure, and so forth, as well as to mitigate personnel resistance to change through training, bringing prochange personnel into positions of influence, and persuading or coercing recalcitrant members to conform to new dicta.

Jail administrators' resistance to change, however, goes beyond internal organizational sources. Invariably, resistance to jail operational changes exists within other criminal justice system components, in local governments, and often with the general public. The jail administrator must take an active role in the formal and informal political systems to influence criminal justice policymakers, local governmental officials, and members of the local public to garner support for new programs and practices. He or she must alter traditional beliefs about the jail's role that determine funding practices and create public attitudes that impede upgrading the jail to conform with current standards of care.

The forces for organizational change emanate from environmental pressures or conflict within an agency (Downs, 1967). Similarly, for jail systems, pressures for change emanate from the external environment. However, environmental pressures opposed to change *do* exist, especially at the local political level, placing proponents of change in a legal and political vise. Working through the contradictory forces, while bringing the agency in line with contemporary professional demands, will require energetic and capable leadership. The jail administrator must alter the inner workings of the jail system while manipulating political and legal forces to advantage. Change in jail systems across the country, in the long term, is inevitable. The issue for jail administrators, sheriffs, and local officials is the extent to which they will participate in the inevitable change.

In conclusion, a lack of clearly articulated often ambiguous, and frequently unenforceable public, judicial, and jail policies exacerbates issues involving jail inmates' mental health care. As a matter of public policy state legislatures must clarify the jail's role in contemporary society. Jails confine a variety of clients, including those accused and those convicted of crimes. Yet these criminal acts are often emphasized to the detriment of more fundamental social issues, including mental health problems. State legislatures must articulate new values, policies, and standards for dealing with such problems.

Many states have promulgated jail standards; however, it appears that their effectiveness has not been universal (Thompson and Mays, 1988b). This may be due to (1) the lack of a clear jail mission statement and (2) the inconsistency between new standards and traditional guidelines (as well as our customary image of jails as warehouses for society's "riffraff").

Legislatures must clearly articulate a new mission statement that recognizes the jail as a community confinement center for social problems that cannot be managed by other social institutions. Policies, standards, and state jail regulations that stem from murky or traditional thinking about jail usage, rather than from a clear mission statement prescribing the jails' contemporary mandate, will be ineffective. Traditional policies that attempt to tack on or incorporate current standards will be contradictory and thus confound implementation. Simply stated, jails are not jails any more. While "jailing" is a part of the business, jails also confine individuals that fall into the criminal justice system's web and who require relatively sophisticated care, support, and treatment. To the extent this broader mission is not recognized by the polity, jail standards will not be enforceable.

Edelman (1964) informs us that symbols are powerful statements that inform and control the thinking of the polity. To the extent this is true, the very word *jail* evokes a picture of bars, concrete, criminals, and punishment in the minds of members of the formal political system, the public at large, and criminal justice policymakers. We would argue that the understanding evoked by the "symbolic" jail limits efforts to implement and enforce new standards and state jail regulations.

Conformity with the traditional or "commonsense" understanding of the jail's role sets the political stage for lax implementation and enforcement of the new standards and rules mandated by the courts and professional associations. Implementation and enforcement of new jail standards and rules easily can become viewed as an attempt to put square pegs into round holes. Outmoded thinking about jails diverts us from articulating public policy that conforms to current inmate care standards and limits the resources and support needed to bring jails into the 1990s and beyond.

NOTES

1. While one state's mental health code may be somewhat different from another's, most are essentially similar. In Michigan's code, for example, mental illness ". . . means a substantial disorder of thought or mood which significantly impairs judgment, behavior, capacity to recognize reality, or ability to cope with ordinary demands of life" (1986, Section 330.1400a). This differs from a person requiring treatment, defined in Michigan's code as "A person who is mentally ill, and who as a result of that mental illness, can reasonably be expected within the near future to intentionally or unintentionally seriously physically injure himself or another person, and who has engaged in an act or acts or made significant threats that are substantially supportive of the expectation" (1986, Section 330.1401a). Other sections address persons who are mentally ill and who, as a result of the mental illness, are unable to attend to their basic physical needs and whose judgment is so impaired that they are unable to understand their need for treatment. At least 15 states have rewritten their mental health codes to allow for somewhat easier institutionalization of the severely mentally ill. Yet, in spite of the fact that lawyers, not doctors, decide when someone should be hospitalized, civil libertarians and some former patients believe that legal reform is dangerous. They believe that a person who has not committed a crime and is not a danger to self or others should not be incarcerated (Goode, 1989).

2. This is based on the authors' reanalysis of data from the National Survey of Jail Inmates, 1983, collected by the Bureau of Justice Statistics. Given the increased numbers of inmates being confined and reflecting involvement in drug use since 1983, this figure may be conservative.

3. Values should underscore programs; that is, they should be the force that leads to policy statements, procedures, and ways of molding subordinates. All organizations have values. They may be implicit or explicit and often may conflict with one another. For example, loyalty to peers is an implicit value that may cause police officers to close their eyes to incompetent or corrupt colleagues. The task for change-oriented, or proactive, administrators is to clearly identify values and articulate them "persuasively and unambiguously," with a goal of shifting emphasis from mere rule compliance to quality action (Kelling et al., 1988).

4. A key problem in many criminal justice training programs is often the lack of a clear objective. That is, there is little clear understanding of whether the trainee should end up with a change in (1) knowledge, (2) attitude, (3) ability, or (4) performance. As a result, training programs often

do not address all the conditions needed to ensure that the objective is achieved: (1) the primary work-group culture, (2) the formal organizational climate, (3) the leadership climate, (4) learning effort, and (5) participant characteristics (House, 1967). Similarly, traditional reliance on lectures or lecture-discussions tends to perpetuate a gap between training and job performance (Lombardo, 1986).

5. Relevant standards for the observation of suicidal inmates range from "... continuing observation" (American Correctional Association Standard 4182–3, added August 1983) through local rules construing fifteen- or thirty-minute checks to be sufficient. Because an inmate could hang himself or herself in about five minutes, checking a suicidal inmate every fifteen minutes clearly is inadequate. As a result, most experts in jail suicide prevention stress the need for constant "eyeball-to-eyeball" supervision or "constant supervision, not the use of CCTV [closed circuit television], but real human contact" of those inmates identified as high suicidal risks (Atlas, 1987; Kalinich and Embert, 1987; Rowan and Haynes, 1988).

6. The use of closed circuit television has been shown to be counterproductive in dealing with a variety of jail issues. Assaults, lawsuits, damage to jail property, the passage of contraband, and fires, as well as inmate suicide attempts, seem to increase with reliance on CCTV (Special Focus on Closed Circuit Television, 1985).

CHAPTER 6

Public Policy Issues in the Delivery of Mental Health Services in a Jail Setting

JEANETTE M. JERRELL AND
RICHARD KOMISARUK

The predominant theme of federal and state mental health policy during the past twenty-five years has been the deinstitutionalization of persons with mental illness, that is, hospitalizing fewer severely ill people and shortening their stays after they are confined. Mental health planning included the development of appropriate alternative care or aftercare mechanisms for persons who formerly would have been institutionalized. However, numerous program and policy evaluations concerning effects of deinstitutionalization indicate that, although the number and length of state and local hospital stays decreased dramatically during this time period, the social supports required to maintain these patients in the community failed to materialize. Thus, local communities have been saturated with psychiatrically marginal people who cannot be maintained adequately by the mental health system. Many of these persons are in need of twenty-four-hour care and previously would

We are indebted to Kenneth Meinhardt, M.D., for his support of this research, to Susan Chapman, J.D., for her professional and personal assistance in completing this report, and to Kim Musci, whose assistance enabled us to collect and report these data.

have been institutionalized, but now they are homeless, substance abusers, or criminal offenders.

A major impact of deinstitutionalizing the seriously mentally ill has been the alarming overlap of this group with the criminal justice system. Because of limited local psychiatric hospital resources, some of these persons are being incarcerated in jails as one alternative to a lack of treatment resources and to restrictive civil commitment laws. Studies in California and elsewhere have demonstrated that 5 percent to 8 percent of jail populations are psychotic (Lamb and Grant, 1982; Swank and Winer, 1976).

This increasing mental health and criminal justice population overlap poses numerous public policy concerns for local officials. Unfortunately, compared to other criminal justice agencies, jails have received little attention in terms of information collection and program development. In one of the most comprehensive examinations of local jail problems, Dunn and Steadman (1982) outlined several of the issues concerning mentally ill persons in local jails, including the need for descriptive information on their numbers, the nature of the services delivered to these offenders, and the types of improvements needed in these services and in the relationships of public agencies providing the services. The authors recognized, however, that impediments to program development could be addressed only at the local level by performing evaluative research to examine specific questions regarding these services, which would then be used to take informed action to ameliorate inadequacies.

This chapter reviews some of the major public policy issues presented by this trend and describes the mental health services that have evolved in Santa Clara County, California, for addressing jail inmates' mental health needs. Data are presented from a study of mental health services in the county jail that examine many of these policy questions.

Public Policy Issues

Nature and Extent of Mental Health Problems

A definition of the numbers and types of inmates referred for and receiving mental health services is important for two reasons. First, these inmates must have a demonstrated need at least equivalent to that of persons outside the custody setting, lest there be powerful public sentiment concerning possible "coddling" of criminals and avoidance of criminal consequences by those who hide behind mental illness. Second, information about the level of need and the number of inmates in need of services informs administrative decisions about service amounts and types to be delivered.

Our experience in providing forensic mental health services has demonstrated that jail inmates who need mental health services fall into three subgroups. Of highest priority to mental health officials are persons diagnosed psychotic, whose crimes warrant incarceration but who cannot be housed with other inmates because they present a danger to themselves or others and need extensive, ongoing psychiatric treatment. A second inmate subgroup, potential beneficiaries of specialized mental health services, includes nonpsychotic persons incarcerated for the first time whose charges warrant jail but who experience severe difficulties in adjusting to incarceration. These inmates pose a high risk of self-destructive behavior but usually need specialized services only for a brief period early in their incarceration. A third subgroup includes psychotic persons who are booked for misdemeanors and who, in the arresting officer's judgment, need twenty-four-hour care. For various reasons, however, such care is not available, so jail incarceration provides the only alternative to leaving them to wander the streets unable to care for themselves. These incarcerations often are referred to as "mercy bookings." Although "mercy bookings" are widely discussed by law enforcement staff, it has been impossible to obtain a specific tally of inmates booked for this reason. Consequently, opinions vary widely about the extent of the practice, and no effective action to pursue alternative steps can be undertaken. Obviously, if these services can be made available outside of the criminal justice system, these mentally ill persons need to be diverted and managed in mental health facilities, thereby reducing the work load for both the jail's custody and mental health staffs.

Previous reviews have demonstrated a dearth of information regarding the nature and extent of jail inmates' mental health problems. As Brodsky (1982) concludes in his review, psychotic disorders have a fairly low prevalence in the general jail population, and the reported rates are only slightly higher than those for the general population. Prevalence rates for less-serious mental disorders, on the other hand, have ranged from 15 percent to 85 percent of the jail populations studied (Brodsky, 1977; Kal, 1977; Petrich, 1976; Swank and Winer, 1976); however, the presence of substantial methodological problems attenuates generality of these findings. Regardless of the specific prevalence rates at each site, it is clear that a sizable percentage of persons incarcerated in local jails have some degree of mental disorder.

Provision of Suitable Care

Once jail inmates with mental health needs have been identified, a second major public policy issue can be addressed: the provision of suitable care. This issue evokes several policy concerns that must be translated into administrative actions. The first of these is the adequacy and comprehensiveness of available treatment within the jail or the availability of transfer to suitable outside resources when proper treatment cannot be provided in the jail. In this regard, psychiatric treatment in the jail is an aspect of overall medical service for the inmate population. Numerous civil class-action suits have been filed by inmates across the country demanding that jail medical services be upgraded to bring them in line with community standards of practice (Singer, 1982). Many counties, including Santa Clara, have been ordered to expand services significantly, under court supervision. While court decisions related to this litigation mandate that medical and psychiatric services be compatible with local community standards, community standards of care vary greatly across counties. Furthermore, although various professional groups have developed standards of care concerning medical services, these are not comparable in their format, content, or application to mental health services; thus, no one set of standards has emerged as definitive (Singer, 1982).

However, several aspects of community standards for health care cross local boundaries and may be applied to psychiatric services. First, emergency assessment services must be available for inmates meeting involuntary commitment criteria. Second, acute beds must be available to house and provide treatment for these inmates, including both psychiatric and twenty-four-hour nursing care. Third, outpatient services must be available for inmates who need treatment but not separate housing or staff coverage on a twenty-four-hour basis. And finally, there must be psychiatric supervision of these services and case consultation available. An enriched program environment might include assessments, group therapy, and more aggressive jail diversion and aftercare planning, provided by clinical psychologists or psychiatric social workers, but these services go beyond basic care standards.

Structure and Operations of Mental Health Services in Jails

The third and closely related public policy issue is how to structure and operate custodial mental health services in the most cost-effective manner. While standards such as those noted above generally are accepted among hospital administrators, there are no specific standards for structuring and operating forensic psychiatric care except stipulations about maintaining confidentiality of psychiatric records and prevention of self-destructive behavior. Key decisions regarding the provision of these services (i.e., the level and amount of service delivered, treatment modality types offered, and staffing types and levels) are left to local authorities' discretion. These questions all must be addressed in establishing and maintaining custodial care quality standards for inmates with psychiatric problems.

Constraints imposed by the custody setting itself also are important concerns in structuring forensic mental health services. Even when the mental health unit has primary administrative responsibility for inpatient service, the correctional environment makes it most difficult to operate a quality treatment unit that includes an array of treatment modalities available in psychiatric hospital settings. A major task in planning and managing these services cost-effectively is to bring to bear external mental health services as needed, in an efficient manner, without substantially duplicating these services within the jail. Service delivery models employed by jails have been described previously by Morgan (1982) and Brodsky (1982).

Internal structure and operation of programs are not the only important service provision elements. Usually, the relationship of forensic mental health services with both acute and outpatient services in the local community and with general medical services and the custodial administrative hierarchy are just as critical. The primary link is through the psychiatric services medical director, who must ensure that standards of care, whether imposed by court decree or by local authorities, are met. This individual also must address administrative issues such as training custody staff to make referrals, ensure the efficient identification and transfer of inmates needing mental health treatment, and work out shared roles and responsibilities for non–acute care staff with medical staff, e.g., having medical unit nurses pass medications in outpatient housing, or with custody staff having uniformed deputies on each unit. Issues specifically related to the interdependency of staff from these different agencies have been studied by Steadman et al. (1985).

Access to Mental Health Services

Jail inmates' access to services is a fourth major public policy issue. In making custodial mental health services available, it is important to understand which inmates have access to them and at what point in their incarceration. Inmates identified by custody or medical unit staff may be afforded closer scrutiny than those who are self-referred or referred by other inmates. Inmates may be differentially perceived as being in need and referred by custody staff due to lack of training or cultural bias. Similarly, once inmates are referred and screened by mental health staff, different rates of acceptance may exist because of exclusive administrative guidelines or because some behavior may be viewed even by trained staff as aberrant when in fact it is culturally related. Gender or ethnic bias may exist, as well as bias related to behavior deemed violent or aggressive and threatening to custody staff. All these aspects of service accessibility should be monitored in providing quality care.

Control of Self-Destructive Behavior

A fifth major public policy issue is prevention of self-destructive behavior. Studies of self-injury have demonstrated a higher incidence in local jails than in other criminal justice facilities (Esparza, 1975; Gibbs, 1978; Heilig, 1973), and prevention of this behavior demands the cooperation of both mental health and custody staffs. The mental health service delivery goal typically is to identify the potential for decompensation early and to intervene. To do this, custody and mental health staffs need to be knowledgeable in their assessments of the potential for self-destructive behavior, not only suicidal behavior but self-mutilation as well. Thus, identification needs to be immediate and treatment direct whenever the risk exists and when a disorder is clearly beyond the custody staff's capacity to manage. Self-destructive behavior control is a grievous and difficult problem for mental health and custody staffs in correctional facilities. Completed jail suicides call attention to staffing and procedural inadequacies, raising appropriate questions as to inmate safety.

Mental Health Services in the Santa Clara County Jail and
Policy Questions to Be Addressed

Dealing with these public policy issues raises specific questions for local administrators. Many of these questions have surfaced in Santa Clara County as mental health services in jail facilities have evolved. This section provides an overview of service
evolution and the types of administrative questions to be answered
through evaluative research.

In Santa Clara County, prior to about 1970, very few county
jail inmates were identified as mentally ill, and even fewer noted
to be in need of immediate and ongoing mental health treatment
while in jail. These few were brought to the psychiatric emergency
service from time to time for evaluation. As their numbers rose,
mental health staff began visiting the jail for a half-day each week
to see inmates. Over a twenty-year period, psychiatric services for
mentally ill inmates in the Santa Clara County Jail system have
developed from what was initially an intermittent consultative
function into a twenty-four-hour, twenty-bed infirmary in the maximum security facility, operated and staffed by the Mental Health
Bureau. In addition to the infirmary, segregated housing is available for eighty inmates requiring mental health observation or
treatment, which is under the custody department's direct supervision. Similar increased demand surfaced in the women's and
men's units at the minimum security facility. Currently, mental
health services are provided to about 15 percent of the incarcerated population.

A striking advantage of the availability of a contained psychiatric unit within the jail (an arrangement Santa Clara has in common with four other large California counties) is the opportunity
to provide brief treatment for nonpsychotic offenders who have
been overwhelmed by the circumstances leading to their arrests
and who are unsuitable for housing in a general jail population at
the inception of their incarceration. Access to prompt evaluation
and treatment also can make a substantial difference in managing
a first psychotic episode, the clinical manifestations of which include criminal conduct. Having mental health staff located within
the main facility provides an efficient link between triage services
and ongoing treatment because staff can be dispatched to perform
assessments as the need arises and provide ongoing treatment services for psychotic inmates within the mental health unit.

Mental health staffing in the main jail consists of psychia-
trists, psychologists, psychiatric social workers, licensed counse-

lors, nurses, and psychiatric technicians. Their principal task is to assist in the expedient and efficient processing of a large number of people in custody, many of whom have emotional problems beyond the custody staff's capacity to handle without professional mental health assistance. A by-product of this shared goal has been the development of interdependence between the custody and mental health staffs. This interdependence has increased especially as program operations standards have been defined, in part as a response to ongoing civil litigation relating to jail overcrowding and adequacy of custodial care.

The principal function of mental health staff is evaluation and possible acceptance for treatment of arrestees in the jail's mental health units. Referrals to the mental health unit originate with sheriffs' deputies, who either observe aberrant behavior at the time of booking or obtain historical data indicative of past psychiatric treatment, especially hospitalization. Alternatively, referrals may stem from the jail medical department, for similar reasons or at inmates' direct request.

In most cases, those detained by custody staff and referred for mental health services are seen first for evaluation by a psychiatric technician, who interviews the individual and obtains a psychiatric history under the supervision of the nursing and clinical staffs. One of the questions that has vexed the mental health administration in the past is the inadequacy of this initial contact. Of particular concern has been the fact that the majority of those arrestees seen for intake evaluation are not accepted for any level of mental health treatment within the jail. Thus, there is considerable reliance on the initial evaluator's experience, but hitherto there has been no means of checking on the reliability of the intake evaluation.

Suicide prevention is an important goal of jail mental health services. Eliciting information as to past suicidal behavior is vitally important at intake. Correctly assessing the suicidal tendencies of arrestees who are depressed as a result of their incarceration is a skill that must be mastered by the psychiatric staff and imparted to the custody team. Suicidal verbalization and a history of prior attempts are seen as clear determinants for acceptance into mental health housing at the time of referral. A previous psychiatric hospitalization history is the other primary identifying characteristic of those inmates accepted into the mental health unit, especially if the inmate was admitted involuntarily due to grave disability.

Although psychiatric diagnostic accuracy is important from

many standpoints, the mixed and changeable clinical picture often presented by the inmate population results in a de-emphasis of nosology. The jail mental health staff's efforts and expectations focus more on restoring and maintaining a level of functioning sufficient to facilitate the detainee's passage through the criminal justice process. Thus therapeutic goals are inclined to be short term, and there is an emphasis on crisis and medication therapies to the exclusion of other intervention types. Thus, offering these custodial services is expedient in terms of processing inmates in need of service, but this structure sacrifices elements of a richer program that might be offered in a secure psychiatric hospital setting.

The decision to utilize the criminal justice system, as opposed to the mental health system (e.g., a psychiatric emergency room), for aberrant behavior is made by the arresting officer, whose experience and training are influential in interpreting the behavior observed. Jails and mental health facilities share the serious social burden of overcrowding and quantitative service deficiency. Efforts to offset the overlap of criminal justice and mental health problems in the jail by attempting to divert those inmates who deteriorate in the jail setting despite available jail mental health intervention, are welcomed by the jail administration when security considerations permit such placements. Santa Clara County has developed such a diversion program, especially for inmates who are under mental health conservatorship because of grave disability and who would benefit from a treatment period in a subacute psychiatric facility. An additional program provides supervision in special housing for certain arrestees who otherwise would not qualify for release on their own recognizance.

Overview of Study and Description of Methods

This study was designed to address six policy concerns: (1) describing the number and types of clients being screened following referral to the mental health unit in terms of their psychiatric symptoms and need for specialized, intensive mental health care; (2) comparing the need for service rates among these inmates with the general population rates for Santa Clara County obtained in a series of previous studies (Meinhardt et al., 1987; Meinhardt and Vega, 1983; Vega et al., 1984); (3) determining whether referrals for mental health crisis assessments from custody staff were appropriate; (4) determining whether the inmates screened were being assigned to an appropriate service level based on the interviews; (5) identifying client subgroups with similar patterns of problems among those screened and either accepted or rejected for mental health services, to better assess the service level required compared to the current service level provided; and (6) determining the prevalence of the "mercy booking" phenomenon.

Data collection was conducted in the following manner. For all inmates screened, the crisis screening form already in use was completed by staff. Two symptom/dysfunction scales—the Depression Scale and the General Psychopathology Scale—were added to the crisis screening usually conducted by the main jail's mental health staff to assess inmates' levels of psychological distress. These scales have been used in epidemiological studies conducted elsewhere (Schwab et al., 1979) and have been found to be valid and reliable reflections of the need for specialized mental health services. The Depression Scale also has been used in Santa Clara County to obtain estimates of the general population's need for mental health services. Data regarding the General Psychopathology Scale were available from sites outside Santa Clara County for comparison purposes. Information on the inmates' employment status, major source of income, and living situation at the time of arrest also were gathered.

Inmates were then determined to be in need of psychiatric housing and treatment within the jail (accepted for service) or not in need of psychiatric services (returned to the general jail population). Based on a listing of all inmates screened by mental health staff, a random sampling procedure was instituted to choose inmates for more intensive psychiatric interviews. For inmates rejected for mental health services, about one-third were randomly chosen to receive follow-up interviews. For inmates accepted into psychiatric housing and treatment, a two-thirds sample was selected for follow-up interviews. These procedures netted a group of over 100 inmates screened per month, 322 for the entire study period, and a sample of 35 inmates per month who received intensive follow-up interviews, with a total sample of 108 follow-up interviews during the three-month study. For all inmates who were not admitted to a mental health service after the initial screening, a consent form was used to obtain their permission to conduct the interview and to gather additional data related to their booking charges. About 30 percent of the inmates referred for crisis screening or contacted about a follow-up interview refused to participate.

Comparison to Main Jail Statistics

During the three-month study period, 18,318 bookings occurred at the main jail and the annex. Between March 1 and May
31, 628 inmates were referred for mental health screenings: 118
were booked and released, and 510 were incarcerated inmates. For
this time period, then, 3.4 percent of those booked into the main
jail and annex were referred for psychiatric screenings. However,
data from 1986 indicate that 78 percent of all those booked were
held in custody less than one week; thus, taking into consideration
the average length of incarceration, about 8 percent of those incarcerated at any time in the jail were seen for psychiatric evaluations.

For the 628 inmates referred for psychiatric screenings, 19
percent were cited and released, whereas 81 percent were incarcerated. Of the 118 screened, booked and released, 32 (27 percent)
were sent directly to the emergency psychiatric service (for mental
health evaluations outside the jail setting), while 86 (73 percent)
were cited and released without additional follow-up (neither
found to warrant incarceration nor to be in need of involuntary
mental health services). This information seems to indicate that
the deputies performing the bookings sense that mental health
problems are evident among some of those booked, but they also
know that the person's criminal charges do not warrant incarceration. Thus, the custody staff seems to be doing a good job of discriminating between the two.

Of the 510 incarcerated inmates referred for mental health
screenings, about 33 percent were accepted for psychiatric services. Overall, then, about 30 percent of those referred for mental
health screenings were found to be needing additional intervention, either in or out of the custody setting. These acceptance figures represent about 1.1 percent of the total bookings for that time
period compared to the 1.4 percent of the general population
treated throughout the County Mental Health Bureau.

Need for Mental Health Services

Among the inmates screened in the main jail from early
March through the end of May 1987, 53 percent had scores on the
Depression Scale one standard deviation above those for the gen-
eral population. In the same group, 41 percent had scores on the
General Psychopathology Scale one standard deviation above the
general population. We can estimate the percentage of respondents

who would be classified in the "high need for treatment intervention" category by calculating the percentage of inmates who score
two standard deviations above the mean on each of these scales.
Thirty-six percent of the inmates screened scored two standard deviations above the general population mean on both instruments
compared to the general population figure of 5.3 percent. These results indicate that inmates being referred by custody staff for
screenings are quite symptomatic compared to the general population and thus are appropriate referrals.

Use of Screening Information to Accept or Reject Clients

A series of analyses were performed to identify (a) systematic
differences between the inmates accepted and those rejected for
mental health services and (b) the subset of screening criteria that
best predict whether inmates were assigned to mental health services. In these analyses, individual item scores on the Depression
and General Psychopathology scales as well as the total scale
scores for each instrument were compared across two groups,
those "accepted" for mental health services, that is, assigned to the
infirmary or outpatient units in the main jail, and those "rejected"
for service and assigned to the main jail's general population.

The results of these analyses indicate that the scores of inmates accepted into the mental health units did not differ significantly on either the Depression Scale or the General Psychopathology Scale from those of inmates assigned to nonpsychiatric
housing. Further comparisons indicated that those accepted for
mental health services reported significantly greater hallucinatory
behavior than did those rejected for service, while those rejected
for mental health services reported significantly greater self-blame
and negativism about the future. Comparisons across those accepted and rejected for service on demographic and related clinical indicators demonstrated significant differences concerning the
reason for referral, diagnosis, types of criminal charges, and alcohol use history. A higher percentage of those not accepted for service were self-referred or referred for exhibiting behavior disturbances, while those accepted for service had psychiatric treatment
histories. Proportionately more of those accepted for service had
psychotic diagnoses, whereas those not accepted were more likely
to have antisocial personality disorders or to have no definable diagnosis. In terms of criminal charges, those accepted for mental
health services tended to have fewer misdemeanor charges, on average, but there was no difference in the number of felony charges

between the two groups. The groups were not significantly different in terms of average age or ethnic background (white/nonwhite) or in terms of drug abuse histories. There was, however, a higher proportion of inmates with alcohol use in the group not accepted for service.

To clarify which screening criteria were most closely associated with an inmate's being assigned to mental health services, a discriminant analysis was performed using several clinical indicators such as reason for referral; previous mental health treatment; and history of medications, suicide, self-injury, or assault; as well as a subset of the depression and psychopathology items to predict acceptance into mental health services. These analyses clearly demonstrate that the most powerful predictors of acceptance into the mental health units are those indicating prior psychiatric treatment, hallucinatory behavior, and negativism about the future. These factors can be used to assign correctly 65 percent of the cases to the two groups ($X^2 = 29.22$, $p = .0000$, canonical correlation = .32). These results are encouraging because they indicate a balanced clinical perspective, which takes into account psychiatric history, psychotic symptomatology or conspicuous bizarreness, and a depressive orientation toward the future as primary criteria for acceptance into the mental health unit.

Follow-Up Intensive Psychiatric Interviews

Another purpose of this study was to determine the extent to which mental health staff performing the initial screenings was assigning inmates to the appropriate service level. To address this issue, more intensive follow-up interviews were conducted with a sample of those accepted for service and a sample of those rejected for service by professional mental health staff. The Brief Psychiatric Rating Scale (BPRS) (Overall and Gorham, 1962), the Psychiatric Status Schedule (Spitzer et al., 1970), and the Antisocial Personality Disorder Scale of the Diagnostic Interview Schedule (Robins et al., 1986, Version 3) were used to structure the interviews and rate inmate responses. In order to establish inter-rater reliability for the study, all four raters—a psychiatrist, a doctoral psychologist, and two psychiatric social workers—conducted ten interviews as a group but performed their ratings of each respondent individually. The results of this analysis indicate that interrater reliability is very high, ranging from .90 to .93 across four subscales on the BPRS. Since follow-up ratings would be performed by only one staff per client, we estimated the intraclass reliability coefficient for each rater (Shrout and Fleiss, 1979); these reliability estimates ranged from .60 to .74, which still is acceptable.

Interviews were completed on 108 inmates; 56 had been accepted for mental health treatment, and 52 had been rejected and returned to general jail housing. Each of the instruments contained several subscales and scores on each of these subscales were computed before the comparative analyses were performed. Symptomatology was significantly higher among those inmates accepted for mental health services on three of the twenty-six items: hallucinatory behavior, denial of illness, and overall illness severity. Symptomatology among those rejected for psychiatric services was higher on two of the twenty-six items: guilt feelings and assaultive actions. Furthermore, clinical ratings were higher for the group accepted into mental health services only on one of the subscales of the PSS, that reflecting behavioral disturbance in terms of memory impairment, disorientation, emotional withdrawal, and strange mannerisms and posturing.

Using the five symptomatology items from the follow-up interview, we were able to classify correctly 67 percent of those inmates in the follow-up interviews into the "accept" or "reject" group ($X^2 = 25.01$, $p = .0001$, canonical correlation $= .46$). Each of the discriminant functions derived to describe differences between the accepted and rejected groups only predicts assignment of two-thirds of the cases for each group, that is, they contain a sizable "noise" or error component. Therefore, the results of the follow-up interviews by professional mental health staff indicate that inmates are being screened and assigned to an appropriate treatment service level by initial interviewers, as indicated both in the statistical analyses and in the reports of the clinical staff performing the follow-up interviews on the inmates rejected for specialized treatment.

Indicators of Mercy Bookings

The final important question raised in both mental health and criminal justice sectors concerns the extent to which psychiatric patients are becoming increasingly a part of the criminal justice system. The major indicator of this phenomenon in Santa Clara County custody facilities is defined to be the number of inmates with extensive mental health service histories who are incarcerated in county jail facilities on misdemeanor charges and continue to receive mental health services through the jail. To address this issue, a comparative analysis was performed on data extracted from the Mental Health Information System for fiscal years 1985–86. Comparisons were made across the two groups, those accepted and those rejected for mental health services, for nine types of services: inpatient, day treatment, outpatient, medication visits, case management, emergency psychiatric service visits, jail inpatient, jail medication visits, and jail outpatient services.

Those inmates accepted for mental health services in this study had received significantly greater amounts of inpatient services, day treatment services, medication visits, and emergency psychiatric contacts in the regular mental health service system during FY 1985–86 than those in the rejected group. Furthermore, they also received significantly greater amounts of inpatient, outpatient, and medication services in the jail in FY 1985–86. Thus, inmates accepted for mental health services were more severely impaired and received services both in and out of the custody setting.

Of the 322 cases analyzed in this study, twenty-four inmates received more than three days of inpatient mental health services (the average for all inmates in 1985–86). This group had the following characteristics: 83 percent were diagnosed psychotic; 75 percent were referred to mental health staff by deputies for having previous psychiatric histories; 66 percent had scores on the Depression Scale well above one standard deviation in the normal population (i.e., 1.50 to 5.20); 50 percent had scores on the General Psychopathology Scale well above one standard deviation in the normal population (i.e., 1.26 to 7.44); and 67 percent had more than one misdemeanor charge and one or more felony charges for which they were serving time. Based on this information about these inmates' severe psychiatric impairments and the nature of their charges, we conclude that the phenomenon of mercy bookings is not present to any perceptible extent in Santa Clara County; these inmates are being served by mental health services both inside and outside the jail, and their charges are serious enough to warrant incarceration.

Conclusions

This study provided data pertinent to several major policy questions facing local mental health and custody officials. Of primary concern was the number of inmates in need of psychiatric services and the gravity of their need. Our results demonstrate that the percentage of inmates referred for mental health services inside the jail is about equal to the percentage for the general population. Furthermore, inmates' needs for mental health services are not only clearly evident, they exceed our previous estimates for the county's general population, thus dispelling the myth that incarcerated inmates are being "coddled" by mental health services. It is also evident that front-line custody staff are making appropriate referrals; that mental health staff performing inmates' initial assessments are screening properly, as confirmed by follow-up interviews by professional staff; and that inmates are receiving a level of care appropriate to their needs. Furthermore, sheriffs' deputies are not using the jail for "mercy bookings," but both custody and mental health officials must carefully assess the extent to which severely psychiatrically impaired inmates could benefit from diversion programs during their incarceration, in order to minimize their lengths of stay in the custody mental health units.

We feel that the analysis of the public policy issues discussed in this chapter and the evaluative data presented to address lingering policy questions regarding adequacy of mental health services are important in understanding the context of mental health service provision within a jail setting and in demonstrating to local officials and scholars in the field that policy questions can be systematically addressed through careful research.

CHAPTER 7

AIDS in Jail

JAMES E. LAWRENCE AND VAN ZWISOHN

No issue in contemporary corrections has aroused greater interest and concern than the management of jail inmates known or thought to be infected with the human immunodeficiency virus (HIV), believed to be the causative agent of acquired immunodeficiency syndrome (AIDS). This issue arises in a broad range of contexts: medical care delivery, security, employment conditions, inmate classification and housing, staff and inmate safety, allocation of correctional resources, and criminal justice policy formulation. Significant concerns have been raised by inmates, officers, advocacy organizations, the legal community, politicians, correctional administrators, and medical care providers. Each of these constituencies fosters polarized positions that often appear to be based on mixtures of available scientific research and profound ignorance, compassion and contempt, reasonable concern for personal safety and unreasonable fear.

HIV Disease in the Criminal Justice System

Human immunodeficiency disease occurs in persons who are infected with the human immunodeficiency virus. This virus attacks a type of white blood cell, the T4-lymphocyte, which is responsible for a major portion of the human immune system. Over a period of eighteen months to seven years or more, HIV impairs and finally destroys this part of the immune system. During this period, victims develop increasingly numerous and severe symptoms and abnormal laboratory test results that indicate HIV activity and/or immune system damage. The presence of these groups, or "complexes," of symptoms is referred to as AIDS-related complex (ARC). Finally, immune deficiency is complete and victims contract rare infectious diseases that rapidly overwhelm them with fatal results. This is the end stage of HIV disease, known as acquired immunodeficiency syndrome, or AIDS.

Several behaviors place persons at risk for HIV infection, but the one of primary importance to correctional administrators is intravenous drug abuse. Ninety-five percent of all inmates in New York who died from AIDS had an admitted history of intravenous drug abuse (New York State Commission of Correction [NYSCOC], 1988). Therefore, the management of HIV disease in correctional facilities is largely governed by two important principles:

1. HIV disease represents a broad spectrum of illness, which begins with HIV infection and progresses to AIDS, often years later; and
2. In correctional facilities, HIV/AIDS is primarily a disease of drug abuse.

How significant is the problem of HIV in local jails? It is difficult to say with any degree of certainty. Epidemiological estimates of the incidence and rate of disease transmission vary widely. Differences in reporting procedures, changing medical definitions of the disease, its confusing array of symptoms, and legal protections of personal privacy make precision difficult. According to the Centers for Disease Control (CDC), however, it is clear that no region of the nation is completely free of the disease's impact. But equally clear is that the impact is geographically disparate, both in real numbers and in prevalence rate.

It is to be expected that the incidence of HIV disease in jails and prisons would follow the incidence in their host communities. Nearly a decade of study of the demographics of HIV has confirmed this linkage. Study of AIDS incidence in the United States (CDC, 1989) reveals that AIDS (and therefore HIV infection) rates are highest in the mid-Atlantic, south Atlantic, and Pacific regions of the United States. New York State ranks first in the nation with an annual AIDS incidence rate of 36.9 cases per 100,000 population, followed by New Jersey, Florida, California, Georgia, and

Texas. Washington, D.C., now reports the highest AIDS incidence rate of any city in the nation with 84.5 cases per 100,000 population followed by San Francisco, New York, Newark, and Miami.

Two national studies of jails and prisons (National Institute of Justice [NIJ], 1988; NYSCOC, 1988) reveal that HIV/AIDS incidence in correctional facilities parallels that in the general population. One study (NYSCOC, 1988) revealed the incidence of all forms of HIV disease in state prisons was highest in the mid-Atlantic, southern New England, south Atlantic, and Pacific regions. New York, Massachusetts, New Jersey, North Carolina, South Carolina, and Nevada all reported more than 700 cases of all types of HIV illness per 100,000 inmates. The National Institute of Justice reported that 90 percent of all AIDS cases in local jails were concentrated in the mid-Atlantic, south Atlantic, and Pacific regions (NIJ, 1988).

The rate of inmate AIDS cases in New York is significantly higher than the national inmate AIDS incidence rate, while paralleling that found in New York's general population. By the end of the 1980s, more than 1,000 New York inmates had died from AIDS. Fourteen percent of those deaths occurred in local jails, and 95 percent of the cases had a documented intravenous drug abuse history. Blacks comprised the largest ethnic group (45 percent of all deaths) with whites and Hispanics accounting for 11 percent and 44 percent, respectively, of all deaths (NYSCOC, 1988).

The relatively small percentage of deaths in local jails is deceptive. Since 1981, an average 13 percent of all AIDS mortality cases in New York State prisons were held in upstate suburban/rural jails prior to transfer to state prison. Of the remaining cases, all but 2 percent were held in the New York City jails. A survey conducted by the NYSCOC (1989b) revealed that 396 inmates were diagnosed with some form of HIV disease in local jails (excluding New York City) in 1988. Moreover, the growth in the AIDS incidence rate is about 12 percent annually in metropolitan New York, while four populous counties in the suburban/rural upstate regions report an average annual increase of AIDS cases of 25 percent (New York State Department of Health [DOH], 1988a). Blind epidemiological studies done in New York yielded an inmate seropositivity rate of 17.4 percent (DOH, 1988b). The average seropositivity rate in six other state studies was 4 percent (NIJ, 1988).

Based on the demographic and epidemiological trends of the 1980s, it is increasingly evident that a large and growing HIV pool is cycling through the criminal justice system. It is estimated that 40 percent of those inmates newly admitted to jail and prison with

HIV infection will become ill during incarceration, while the rest will be discharged back to their communities, many without having been diagnosed.

Health Care Delivery in Jails

Jails are, with few exceptions, operated by elected sheriffs. Although there are some general similarities, each county jail is unique, particularly with respect to health care delivery. Each New York County, for example, is required by law to appoint a jail physician and, by state regulation, to conduct inmate health appraisals; provide no medical treatment unless authorized by a physician; make provision for prompt hospitalization in the event of a medical emergency; and maintain adequate medical records. Beyond that, jails are on their own. Some jails have exemplary health care delivery systems, while others have virtually no organized system. Health care budgets are uniformly limited, with wide variation from county to county. A small county jail (average daily census 50 to 100) may spend $15,000 to $20,000 per year. A medium-size facility (average daily census 100 to 300) may spend $100,000 to $120,000 per year. These two categories include 85 percent of New York's jails (NYSCOC, 1988). A few facilities contract services, but catastrophic illness is often excluded from contract coverage. About half of the medium-size facilities have part-time allied health care support. None have contractual agreements with hospitals. Few have in-house infirmaries.

Therefore, about 85 percent of local facilities cannot cope with even one AIDS case for an extended time. A single case over a six-month period could entirely consume a typical jail health care budget. At present, because of short average lengths of incarceration, the problem is limited. However, as previously mentioned, new AIDS cases are now being reported outside the large metropolitan areas at a greater rate than within them.

Clearly, jails have an enormous stake in achieving at least nominal management of HIV/AIDS in a cost-effective manner. This necessarily requires a planned, comprehensive approach. The essential elements of a comprehensive jail system for management of HIV disease in jail are sixfold:

1. early detection and diagnosis
2. medical management
3. inmate classification
4. transmission risk reduction

5. education and training
6. resource allocation

Early Detection and Diagnosis

The HIV Antibody Test. Within four to twelve weeks after exposure to HIV, infected persons develop antibodies to the virus in their blood sera. These antibodies can be detected by the HIV antibody test, which is conducted in two stages. The first stage, known as the Enzyme-Linked Immunosorbent Assay (ELISA) is a general screening test. The second stage, known as Western Blot, confirms ELISA specifically for HIV antibodies. The test detects only antibodies to HIV. It does not detect the virus itself, nor does it predict development of HIV disease in apparently healthy persons who test positive.

In general, those states with the preponderance of AIDS cases have established centralized or regionalized control of HIV antibody testing, administration of the process, and dissemination of the results (NIJ, 1988). California, New York, and Massachusetts have enacted highly restrictive laws. Authority to perform the test often is licensed or proscribed by state health departments, and provisions for informed consent and confidentiality of results may be prescribed by statute. In New York, it can constitute a crime to perform an HIV antibody test without the patient's informed consent or to inform anyone not specifically identified in the statute of the results (New York Public Health Law, Section 2783, 1988). Although mass compulsory testing for HIV remains the subject of heated debate, the general trend in high AIDS–incidence states is away from mass testing (NIJ, 1988). Although some jurisdictions permit mass or compulsory testing, such programs have proved unwieldy, unreliable, and excessively expensive. The following guidelines for HIV antibody testing as part of an early detection program for HIV/AIDS are consistent with applicable laws and prudent correctional practices:

1. Inmates who exhibit symptoms consistent with HIV infection and/or impaired immunity, and those known to have been exposed to HIV should be consentually tested as part of a medical diagnostic workup for suspected HIV/AIDS.
2. Inmates who believe they have been exposed to HIV, relate a history of behavior that places them at risk for HIV infection, and who request a test should be afforded the test.

3. A written, informed consent should be executed with each inmate tested.

4. A pretest and posttest counseling session should be conducted and documented by qualified health care providers in each case. Pretest counseling focuses on the nature of the test and informed consent. Posttest counseling involves transmission risk reduction, available medical care options, the potential social consequences of HIV infection, and the applicable legal rights and protections.

5. The HIV antibody test results should be filed in each inmate's individual facility medical record and in no other location—access to this record should be strictly limited.

6. In cases where inmates are referred to an infectious disease specialist or hospital outpatient diagnostic center for suspected HIV disease, the referring jail physician should request HIV antibody testing as part of the consultation, and request the results.

Admission Health Screening. While HIV disease is not considered curable at present, it is now generally regarded as a treatable disease (Yarchoan et al., 1988). A variety of therapies presently are available that can extend the duration and quality of life for HIV victims. Some treatments may be more effective early in the disease's course, before immunity is permanently destroyed. Therefore, there is a growing consensus that the jail medical department may not ignore the health care needs of inmates with HIV disease merely because they are thought to have a terminal illness. As time and medical science progress, the measure of the adequacy of care may be the effectiveness of the jail's early detection protocol.

Each new inmate should undergo medical and mental health screening upon admission to the jail. All inmates should be questioned concerning a history of risk behaviors known to be associated with HIV infection. Paramount among these is intravenous drug abuse.

Medical Management

Admission Physical Examination. Each newly admitted inmate should receive a medical history and a physical examination within fourteen days of reception. Inmates at risk for HIV disease, particularly intravenous drug abusers, should be examined for clinical evidence of HIV infection or immune deficiency, particularly for the following: chronic fever; chronic cough; shortness of breath; unexplained weight loss; weakness/fatigue; intestinal problems, e.g., diarrhea, nausea, vomiting, or abdominal pain; chills; night sweats; chest pain; swollen lymph glands; headache; chronic flulike illness; fungal infection of mouth or throat (candidiasis); chronic rash; and altered mental status. Inmates who present one or more of these complaints should be evaluated carefully for possible HIV disease, particularly if the patient is a known intravenous drug abuser (NYSCOC, 1988).

Medical Follow-Up and Treatment. Management and treatment of HIV in local correctional facilities requires close coordination with the outpatient infectious disease or immunology clinic of a medical center or with other specialists qualified to treat infectious diseases. Treatment plans should be formulated at such clinics and followed by the facility medical department. HIV disease patients require regular re-evaluation at such clinics.

Nutrition. The nutrition of inmates with HIV disease is affected by their underlying constitutional disease, specific infectious diseases, and the therapies used against them. Constitutional disease (e.g., "wasting") and infectious disease are separate and distinct entities. Therapies are different and have different nutritional implications. Inmates with HIV disease frequently are unable to maintain body weight and require special nutritional support to do so. Medical diets prescribed by a physician should be afforded to inmates.

Psychosocial Services. Services to identify, assess, and manage the social and mental health problems related to illness are a necessary component of managing inmates with HIV disease. These services usually are provided by qualified social workers and will require the county mental health department's involvement.

Inmate Classification

Conditions related to HIV cover a wide continuum. At one pole are inmates whose histories or institutional behaviors involve engagement in two primary risk factors known to be associated with the disease: intravenous drug use and homosexual intercourse. These inmates may warrant housing and supervision designed to reduce the opportunities for such behavior while incarcerated. At the opposite pole are inmates diagnosed as having AIDS who are in the disease's terminal stages. They may present

FIGURE 7.1

The HIV Disease Continuum

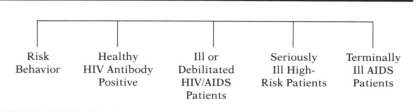

| Risk Behavior | Healthy HIV Antibody Positive | Ill or Debilitated HIV/AIDS Patients | Seriously Ill High-Risk Patients | Terminally Ill AIDS Patients |

few security problems but will require extensive medical care and supervision.

As illustrated in figure 7.1, between the poles are certain distinct categories of inmates: healthy but antibody-positive inmates; chronically ill or debilitated inmates with various, often relatively mild, degrees of HIV-related illness; and very ill, high-risk inmates. Each presents different classification issues.

Apparently Healthy HIV-Positive Inmates. Inmates known to be infected with HIV but who are without signs of major illness need not be segregated from other inmates. Indeed, arbitrary segregation of such inmates for no reason other than asymptomatic or mildly symptomatic HIV infection may violate regulations that prohibit discriminatory treatment.

Ill or Debilitated Inmate HIV/AIDS Patients. Inmates who have developed ARC or AIDS and are chronically ill or debilitated but not sufficiently ill to be hospitalized will require special care at the facility. In general, these patients will require an infirmary setting with a hospital bed, sufficient space to provide direct care, sufficient equipment, and the availability of nursing care. Flexibility in work and educational and recreational programs is needed, and medical monitoring is required when the inmate is not receiving direct medical supervision. These inmates may need assistance with ordinary daily living activities. The security issues may involve dealing with the hostility of other inmates and staff (at this stage, the inmate is likely to have been identified as an AIDS patient); aggressive behavior; and suicide attempts.

Seriously Ill High-Risk Inmates. Inmates who are incontinent, have a communicable or highly communicable infection, are experiencing altered mental status in which there is a risk of danger to self or others, or who are receiving oxygen on a regular basis require a private room apart from the general population and other inmates. Such a room must be equipped to provide necessary care, and nursing staff must be present on a twenty-four-hour basis.

Safety and Security. The foregoing classification recommendations should be interpreted in light of the paramount necessity of maintaining the security of the facility and the safety of the staff and inmates, including an affected inmate. A reasonable appraisal of the risks posed by any inmate with HIV disease should govern classification decisions.

Transmission Risk Reduction

The bloodborne infection caused by HIV is transmitted by direct inoculation of infected blood or body substances containing infected blood products into the circulation or onto mucous membranes of an uninfected person. Significant-risk body substances are blood; semen; vaginal secretions; breast milk; tissue; and the following body fluids: cerebrospinal, amniotic, peritoneal, synovial, pericardial, and pleural (New York Codes, Rules and Regulations [NYCRR], Title 10, Part 63).

The following circumstances constitute significant risk of contracting or transmitting the virus.

1. sexual intercourse that exposed an uninfected person to the semen or vaginal secretions of an infected person
2. sharing of needles and other paraphernalia used for preparing and injecting drugs between infected and uninfected persons
3. gestation, birthing, or breast feeding of an infant by an infected mother
4. blood transfusions or organ or tissue transplants from an infected to an uninfected person
5. direct contact of a significant-risk body substance with an uninfected person's mucous membranes (i.e., eyes, nose, mouth), nonintact skin (open wound, skin with a dermatitic condition, abraded areas), or the vascular system—arising from, but not limited to, needle stick or puncture wound injuries and direct saturation or permeation of these body surfaces by the infectious body substances

Circumstances involving a significant risk of HIV infection specifically do not include exposure to urine, feces, sputum, nasal secretions, saliva, sweat, tears, or vomitus that does not contain blood that is visible to the naked eye. Nor does significant risk include human bites where there is no direct blood to blood contact, blood to mucous membrane contact, or exposure of intact skin to blood or any other body substance (NYCRR, Title 10, Part 63). Significant risk is not present in occupational settings where scientifically accepted universal barrier precautions (such as gloves) and preventive practices are routinely used (CDC, 1988).

Correctional personnel should be aware of the risks attendant to any inmate contact. Knowledge of the precise nature of an individual prisoner's medical diagnosis is far less important than knowledge of safety precautions to be taken when interacting with inmates during the various operations that comprise correctional supervision and security. Correctional personnel should be aware that HIV is only one risk among many, including exposure to many other serious and potentially life-threatening diseases.

Education and Training

No single effort will have a more beneficial effect on a jail administration's capability to manage HIV/AIDS-related issues than an effective education and training program. To be effective, such a program must be credible, relevant, and ongoing. For staff, this means that basic training curricula include adequate coverage of HIV/AIDS-related issues including the etiology and spread of the disease, clinical manifestations of the disease's various stages, transmission methods, preventive measures, available treatments and therapies, testing issues and policies, confidentiality issues and policies, classification and program assignment policies, and supervision issues including transportation and inmate movement.

This material should be taught by an outside presenter thoroughly prepared on the issues, familiar with corrections but outside the direct chain of command so as to create an atmosphere supporting frank and open discussion. An outside medical expert unaffiliated with correctional management and experienced in establishing educational rapport with laypersons would be a good choice. The curriculum should be revised as new information becomes available.

Periodic inservice training should be provided to all facility staff for several reasons. It serves to reinforce the basic training material, provides updated information, and affords an opportunity for discussion of practical problems. Ongoing inservice training provides feedback to administrators concerning staff attitudes and an opportunity to evaluate operating policies and procedures. Such training can relieve stress as well as impart information. Staff concerns or fears can be aired and addressed, rumors controlled, and incorrect information or beliefs corrected.

Inmate education is also important. Risk behaviors should be identified and consequences made clear. Inmates should be made aware that their safety is an essential part of the correctional mission and that reducing or preventing the spread of AIDS is important to that mission. Testing policies should be explained, as well as the availability of medical and mental health services. Symptoms and the progression of the disease should be described, and modes of transmission and prevention should be thoroughly discussed; this may include the effectiveness of condoms and sterilized needles.

Of the greatest importance is the degree to which inmates can be reassured about the maintenance of confidentiality. Printed, multilingual materials prepared by credible, nonjudgmental sources should be distributed and explained at admission and at regular intervals thereafter. Inmates should be encouraged to provide releases when appropriate for medical records and informed consent for testing.

In sum, training and education of both inmates and staff should serve to provide the basis for behavioral restraint, accurate knowledge, and mutual respect. Where HIV/AIDS is concerned, we are all in it together.

Resource Allocation

Medical care costs for AIDS patients, inmates or not, can be staggering. These costs have been known to reach $1,000 per day (Sullivan, 1987). For example, zidovudine, marketed as Retrovir, is an effective agent against HIV. Formerly known as AZT, it has been shown to prolong the quality and duration of life for those infected with HIV. This drug is exceedingly expensive: therapy for a single patient can cost from $2,500 to $3,600 annually. A joint federal/state financial assistance program, ADAP, unfortunately specifically excludes inmates. Because jail budgets are usually a local, rather than a state, obligation, and because the financial resources devoted to corrections are universally viewed as inadequate, corrections administrators and planners must be prepared to aggressively advocate for sufficient funds to meet both current and future needs. Those requests for resources must be linked to management plans, which are viewed as cost-effective. Projections for AIDS incidences for the particular jurisdictions that drive inmate populations must be made in consultation with federal, state, and local public health authorities.

The burden likely will fall, as it does with so many criminal justice and corrections issues, on the facility administrator. Extensive planning and comprehensive needs assessments cannot be implemented without necessary resources and the support of the other actors whose involvement is crucial to the proper management of HIV. Policy made at other criminal justice system decision points—crime control planning, drug policy, arrest coordination, prosecution selection, and sentencing—all have a significant impact on correctional management; yet none are directly within correctional managers' control.

Each of the areas outlined as essential elements of HIV/AIDS management—early detection and diagnosis, medical management, inmate classification, transmission risk reduction, education and training, and resource allocation—have implications not only for the basic task of corrections, that is, institutional safety and security maintenance, but they also require noncorrectional expertise and cooperation. In order to implement an HIV/AIDS management policy consistent with medical and correctional goals, the following must be done:

Develop a Network of Medical Expertise. Depending on the demographic nature of the correctional jurisdiction—urban, suburban, rural; long- or short-term custody; anticipated rate of incarceration of risk-behavior inmates—sources of medical and epidemiological information should be accessible to correctional management. In an urban area, such sources usually can be found within the immediate jurisdiction. In a rural county where HIV disease has been rare, university medical schools, state health departments, or even federal health officials may be available sources for information and advice. This serves two functions: it assures corrections professionals of reliable data and, just as important, familiarizes the noncorrectional medical community with the problems facing jails. Time spent developing this network will yield long-term benefits.

Maintain Close Communication with Facility Medical Providers. In jail, medical management and security management are necessarily closely related. It is axiomatic that conflicts between them will arise. Because correctional managers most frequently come from a security background, it is important that they regularly communicate with other service providers present in the facility to prevent such conflicts from interfering with either security or medical management. Effective inmate classification relies on information regarding both medical and security characteristics. The closer the linkage is between security decisions and medical service imperatives, the better the classification decisions will be and the more appropriate the level of service provided.

Politics, Politics, Politics!

It has been noted even by casual observers that the term "criminal justice system" is something of a misnomer. In an era of scarce public resources, what is given to one part of the "system" frequently is taken from another. If corrections managers are to provide (1) effective education and training to the staff and inmates, (2) the type of care made necessary by the presence of HIV, and (3) cost-effective security for officers, prisoners, and the community, then increased advocacy among all the jurisdictions' decision makers for correctional resources is a necessary part of the jail job. That this is the case not only must be *accepted* by administrators—who long have known it—but *communicated* to staff and the community as well.

Issues related to HIV/AIDS will continue to create challenges for correctional practitioners. Correctional facilities contain a concentration of persons whose behavior and attitudes create a high degree of risk. Adequate management of HIV/AIDS-afflicted inmates requires a cooperative, collegial effort among administrators, security personnel, program staff, and medical care providers. An environment free of ignorance, fear, and hostility is essential. In corrections, HIV is a fact of life. Only through awareness and planning and utilization of good correctional practices will correctional professionals be able to weather this storm.

SECTION THREE

CROWDING AND MANAGEMENT ISSUES FACING THE AMERICAN JAIL

The most severe problem facing contemporary American jails is crowding. State legislatures continue to enact politically popular legislation requiring mandatory sentences without regard for the impact on the corrections system. The result is that local jails have filled to capacity and are overflowing. Between 1972 and 1985, jail populations grew from 141,588 to 233,551 inmates, an increase of almost 84 percent, while the rated capacity of jail space grew by less than 20 percent. Prison populations more than doubled during this same period with one result being that nineteen states now report that some state inmates are "backed up," i.e., being held in local jails. Rarely does a day go by that one does not read news accounts of another sheriff being forced by the courts or state prison officials to accept more inmates in an already overcrowded facility. Estimates and survey results vary, but approximately one in four large jails is under court order to expand capacity or reduce inmate population.

Crowding is a problem in and of itself, but it also exacerbates other problems: access to medical, counseling, educational, and recreational programs; proper classification; jail management;

and overall safety and security. Wayne Welsh and his colleagues discuss an important cause of jail crowding—local politics, which too often operates in an environment clouded by public misperception of the jail and its operation. Also, local policymakers too often are influenced by a small, but vocal, segment of the population. They recommend that local officials (1) be more sensitive to the complexity of public opinion, which they find to be less punitive and more diverse than commonly believed and (2) use media and public information resources more aggressively to present jail problems and potential solutions to the public.

Michael Welch explores the question of whether makeshift jails are necessary because of the continued misuse of our main jails. Makeshift facilities may help in the short term, but Welsh is not optimistic about current efforts to find lasting solutions to the problem of crowding. He notes that crowding usually is viewed as a "temporary problem," while in reality it always has been a problem and will continue to be until long-term strategies are developed.

The last two chapters in this section offer some potential remedies for jail problems in general, and crowding in particular. Eric Poole and Mark Pogrebin call for a reconceptualization of jail organization and management as each relates to improved utilization of personnel. Jails are not working very well, and we must be more humane, more creative, and more willing to take risks in our management approaches. They recommend more flexibility in organizational form; more active participation by jail managers in personnel issues; steadier communications between line staff, managers, and those engaged in developing personnel policies; and, overall, greater commitment to long-range planning. These changes would make the jail a less stressful place to work, resulting in reduced turnover and better staff-to-inmate relations.

Linda Zupan and Ben Menke also argue for greater attention to the selection, training, and retention of jail personnel and for the development of a career officer orientation. Traditional supervision styles, in conjunction with traditional architectural designs, are a serious impediment to formal and legitimate institutional control of inmate behavior that may encourage violent and destructive behavior. They advocate the "new generation" approach to jail construction and management that may provide a safer and more humane environment for both inmates and staff.

CHAPTER 8

The Politics of Jail Overcrowding: Public Attitudes and Official Policies

WAYNE N. WELSH, MATTHEW C. LEONE,
PATRICK T. KINKADE, AND HENRY N. PONTELL

Overcrowded penal facilities represent the single largest dilemma facing modern American penology. In 1984, twenty-five states had at least one prison under court order or consent decree to improve confinement conditions, including overcrowding, while six other states were operating their entire prison system under court order (Bureau of Justice Statistics, 1988a). Overcrowded institutions, however, are not limited to state and federal prisons. Jails, more numerous than prisons and more local in nature, also are coming under judicial scrutiny because of problems associated with housing and processing large numbers of pretrial (legally innocent) detainees and sentenced offenders. In 1987, 33 percent of the nation's large jails were under court order to improve confinement conditions, including overcrowding (84 percent of court orders) (Bureau of Justice Statistics, 1988b). Despite stepped-up jail construction, it is unlikely that we simply can build our way out of the overcrowding crisis (Busher, 1983; California Board of Corrections, 1985; Pontell, 1984).

Despite the enormity of the jail overcrowding problem, solutions are not readily apparent. Important areas of influence to be examined are the interaction between public opinion and governmental policy development regarding jails and how public reactions impact on measures designed to alleviate jail overcrowding.

In examining the relationships among penal policies, jail over-crowding, and public opinion, we delineate three main areas: (1) public attitudes toward punishment and the use of alternatives to incarceration; (2) discrepancies between the views of policymakers and the public; and (3) public opinion and the siting of additional correctional institutions.

First, it is suggested that official ideology and public opinion regarding the purposes of incarceration historically have alternated between rehabilitation and retribution. Although numerous alternatives to incarceration have been proposed to help alleviate current jail and prison overcrowding (e.g., Petersilia, 1987), negative public attitudes have, in the past, severely limited such practices (Smykla, 1981).

Second, an important issue regards the accuracy of policymaker perceptions of public opinion (e.g., Cory and Gettinger, 1984; Cullen et al., 1985). If policymakers misperceive or misinterpret public desires, then claims by public officials that they simply are fulfilling the public will are misleading. Among the costs of exaggerated perceptions of public punitiveness are jail and prison overcrowding, expensive lawsuits, and the issuing of court orders declaring that confinement conditions are unconstitutional.

A third major area impacting jail crowding concerns public opposition to proposed jail and prison sites, which has thwarted official attempts to build new facilities. Attempts to choose a correctional institution site typically result in a "not in my back yard" (NIMBY) impasse (Peele, 1985). Although obtaining local constituents' support would seem to be an integral part of effective planning, officials instead attempt to "dump" a jail on someone else's constituency, which results in local outrage but quiet condonement by the rest of the county (glad, of course, that the jail is not near them). Although demonstrating a desire for new or improved facilities in which to incarcerate offenders, the public is at the same time actively preventing their siting and eventual construction.

Jail Overcrowding: One County's Experience

California's jail system is the country's largest. Between 1974 and 1984, California's jail population nearly doubled (Kizziah, 1984). As of August 1987, there were 60,802 California jail prisoners, 35 percent over the combined rated capacities of 45,085 (California Board of Corrections, 1988).

Our analysis of jail overcrowding, using data drawn largely

from Orange County, California, underscores the complexity of interactions among public opinion, official policies, and jail overcrowding. Orange County has the state's third largest jail population, behind Los Angeles and San Diego (California Board of Corrections, 1988) and the nation's eighth largest (Bureau of Justice Statistics, 1988b).

The American Civil Liberties Union (ACLU) filed a class-action lawsuit in 1975, alleging violations of inmates' constitutional rights due to overcrowding and poor confinement conditions. The Orange County Central Jail's average daily population had reached nearly 2,000, far in excess of its state-rated capacity of 1,219 (Hicks, 1985). In 1978, a U.S. district court judge ordered standards including a bed for each inmate detained more than 24 hours, a minimum of eight hours sleep per night, regular showers, and a twice-weekly clothing change. Procedural changes regarding recreation, visitation, and inmate handling also were specified. Later, a population cap of 1,400 was set for the central jail (Reyes, 1985).

In 1985, the same judge found the sheriff and county board of supervisors in contempt of the court order. Mandated changes had not been implemented and, at times, over five hundred men were still sleeping on the floor. The county was fined $50,000 (to be used to hire a special master to oversee compliance) and levied an additional charge of $10 per day for each inmate who slept on the floor for more than one night.

To meet the court order's demands, Orange County took various measures to reduce jail populations. The sheriff discontinued housing state and federal prisoners (e.g., parole violators) awaiting hearings or transfers, as well as inmates returning to local courts to testify. Inmates also were released up to five days early to balance jail population counts, under Section 4024.1 of the California Penal Code (Perlman, 1986). Finally, under the Penal Code's Section 853.6, all misdemeanor suspects with warrants under $5,000 were cited and released after signing a promise to appear in court.

The special master's recommendations included implementation of two alternatives to incarceration. The first was development of a home-confinement program for those assigned to the county's work furlough program (Needham, 1987a). A one-year pilot Supervised Electronic Confinement program (SEC) was implemented in October 1986, supervising 133 inmates (Schumacher, 1987). The program was projected to have saved 5,759 jail bed days in the twelve-month period and was expanded due to its demonstrated success. The second suggestion was that the county increase its use of the county parole program, under which inmates may apply to a local parole board for early release under certain conditions (California Board of Corrections, 1985). Although the county has considered this alternative, it has been used sparingly (County Administrative Office, 1986).

Numerous construction projects have been planned to increase jail capacity, although none has been initiated due to a tangle of legal problems and community opposition. Lawsuits brought by cities and community groups are pending over all of the projects, and needed funding has not been secured. A proposed sales tax increase to raise jail funds is not expected to pass if it is put up for vote, and the board of supervisors has postponed this course of action until a more effective campaign to gain public support can be formulated (Knap, 1988a). As a result, jail construction may be delayed by as much as two years (Knap, 1988b).

The court order was removed on July 1, 1988, because the judge felt that the county was taking "sincere and sufficient steps" to reduce overcrowding (Dawson and Warner, 1988). The ACLU, which filed the original class-action suit resulting in the court order, argued that many constitutional violations remained at county facilities (Dawson, 1988). New charges of brutality toward inmates were filed in federal court on August 12, 1988 (Weikel, 1988).

Methodology

In examining interactions among public opinion, penal policies, and jail overcrowding, this study utilized an "elite interview" methodology (Dexter, 1970; Lofland, 1971). Key policymakers' perceptions are crucial determinants of how policies actually are formulated, initiated, and carried out by those in positions of power (Berk and Rossi, 1977; Gottfredson and Taylor, 1987). Sampling of officials, therefore, was based on the knowledge of key actors either employed in the county criminal justice system or directly involved in policy decisions affecting county jails. We interviewed officials in the following agencies: sheriff's department (n = 2), judges and court officials (n = 9), prosecutors (n = 4), public defenders (n = 2), county board of supervisors and aides (n = 7), probation officials (n = 6), local police chiefs (n = 18), one professional corrections consultant, and state legislators directly involved in jail and prison issues (n = 15). Overall, sixty-four key policymakers were interviewed.

Interview questions were based on jail and prison literature reviews, technical reports, newspapers, and archival data. Questions were centered on perceived causes and effects of jail overcrowding, as well as on potential solutions. The interviews ranged from thirty to ninety minutes.

Public Attitudes toward Punishment and the Use of Alternatives to Incarceration

The "get tough movement" (Cullen et al., 1985) often has been presented as an example of democracy in action: the public gets what it wants; namely, a tougher response to crime. While clearly it is debatable that tougher laws and enforcement actually have fulfilled their goals or added substantially to public safety, public opinion cannot by itself account for the present retributive climate. In order to account for the present climate, one must examine the historical background of public and policymaker attitudes toward incarceration, in conjunction with elected officials' attempts to respond to and shape public perceptions about crime and criminal justice.

Ideological swings have shaped correctional policy throughout modern American history (Rothman, 1980). A progressive reform movement supportive of rehabilitation occurred in the early twentieth century, leading to the development of probation, parole, and indeterminate sentencing.

Early support for rehabilitative ideals can be seen as a result of the interplay between "conscience and convenience" (Rothman, 1980). Conscience described reformers' well-intentioned belief in the state's ability to transform criminals into productive members of society. However, the widespread acceptance of rehabilitative ideals by public officials was also a matter of convenience: ideals accepted were those that increased official discretion and supplemented efficient offender processing.

Progressive reform did not live up to its high goals, however. Crime was neither reduced nor eradicated. In addition, administrative demands for secure custody compromised rehabilitative program quality. As Rothman (1980: 10) maintains: "In the end, when conscience and convenience met, convenience won. When treatment and coercion met, coercion won." Disillusionment, combined with harsh economics and the rising crime rates of the 1920s and 1930s, facilitated a shift toward retributive policies, epitomized by scathing attacks on the probation and parole systems. The legacies of probation, parole, and indeterminate sentencing, however, remained (Rothman, 1980).

Rehabilitative goals were not so widely expressed by public officials again until the 1960s. The Law Enforcement Assistance Administration (LEAA) spent millions of federal dollars on community corrections programs during the late 1960s and early 1970s (Blackmore, 1986). Advocates argued that community-based programs (e.g., reintegration programs, work furloughs, and educational programs) would be more humane, less expensive, and more effective in reducing recidivism than would monolithic correctional institutions. The use of community corrections, while exemplifying rehabilitative ideals, also allowed the state a certain amount of "convenience": alternatives apparently became supplements to, rather than replacements for, jails and prisons (Austin and Krisberg, 1982; Chan and Ericson, 1981; Hylton, 1982).

In his analysis of "decarceration," Scull (1984) suggests that community corrections rhetoric merely provided ideological camouflage for the state to reduce its expenditures on institutional incarceration. He argues that the attractiveness of community corrections to policymakers resided more in its perceived cost-effectiveness than in its potential rehabilitative value.

Although offender reintegration into the community was to be a primary purpose of community corrections (President's Commission, 1967), available evidence suggested that the public did not desire to be integrated with offenders. Homeowners strongly resisted proposed community correctional facilities, citing threats to public safety and decreased property values (e.g., Blackmore, 1986; Smykla, 1981).

The new rehabilitative rhetoric of community alternatives also was dampened by an increasingly conservative political climate and rising crime rate of the late 1970s (Gross, 1982). Ronald Reagan was elected president in 1980 partly on a law-and-order platform, which placed responsibility for social ills on weak and permissive leadership and evil individuals who comprised the "crime problem." In a 1981 speech to the International Association of Chiefs of Police, Reagan criticized the "social thinkers" of the 1960s and suggested that only "deep moral values" could hold back the "darker impulses of human nature" (Gross, 1982).

Neither the effect of official rhetoric nor public opinion is unidirectional, however. Public opinion, policy decisions, and media coverage interact and feed on one another to influence the social response toward crime. One study, for example, shows the effects of official policies and media pronouncements on public opinion and the creation of "moral panics." In an analysis of the mugging panic in Great Britain, Hall et al. (1978) suggested that repressive crime control policies, coupled with selective media coverage focusing on extreme instances of newly defined threats to public order, helped define and shape a crisis. Paradoxically, this perceived threat led to increased law enforcement, greater detection of crime, and increased, rather than decreased, public fear. Public fear led to further calls for tougher law enforcement, regenerating and perpetuating a vicious cycle.

In recent years, the Reagan administration helped shape a punitive public response toward criminals, which resulted in reduced support for rehabilitation and the use of alternatives. One local official pointed out that national crime policies and programs probably affected local criminal justice systems in fundamental ways:

> If you look at national trends, about 1980 is when the populations in prisons and jails started to go. Anything else happen in 1980? What happened in Washington in 1980? We got a new President. We got a new justice system. We got a new Attorney General. And some of the philosophy changed. (Personal interview).

A contributing factor to overcrowding, outside of criminal justice system control, was a large increase in the younger more crime-prone age groups, brought about by the maturing of the postwar baby boom generation (Blumstein, 1988). The changing population age composition, however, intersected with increasingly conservative political agendas.

The preferred course of action was to "get tough" by increasing law enforcement expenditures, restricting parole, increasing sentence lengths for certain crimes, and building more correctional institutions (Cullen et al., 1985). One official suggested that the public had contributed to more severe sentencing policy by exercising their electoral prerogative:

> . . . how many judges got knocked off by tough-ass DA's who were saying that so-and-so was weak on crime? Well, you don't have very much of that happening [now] because every single one of these guys has got their foot to the floorboard in trying to send everybody up for life sentences regardless of what their crime was. (Personal interview)

Out of necessity, however, conservative ideology has begun to turn on itself. As jail and prison populations overextended available capacities, and as court orders to reduce correctional populations proliferated, the expanded use of alternatives once again has become politically feasible and even necessary. As one official noted:

> I think that even Republicans who have never been fans of rehabilitation and tend to be more on the "law-and-order" side of things are coming to realize that we cannot continue to construct jails and prisons fast enough to keep up with the increased penalties that put more people in those institutions. So, I think that there will be movement across the political spectrum to support alternatives. (Personal interview).

At the same time that alternatives to incarceration are becoming more politically and fiscally feasible, another revelation has begun to surface that may increase even further their political viability: public attitudes may not be as uniformly harsh as is often thought. In the 1984 Orange County Annual Survey (Baldassare, 1984), 64 percent of those polled favored longer prison sentences, and 68 percent disagreed that probation and parole should be used as alternatives to prison. However, the same survey also found that 66 percent responded that prison conditions needed to be improved (Baldassare, 1984). Similarly, Cullen et al. (1985) found that a majority of Texas residents polled felt that the courts were too easy on criminals (77 percent) and that prison inmates should serve their full sentences (58 percent). However, many of these same respondents said that rehabilitation was an important prison function (79 percent), and 72 percent favored some type of community-based corrections instead of simply "building as many prisons as needed." In surveys of two Ohio cities, Skovron et al. (1988) found that most respondents (80 percent and 70 percent for the two cities) favored allowing prisoners to earn early release credits through good behavior and to participate in education or work programs while in prison. A large majority (90 percent and 87 percent) also favored the development of local programs to keep nonviolent and first-time offenders active and working in the community.

Other research supports the notion that the public is less retributive and holds more complicated attitudes than public officials give them credit for. Doble (1977), using a focus-group survey and interview method, explored public attitudes toward crime and punishment. Focus groups are directed discussions of public policy issues among small groups of people representative of their fellow citizens:

> Focus groups are designed to probe issues more deeply than public opinion surveys can, allowing participants to explain their opinions in order to surface the assumptions that underlie these perspectives. (Schoen, 1987: 4)

Doble conducted focus groups with a total of 125 men and women in ten U.S. cities.

Considerable support was found for the use of alternatives to incarceration. Rehabilitation was perceived to be a primary goal of the prison system, although respondents thought that prisons presently were doing a poor job in this regard. Respondents supported rehabilitation because they understood that most offenders eventually get out of prison; job training and education were seen as priorities. The use of alternatives to incarceration (e.g., restitution, community service, fines, drug and alcohol abuse treatment, halfway houses) was strongly supported, although respondents thought that certain types of offenders (e.g., violent or repeat offenders) should be excluded and that alternatives should not be unduly "soft."

Sometimes, however, the public simply does not have adequate information on criminal justice issues and may express simplistic opinions in response to questions that overtax their knowledge base (e.g., Krisberg, 1988). One official noted this problem:

> Public opinion is a really difficult thing to weigh because . . . when I'm confronted with a member of "the public" and we talk facts, their facts are so sketchy, or just erroneous, that it's hard to give a lot of weight to the public opinion on technical matters. They just don't have the details. (Personal interview).

These population surveys show considerably more support for rehabilitative goals and the use of alternatives than is generally thought, and a considerable portion of the public appear frustrated with the failure of corrections to rehabilitate and with rising incarceration costs. Several officials perceived public frustration with corrections but anticipated little public support for rehabilitation:

> . . . if the public really understood that in order to keep this person from harassing you permanently, there are some things that we ought to do . . . we can throw him in; but, if we've not rehabilitated him . . . he's going to be right back out, worse than before. The public says get rid of him: put him on a ship that has no bottom to it and let him sink into the ocean. (Personal interview)

Many officials, however, advocated alternatives because of the perceived necessity to reduce overcrowded correctional conditions and because of insufficient time and finances to build new jails and prisons. Alternatives were seen as increasingly viable not as a result of public support but in spite of a shortage of it:

> ... there is neither money nor time to build, or operate the number of beds that the charts all indicate. It is strictly impossible; it will never happen. So, therefore, what will happen? Alternatives will happen. (Personal interview)

Discrepancies Between Viewpoints of Policymakers and the Public

Public opinion is less retributive and more complex than is commonly thought. Political figures probably have overestimated the public's punitiveness and have used this presumed sentiment to enact policies which, although intended to appease the public, contributed to jail and prison overcrowding (Skovron et al., 1988).

Research that investigates the relationship between public attitudes and policymaker perceptions of those attitudes has been carried out in several states. Riley and Rose (1980) surveyed a large segment of the residents of the state of Washington concerning their opinions on correctional issues. These attitudinal responses were compared to previously assessed attitudes of Washington state policymakers, who had evidenced a belief that the public wanted tougher penal measures (Berk and Rossi, 1977). Although the results were somewhat inconclusive, the findings suggested that policymakers exaggerated the punitiveness of public opinion.

Relationships between public opinion and policymaker perceptions were examined in more detail by Gottfredson and Taylor (1987) in a Maryland study. The research included a sample of eighty criminal justice system policymakers and a survey of six hundred state residents. Although numerous findings were reported, the relationship between public support for four correctional goals and policymaker perceptions of such public opinion is particularly relevant to our study. The researchers had resident respondents rank four correctional goals in order of importance: incapacitation, rehabilitation, punishment, and deterrence. Policymakers ranked each goal in terms of how important it was to the public. The correlation between public and policymaker rankings of the four goals measured $-.84$. This relationship clearly indicates serious policymaker misperceptions. Komarnicki and Doble (1986: 121) report similar results.

The get tough movement appears to have taken on a life of its own, supported by two major social realities. The first concerns the vulnerability of those in the public eye who appear soft on crime. As a result, some officials exploit crime and punishment issues for their own political gains. The tradition of getting tough is also espoused by special interest groups, such as MADD (Mothers Against Drunk Driving). These groups, while not necessarily representative of general public opinion, create a sense of accountability in public officials, who already feel duty bound to comply with what they perceive as the public's desire for punishment.

The second aspect of social structure potentially promoting the mismatch between public opinion and policymaker perception concerns the media's role. Reactions to deviance by both the public and social control agents largely are influenced by the nature of information that is available to each (Cohen, 1972). In modern westernized societies, much of this information is secondhand, interpreted and filtered by the media. Even if no conscious attempt is made to distort the facts, the choice of which facts are presented is always guided by the "Will it sell?" notion of newsworthiness. By concentrating news coverage on extreme and dramatic crimes, the news media may create the impression that the problem (and therefore the public's response) is more severe than it really is and may fuel sporadic outbursts by the public or special interest groups that influence policymaker perceptions and responses.

Public Opinion and Correctional Institution Siting

The social impacts of certain types of industries and public facilities are an important issue. These impacts range from threats to public health associated with landfills and toxic waste disposal sites to social, economic, and safety issues related to airports and correctional institutions. There are two basic elements such land uses have in common: (1) they represent utilization of existing land in a fashion that is undesirable to local residents (Locally Undesirable Land Uses, or LULUs) and (2) proper facility siting can make the difference between success or failure of the venture.

Labeling a facility a LULU does not imply that the public does not see the need for these facilities, only that they do not want them in their backyard. This "not in my back yard" (NIMBY) movement has affected the location of numerous industries (see, e.g., Colin, 1984: ch. 7; Popper, 1981, 1985). Concerns such as decreased land values may be real but are generated in many instances by a form of self-fulfilling prophecy (Merton, 1957). Residents' panic may lead to a mass local attempt to sell property quickly, resulting in the reduced land values they feared.

Land value reductions near correctional sites, where observed at all, usually are not nearly as serious as originally thought (Abrams, 1988; Hawes, 1985). Similarly, claims by community opponents that nearby correctional facilities will result in a public safety threat also are suspect. Comparisons with matched control jurisdictions have found equal or lesser crime rates in areas with correctional institutions (Abrams, 1988; Hawes, 1985) and no incidents of physical harm afflicted on residents as a result of escapes (Abrams, 1988).

Two distinctions are crucial to the analysis of jail siting: (1) the purpose of the proposed facility must be identified (i.e., will it be used for the intake and release of inmates, for housing sentenced inmates, or both?) and (2) the security level of the proposed facility must be identified (i.e., will the facility be used to house maximum, medium, or minimum security inmates?).

If the facility in question is primarily an intake/release center, usually it will process new arrestees, check them for outstanding warrants, screen them for pretrial release, provide standard health checks, classify their security risk level, and assign them to a cell pending arraignment or trial. If convicted, the inmate is sent either to a state prison or to a county institution—such as a jail—where the sentence is served. Although many jails serve both functions (intake/release and housing sentenced inmates), this distinction can create different types of controversy.

An intake/release center will experience a constant traffic flow: lawyers waiting to see clients, bail bondsmen, inmates' families and friends, and officers doing initial bookings and inmate court transfers. Facilities for sentenced inmates, however, experience much less traffic, mainly visitors. Such traffic is not without problems, however: community members perceive visitors as potentially dangerous themselves.

Depending on the institution's security level, the public also may perceive a threat from potential escapes of dangerous criminals into their neighborhood. A single dramatic incident has an enormous impact on public opinion. One well-known escape from a California prison that ended in tragedy several years ago still influences the opinions of policymakers and the public:

> . . . we have worked very, very hard to educate the public, but it is also very hard to convince the public, say in the Gypsum Canyon area, who say "Hey, look, we live near Chino, we know what Cooper

did out there and killed that family." We say, "Yeah, but don't you understand a person can't be sentenced to more than a year in a county jail? If you go beyond a year then you go to state prison." People won't accept that; people just come back and say "I don't care." (Personal interview)

From a policymaker perspective, however, some locations are more desirable and efficient than others. These concerns are explained by the concepts of *costs of friction* and *geometry of industrial location*, as first proposed by Adna Weber (1929). The *geometry of industrial location* process originally was formulated to explain the location of industrial enterprises, based on criteria of efficiency and cost effectiveness. Determining location factors included the industry's proximity to the labor market, costs of moving the finished product to market, and costs of moving raw materials to the production site. The costs of moving labor, raw materials, and finished products from one place to another are referred to as the *costs of friction*.

Some jail sites may be more efficient than others. In a large county such as Orange, which is comprised of twenty-six smaller cities (most operating separate police forces), the attempt to centrally locate any facility is extremely difficult. Costs of friction are felt both by local police forces, who book inmates into the jail, and sheriffs' deputies, who transport inmates to court and back. One official expressed this difficulty as follows:

> . . . we need jails that are centrally located because prisoners have to go to all five courts in this county, which means that you have to transport them as far north as Fullerton to Westminster, and all the way to South County, Laguna Niguel. (Personal interview)

In some of Orange County's southern cities, a round trip to the jail intake facility, including the paperwork necessary to book a prisoner, may take an officer a minimum of three to four hours. As one law enforcement official noted, "We can't afford to lose an officer for half a day just to run in a public drunk" (personal interview).

The courts can also play a significant role in jail site selection. One proposed jail site (Katella/Douglas in Anaheim) has been temporarily put on hold since community opponents successfully challenged the validity of an Environmental Impact Report (EIR) in Superior Court. The judge ruled that the report failed to sufficiently discuss possible economic and social effects of the jail on the surrounding community. County supervisors were given six months to submit an amended report (Zoroya and Serrano, 1988).

Community opposition to a proposed jail site also can involve organized attempts to mobilize local resistance. Scare tactics sometimes are used, warning of the loss of family safety and drops in property values. Such campaigns have involved the use of visuals, such as films and posters showing family-oriented persons being criminally victimized by those either released or escaped from the jail (Needham, 1987b). Eventually, partisans begin to suggest better jail locations, with some favoring more remote localities and others insisting on urban sites closer to the courts.

An example of this is found in the case of Gypsum Canyon, the proposed site for a 6,200-bed, maximum-security jail in Orange County, which has met with organized resistance from affluent communities. Residents have complained that they would be able to see the jail from their homes, that it would attract an undesirable element in the form of visitors, and that dangerous offenders might escape into the community. A local group, Taxpayers for a Centralized Jail, has obtained the required 66,200 signatures to put an initiative before voters forcing all new jail construction to be limited to Santa Ana, the county seat (Knap, 1988c). The board of supervisors must now consider this petition before taking any action on the Gypsum site.

Expansion of existing facilities also has met with community and local government resistance. Expansion of a medium-security jail in the city of Orange would have added 300 maximum-security jail beds and 700 medium- to minimum-security beds. Because of local resistance, the board of supervisors decided that only medium-security beds would be built. The city of Orange, however, has launched a lawsuit to prevent expansion of any sort (Zoroya, 1988).

A combination of community resistance and poor planning prevented any further expansion of jail capacity at another site, the James A. Musick Honor Farm in El Toro, originally designated as the county's long-term jail site. The board of supervisors was criticized for allowing private property development alongside this previously "remote" site:

> . . . they went down and bought a sizable piece of property next to the Marine quarter in El Toro, and that got into some political activity that was questionable, and the next thing you know is they say you can't use that 100 acres. This is the only planning we have ever done with the county, because now we have allowed single-family

housing intrusion and industrial intrusion on the site, and we now have all kinds of problems in being able to utilize the only site that we did plan ahead. (Personal interview)

The widespread attempts of citizen groups to prevent jail construction in their neighborhoods exemplify the "toilet assumption" offered by Slater (1976: 21), who claims that the public feels "that unwanted matter, unwanted difficulties, unwanted complexities and obstacles will disappear if they are removed from our immediate field of vision." The toilet assumption's basic premise (out of sight, out of mind) operates on the idea that people prefer not to deal with social problems personally but to remove them as far from their daily existence as possible. It is paradoxical that citizens want a tough response to crime but resist strongly the siting of correctional institutions needed to implement such a policy.

While urban NIMBY groups are fighting to stop correctional construction in their areas, other locations (usually more remote, less populous, and economically depressed) actually have requested to have correctional facilities built in their communities. For example, a state prison has been well accepted in Fresno, California (McClatchy News Service, 1988: B12), and the state of California has been courted to situate a prison in Imperial County (Associated Press, 1988: B11). To their advantage, these sites usually offer cheap and abundant land, a willing (if untrained) work force, and local government support. However, the time and cost of transporting inmates eventually may offset any revenue saved by utilizing a remote site.

Summary and Recommendations

Public opinion affects decisions regarding the use of jails and alternatives in diverse and significant ways. Policymakers have certain perceptions of what the public wants that only partially represent reality. The relation between public opinion and public policy must be seen as both transactional and dynamic. Policymakers, by their actions and public pronouncements, can shape public opinion. Public lobbies, however, also can have an impact on policymakers and policy decisions. These processes are also dynamic in that public and policymaker attitudes fluctuate over time. As such, what was accepted fact yesterday may be historical fancy tomorrow.

There is little doubt that significant, vocal portions of the public have influenced policymaker perceptions of public opinion and have impacted decisions regarding jail site selection and the use of alternatives to incarceration. Elected officials largely blamed the "punitive public" for harsh sentences, tougher laws, and overcrowding, although evidence suggests that such perceptions may be overly simplistic, inaccurate, or even self-serving.

Four major policy recommendations emanate from the preceding analysis:

1. Policymakers should more aggressively use media and public information resources to squarely present correctional problems and potential solutions to the public, rather than simply bending to what they perceive to be the public will (Schwartz, 1989). Attitudes toward alternatives to incarceration and institutional siting or expansion are not shaped in a vacuum.

2. Policymakers must be more sensitive to the complexity of public opinion: the public holds attitudes that are less punitive and more diverse than commonly acknowledged. Public opinion regarding the use of alternatives to incarceration and jail siting should be tapped via competently conducted population surveys, focus groups, or public forums. Care must be taken, however, that special interest groups are not overrepresented in policy formulation. Public disputes need not proceed as hostile "win-lose" encounters but can be managed effectively and fairly (Susskind and Cruikshank, 1987).

3. A comprehensive needs assessment should be done for the particular jurisdiction under consideration. Although detailed discussion of this topic is beyond the scope of this chapter, needs assessments should determine which persons enter the jail, how long they stay, and by what mechanisms they are released. Needs assessments should project long-term jail needs and explore the appropriate use of various alternatives to incarceration (both pretrial and postsentencing). Excellent examples of jail needs assessments are provided by the National Council on Crime and Delinquency (1985, 1988).

Community alternatives can provide a viable means of reducing jail and prison overcrowding and may assist officials in complying with court orders and in reducing future litigation. Alternatives to incarceration also may hold rehabilitative potential, which might lessen recidivism rates. However, careful problem analysis, decision making, implementation, formalization, and evaluation (Feeley, 1983) are needed if community programs are potentially to demonstrate positive effects. Public acceptance of such programs also must be more actively cultivated than has been the case previously (Blackmore, 1986). If such measures are used, and realistic goals and expectations are clearly specified, convenience need not win out over conscience.

4. If a competent and thorough jail needs assessment determines that increased institutional capacity is needed, then various types of jail construction should be explored. Many jails currently under court order are old, outmoded, and inefficient. Modern designs, such as the modular, direct-supervision model, may enable officials to more efficiently and humanely process and house inmates and reduce or avoid litigation (Gettinger, 1984).

It is fruitless to place blame for jail problems solely on the public or those who make policies affecting corrections. Public policy formation is a dynamic political process, fraught with conflicting values and multiple interests. Responsible government, however, cannot merely deflect blame for problems by claiming to follow public will. Neither can moral entrepreneurship (Becker, 1963), insensitive to public demands, be a viable route for policymakers. Any serious progress in solving jail and prison problems will require a rational balance between these two extremes.

Jail crowding is a major criminal justice issue that will long be in the public eye. Jail and prison problems will not be solved by public and official focus on misunderstood and often misperceived crises in the use of incarceration, but by the introduction of systematic research and valid information to inform future directions and policies.

CHAPTER 9

The Expansion of Jail Capacity: Makeshift Jails and Public Policy

MICHAEL WELCH

The jail often is characterized as a "strange correctional hybrid" because it is used as a detention center for suspects, a correctional facility for misdemeanants, and a refuge to hold social misfits (Clear and Cole, 1986: 195). Taking into consideration that most persons held in jails are economically disadvantaged, the jail also is regarded as the "poorhouse of the twentieth century," "the ultimate ghetto," "storage bins for humans," as well as a social "garbage can" used to discard society's "rabble" (Clear and Cole, 1986; Goldfarb, 1975; Glaser, 1979; Irwin, 1985; Moynahan and Stewart, 1980). While prisons have been the target of volumes of research, the jail remains relatively ignored by criminal justice scholars. This lack of attention is particularly disturbing because jails suffer from many of the same problems that exist in prisons, such as poor services, security lapses, and violence. In many cases, jail conditions not only are worse but more often are neglected (Briar, 1983).

While serving as director of the federal bureau of prisons, Norman Carlson maintained that "[p]robably the most pressing problem in the correctional sphere is the tragic situation in our nation's jails" (see Place and Sands, 1975: 29). Given the historical dimension of neglected jail conditions and the current state of affairs, there is little evidence that much has changed.

It is assumed that many jail problems stem directly or indirectly from crowded conditions that often are created by systemic conflicts (Demos, 1984). In fact, Guynes (1988) surveyed jail managers who ranked jail crowding as a more severe problem than prison crowding. Perennial corrections institution crowding imposes an enormous strain on the government officials who are responsible for drafting and implementing public policy. Yet, developing policy that makes fiscal sense, alleviates the community's fear of crime, and meets minimum incarceration standards is a task requiring great ingenuity.

In response to crowding, some policymakers have decided to house misdemeanants and detainees in alternative facilities known as makeshift jails, satellite jails, or jail annexes. In this chapter, the controversy surrounding policy and jail crowding will be discussed as it relates to the use of makeshift jails. The scope of this discussion will remain focused on those problems facing jails in major cities where large jails usually are managed like prisons. In addition to presenting jail crowding in a social and historical context, issues such as architecture, community protest, and the future of makeshift jails will be explored as they relate to public policy.

Jail Crowding and Makeshift Solutions

Given the history of punishment, institutional crowding has been a policy issue since incarceration replaced corporal punishment. In response to the perennial "crowding crisis," government officials have had to find viable solutions; and, due to the urgency of the crisis, many solutions offered are temporary. Makeshift jails, satellite jails, and jail annexes are simply conversions of existing structures that can be used for incarceration or detention. Earlier makeshift jails included suspended cages, municipal basements, dungeons, unscalable pits, holes in the ground, as well as large trees to which the individual would be chained (Johnston, 1973; Mattick, 1974).

Although the use of makeshift jails as a method of creating additional jail capacity is not a new way of dealing with crowding crises, it has gained recent popularity. Today, transforming old buildings into makeshift jails is a convenient and cheap way to continue the rate of detention and incarceration. There are various examples of makeshift jails. The National Institute of Justice (1986a, 1986b) illustrates ways in which prefabricated structures can be used instead of constructing expensive conventional jails. Some county and city correctional departments have converted old school buildings into minimum security detention centers (Mays and Thompson, 1988). North Carolina officials have appropriated $20 million to construct makeshift jails for nonviolent, petty offenders (Healey, 1987).

In Denton, Texas, the county jail system was expanded by converting an abandoned gas station into a makeshift jail. This jail is simply one large room with bunk beds and dormitory-style bathrooms/showers. The jail's population fluctuates between approximately thirty inmates during the week and fifty on the weekends, when many DWI offenders serve their sentences. There is minimal privacy and constant traffic within this nonpartitioned space. Yet, an important advantage for the correctional staff is that this jail can be supervised by one officer.

Historically, a common makeshift arrangement for corrections was the use of penal colonies and islands. During crowding crises, these locations served as convenient and symbolic places to ostracize prisoners. Devil's Island and Australia were two of the most famous penal colonies, and today some islands still function as penal colonies.

Currently, Rikers Island is an example of a large penal colony—holding more than 14,000 inmates (as of May 31, 1989). As New York City's primary jail complex, Rikers Island is strained by having to process an enormous influx of detainees and misdemeanants. One strategy to ease crowding at Rikers Island is to house inmates in a makeshift jail, a floating barge moored at the city's waterfront. Also known as the *Bibby Venture*, the jail barge is leased from England for $19 million, with an option to buy. The *Bibby Venture* has a unique history as a vessel. Prior to its arriving in New York City, the British employed it as their military troop barracks during the Falkland Islands war. Since being converted into a makeshift jail, it has been regarded as only a short-term solution to the city's need for additional jail capacity. As of May 1989, 355 inmates were placed on the barge, and soon it will be accompanied by another jail barge, the *Bibby Resolution*. Meanwhile, New York City's Board of Estimate has approved purchasing an additional barge and is negotiating contracts for construction of a "designer barge" that will hold approximately 800 inmates. Numerous sites on the Hudson and East rivers around Manhattan and Brooklyn are being evaluated as possible sites to accommodate this fleet of floating makeshift jails, causing heated community protest.

The employment of barges as floating makeshift jails is not an entirely new policy for New York City, or other correctional systems for that matter. Even before introducing the barge in New

York City, two refurbished Staten Island ferryboats were moored at Rikers Island to create additional jail capacity. By placing make-shift jails in a larger sociohistorical context, this remedy for crowding has emerged during other crowding crises. In fact, there is historical precedence for placing inmates on ships designed as makeshift jails. Until 1875, Britain used old "convict hulks," abandoned war vessels and transport ships anchored along the banks of the Thames. The hulks also were known as "hell holds" and "floating hells" because they were vermin-infested ships where prisoners were flogged (American Correctional Association, 1983). The use of hulks was England's policy for dealing with prison/jail crowding when the shipping of inmates to penal colonies was terminated (Allen and Simonsen, 1986; Clear and Cole, 1986). Similar applications of vessels to serve as makeshift jails were seen in the United States. During the Revolutionary War, American soldiers were held in prison ships that surrounded New York harbor, and an estimated 12,000 prisoners died while on board. In the 1800s, California used hulks to incarcerate prisoners, and between 1976 and 1980 numerous states (Washington, Maryland, Louisiana, Massachusetts, and New York) made extensive preparations to convert decommissioned warships into makeshift correctional facilities (Allen and Simonsen, 1986; American Correctional Association, 1983).

Architecture as an Expression of Public Policy

Usually, architecture is designed to facilitate the function of a building or structure. Yet the architecture of a prison or jail sometimes goes beyond its obvious function to express a punitive philosophy. For example, European penitentiaries were constructed as "Gothic Monoliths" to promote fear and intimidation (Allen and Simonsen, 1986; Gill, 1962). As imprisonment replaced corporal punishment, prison and jail planning and design became more refined. Numerous architectural developments also are linked to a specific philosophy of punishment, and one of the most analyzed correctional structures is the panopticon. The panopticon has been studied extensively because of its advanced correctional planning that combined philosophy and policy with architecture.

Since Jeremy Bentham introduced the panopticon, it has been analyzed from several interrelated perspectives: punishment philosophy, social control, and observational economics (Foucault, 1975). Bentham planned to build this "ultimate prison" whose architecture would combine his crime and punishment theory (hedonistic calculus) with a prison management technique (systematic inspection). The panopticon, or inspection-house, was designed to maximize prisoner observation by placing the cells in a circular arrangement resembling the spokes on a wheel (Allen and Simonsen, 1986). Referred to as the "totalitarian housing project" by Aldous Huxley, the panopticon was never actually constructed in Europe (Johnston, 1973). Yet, Western Penitentiary (Pennsylvania) and Stateville (Illinois) succeeded in putting Bentham's architectural ideas into practice.

Whereas the panopticon was designed specifically for a prison population, there were jails whose architecture also reflected a highly organized plan for correctional policy. The rotary jail (also known as The Human Squirrel Cage or The Lazy Susan Jail) stands as one of the most innovative jail structural designs (Lunden, 1959). The rotary jail emerged as a facility that complemented security with convenience. In the Midwest, shortly after the Civil War, rotary jails were constructed by combining "cellular" floor plans with state-of-the-art machinery. The rotary jail's basic rationale was to place inmates in small pie-shaped cells of a larger cylinder: three decks of ten radial cells, housing a total of about sixty prisoners. Originally, the architect planned to have the cylinder mechanically rotate within the boxlike building. In fact, patent letters dated 1881 revealed that the large cylinder could be continuously rotated while the jailer was away from his post. Much like the primary "economic" feature of the panopticon, the rotary jail offered optimum surveillance of numerous inmates by a single jailer. The rotary jail, as is the case with contemporary makeshift jails, captured the economic feature of convenience.

There are similarities between the rotary jail used in the Midwest during the post–Civil War era and the jail barge currently employed in New York City. In both instances local governments urgently set out to confront the threatening crime wave. When law enforcement officials introduced the rotary jail, the Midwest was plagued by the lawless raids on banks and trains by such groups as the James brothers (Lunden, 1959). Similarly, New York City uses the jail barge as the "war on crime" intensifies; particularly the "war on drugs" that pits New York's Tactical Narcotics Team (TNT) against urban drug gangs. The immediate consequence of these law enforcement campaigns is the need to find available space for those arrested.

Unlike the carefully designed jails and prisons that have been constructed in Europe and the United States, makeshift jails stand as architectural anomalies because they depart from their original functions. Historically, prisoners have been housed in makeshift jails/prisons that often were structures that had different original functions. At times, the secondary use of structures involves a great deal of planning. An example of the secondary use of structures is development of the underground prison in Simsbury, Connecticut (1773), which was an abandoned copper mine (Dean, 1977). Although this mine was a convenient structure, Allen and Simonsen (1986) note that forcing prisoners to live and work in these mine shafts was reminiscent of the sulfur pits of ancient Rome. A recent illustration of the secondary use of structures is the transformation of the Olympic Village that housed athletes during the 1980 Lake Placid games into a federal prison known as Raybrook. The secondary use of structures offers clear advantages for developing policy geared toward creating additional jail capacity. It makes more sense to modify existing structures than to build new ones, particularly in light of the lengthy process of municipal land approval. Therefore, the underlying themes of the secondary use of existing structures are convenience and costs, which are important components of correctional policy-making.

Convenience is an important jail feature because inmates need to be in close proximity to the courthouses, and detainee transportation must be kept to a minimum. During a recent attempt to ease New York City's jail crowding, inmates were transported upstate to prisons on the Canadian border. In this case, the lack of convenience became an issue due to the distance between the city courts and the upstate prisons. With use of jail barges, not only is convenience reached but greatly improved by another unique feature—barge portability. Portability greatly enhances the convenience feature, which is particularly important if the city decides to move the jail barge because of excessive community protest.

The portability of jail barges also has historical precedence. Foucault (1979: 263–64) described a portable structure used to incarcerate and transport offenders. The panoptic carriage, a movable prison modeled after the panopticon, was a European alternative to the chain gang. The design of this structure was quite elaborate, and one of its functions was to leave onlookers with a lasting impression of the horrors of incarceration. Whereas the carriage primarily was used as transportation to the penitentiary, the three-day journey was difficult to endure. Therefore, the carriage's portable nature not only enhanced its convenience but also reinforced the symbolic value of punishment.

Portable jail wagons also were common in the South during

Reconstruction when prisoners were used as convict labor. These "cages on wheels" provided sleeping quarters for thirty-nine prisoners and transported them from one worksite to another (American Correctional Association, 1983).

Today, the need to create additional jail capacity forces policymakers to consider the use of convenient structures that already exist. Moreover, convenience is greatly enhanced if the structure, like the jail barge, is portable. Policymakers can argue more favorably if convenience is at hand, particularly when costs are taken into consideration. Some policymakers argue that use of jail barges is a less expensive strategy to ease jail crowding. This point, however, is vehemently debated by the opponents of jail barges who favor using alternatives to detention and incarceration.

Society, Jails, and Public Policy

Costs, the public's fear of criminals, and correctional watchdogs are among the concerns facing policymakers when attempting to ease crowding. Budgetary constraints limit the amount of funds required to build or renovate jails. Instead of spending more money building additional jails, there have been some attempts to incarcerate only those deemed imminently dangerous and to supervise low-risk offenders in the community. Although these strategies ease crowding, such alternatives are criticized by politicians who want their constituents to perceive them as being tough on crime (a theme that is understandably important during crucial election campaigns). Hence, numerous systemic crosscurrents impede any attempt to ease jail crowding. A particularly troublesome crosscurrent that complicates jail use is the struggle between different courts. While some courts send suspects and offenders to jail, others demand that inmates' constitutional rights be protected throughout their incarceration. The struggle between different segments of the criminal justice system often creates its own obstruction, which can be broadly interpreted as conflict between the crime control model and the due process model (Packer, 1968).

To confront jail crowding, one must focus on the forces and circumstances that stem from systemic problems. First, the "tough on crime" theme of law enforcement is not created actually to put a dent in crime. Rather, it is used by politicians who realize that many voters respond favorably to images of "tough" leadership. The unintended consequence is jail and prison crowding due to sweeping law enforcement campaigns. Second, as a function of more prison sentences being handed down, jails and prisons are increasingly more crowded. To compound matters, jails and prisons are instructed by courts not to exceed certain population levels. As a result, enormous numbers of state prisoners are housed in local jails, and this creates animosity between local and state officials. The Clark Foundation (1982) reports an incident in Arkansas where a frustrated county sheriff attempted to rid his jail of state inmates by chaining them to the state penitentiary's fence. The sheriff, however, was blocked by state officials who confronted him with shotguns and a court order to return the inmates to the county jail.

A third systemic problem contributing to jail crowding is the antiquated and biased bail policy that keeps people detained only because they cannot afford bail. Goldfarb (1975) reacts strongly to the financial feature of the pretrial system, suggesting that a more logical alternative is to devise a scheme to identify high-risk and dangerous offenders and to avoid detaining suspects simply because they are poor. Furthermore, forcing suspects to suffer in jail violates the fundamental assumption that one is innocent until proven guilty (Place and Sands, 1975).

Generally, major municipal jails functioning below capacity rarely are tolerated, particularly in light of the resurrection of the war on crime. Furthermore, it stands to reason that people are more likely to be detained before their trials if there is jail space available, even if this requires squeezing them into already crowded facilities. Consequently, as the population exceeds the jail's operational capacity, additional incarceration and detention space is required. Not only does the system have to ease *existing* crowding to comply with minimum incarceration standards, but additional space is needed to keep pace with the courts that continue to place more misdemeanants and detainees in jail.

As mentioned, the jail is a unique correctional hybrid that, among other functions, houses persons who do not have the means to avoid detention. Most jail inhabitants are poverty-stricken minorities who share similar characteristics with the debtors, vagrants, and beggars who were detained in fifteenth- and sixteenth-century houses of corrections (Flynn, 1973). Today, most jail inmates disproportionately represent the underclass and primarily are detained because they cannot afford bail. Considering this, public policy and the jail's role cannot be defined properly without keeping the central focus on the types of persons most likely to be detained.

Irwin (1985) claims that very few jail inmates fit the description of dangerous in the sense that they seriously threaten the lives and property of lawful citizens. Rather, jail inmates commonly are detached people who have limited means to survive. Irwin refers to these persons as the "rabble." Because the rabble appear unconventional, they generally are regarded as "offensive" or "threatening" by conventional society. To rid the streets of the rabble, jails are used as convenient social repositories. In many ways, Irwin's analysis parallels that of Spitzer (1975) and Galtung (1968). Spitzer describes the emergence of "social junk" who are harmlessly "offensive" persons detached from conventional society. Moreover, Galtung contends that one function of prisons is social sanitation by ridding communities of the "offensive" element. Arguing that the rabble are among the most frequently jailed, Irwin maintains that it is not so much the severity of their crime as the "offensive" nature of their behavior that makes them more subject to being jailed.

Public Policy and Community Protest

Among the many hurdles confronting policymakers is the community that challenges the placement of jails in their neighborhood. Occasionally, these protests are so well organized that lawsuits are filed, as was the case in New York City. While residents want the local government to arrest and incarcerate criminals, they do not want the facilities in their communities. These "not in my back yard" protests cannot be taken lightly because many of those who make decisions about jail use are elected officials. As a result, these officials are sensitive to the political liabilities of jail placement in or near a protesting community while also being aware that logistical convenience is a vital feature of jail policy. It seems that many policymakers discount the community protest and decide to place jails in these neighborhoods because of the obvious convenience to the courts. However, in selecting these "politically appropriate" sites, policymakers tend to target middle- and lower-class neighborhoods to minimize any political damage. Whereas jails are used as social garbage cans, the community where the jail is placed also appears to serve a similar function.

Advantages and Disadvantages of Makeshift Jails

Public policy must be carefully prepared to deal with societal "emergencies" requiring immediate attention. In terms of crowding, makeshift jails provide an immediate and seemingly plausible solution. One of the advantages of makeshift jails is that as existing structures they do not have to be constructed, but usually need only minimal modifications. This advantage is crucial when government officials have to contend with the political process of approving land use. In the case of the jail barge, the debate over municipal land use and the refurbishing of the barge can take place simultaneously. Because these buildings and structures already exist, their proponents argue in favor of their immediate convenience and fiscal sense, an important consideration when the primary jail is under court order to reduce its population.

One also could argue that the use of makeshift jails can improve inmate population management. By placing smaller inmate groups (i.e., one hundred to two hundred) in a makeshift jail, supervision potentially is improved. This is similar to the line of reasoning in the emergence of the "new generation" jails (Clear and Cole, 1986). Comparing "mini-jails" to large city jails, it appears that makeshift jails can be managed much more like a county jail than a municipal prison.

In balancing the overall picture, the numerous disadvantages of makeshift jails need to be discussed. The issue of lawsuits filed by community organizations challenging the placement of jails in their neighborhoods already has been mentioned. Yet, the obvious disadvantage of such placement of a makeshift jail, which is considered less secure, only adds to future community lawsuits. In search of immediate solutions to the problem, officials have been forced by the sense of urgency to sacrifice secure architecture for convenience. One of the major limitations of makeshift jails is that they can be used only as minimum security units. This is an inherent problem of relying on the secondary use of structures for security purposes, and community leaders often rely on this issue to organize protests. The barge's architecture, for instance, further magnifies the limitations of makeshift jails, which cannot secure high-risk and dangerous inmates. As a troops barracks, the barge was employed to house soldiers, not inmates, and its design reflects that function. Using a barracks for a jail involves modifications and careful planning. Unlike a meticulously designed jail, the barge had numerous deadends and mazelike corridors. This limits the visibility (surveillance), consequently jeopardizing security. During the barge's renovation, many of these architectural problems had to be corrected. Additional dangerous features included exposed hooks, firehose nozzles, and rubber hoses in the showers. Although the jail barge was modified to comply with minimum jail standards, the structure and use of the barge remains controversial.

Whereas the purpose of jail architecture is to enhance the function of the structure (in this case security), makeshift jails do not necessarily add to this overall objective. Because they cannot be used to secure high-risk inmates, correctional managers must carefully select inmates who are classified as low escape risks—not dangerous—and expected to cooperate with the correctional staff. This procedure of selecting appropriate candidates for minimum security is instantly complicated by the "sorting" issue; the fact is, most jails are crowded because there is very little sorting of *which* inmates should be detained at the initial processing stages (Allinson, 1982). Some administrators might refer to prisoners who fit this description as "ideal inmates." The paradox is that those inmates considered appropriate candidates for makeshift jails also are good candidates for community supervision.

Another disadvantage in using makeshift jails is that, unlike primary jails, very few (if any) programs are available. A case in point is the Nassau County Jail (Long Island, New York), where inmates in the main jail are allowed to enroll in substance abuse and educational programs, but inmates in "The Compound" or jail annex are excluded from such programs. Consequently, idle inmates often fight to relieve their boredom.

Finally, convenience has been introduced as a central feature of makeshift jails, but from a policy viewpoint convenience has little to do with security. Rather, it has more to do with the need for immediately available space that is required to keep pace with the war on crime, which is both political and bureaucratic.

Policy Recommendations: Alternatives and Solutions

Persons most likely to be criminally processed and detained in jails are generally those belonging to the underclass. Members of the underclass typically have poor employment/educational histories; drug and alcohol problems; and medical, mental health, and legal services needs. Considering this, the jail has become known as the "social agency of last resort" (Clear and Cole, 1986). Irwin (1985) places jails in a larger social context by demonstrating how they function as an extension of the welfare system (see especially Pivan and Cloward, 1971). One approach to public policy, jail crowding and the use of makeshift jails, is to remain sensitive to the arguments regarding the jail's role in society.

One of the most popular jail crowding solutions is new facility construction. However, this strategy has never kept pace with the incarceration and detention rate and, therefore, is historically in-

incarceration and detention rate and, therefore, is historically in-
defensible. While the building of new facilities requires a long-
range plan, numerous short-term efforts have been considered or
attempted. For instance, the extensive use of "all available space"
in a jail is a common tactic to ease crowding, meaning dayrooms,
gymnasiums, classrooms, and large hallways quickly are transformed into living units. Soon all available space is occupied by
inmates, and this sets the stage for the next logical short-term solution: farming out. This step involves renting bed space from
neighboring jails or prisons, an expensive and logistically difficult
method of increasing jail capacity (Huggins, 1982).

Among the most recent strategies to develop additional jail
capacity is the secondary use of existing structures, or makeshift
jails. Makeshift jails ostensibly are introduced as "temporary" solutions, but they run the risk of quickly being legitimized and institutionalized. In other words, one can speculate that makeshift jails
soon could be uncritically accepted as an appropriate method of
detaining inmates. As a reminder, the English hulks were introduced as a "temporary" solution, yet they were used for 85 years
(Bartollas, 1981). Because makeshift jails, particularly jail barges,
are convenient, portable, and relatively inexpensive, their popularity from a public policy perspective can easily overshadow the disadvantages.

The construction of additional jails should not be taken as a
serious solution to ease jail crowding. There are several strategies
to ease jail crowding without creating makeshift jails. Klofas
(1987) points out that jails can be better utilized by addressing the
policies that guide their use, and he suggests that a cybernetic
approach to jail use can improve planning. This is accomplished
by expanding communication between key decisionmakers such as
judges, prosecutors, and police officials. Perlstein and Henry
(1986a, 1986b) also support this approach and have developed
manuals with guidelines for judges and prosecutors to encourage
more effective detention space usage.

Due to the lack of clear policies that can guide jail use, jail
crowding is further compounded by the incarceration of low-risk
misdemeanants who are not regarded as dangerous. The majority
of inmates in makeshift jails, particularly the jail barge, are considered ideal inmates. Many of them are serving brief sentences
and are such low risks that they usually are assigned work release
only to return to the barge to be supervised while asleep. Ironically,
they are trusted enough to work in the community during the day
only to be incarcerated at night. Considering the characteristics of
these work release inmates, they probably are good candidates for

community supervision. A more reasonable policy is to incarcerate only those considered high escape risks or dangerous. Crowding could be reduced quickly if jails were used to house those who really belong there. Whereas the larger problem exists in the misuse of primary jails because officials fail to classify and sort inmates properly, there is a systemic paradox with the use of makeshift jails. Due to the nature of these facilities they can function only as minimum security units; it may make more sense to supervise these types of individuals in the community.

There are many ways to use community resources in dealing with those awaiting trial or serving sentences for misdemeanors. Work and educational programs, house arrest, day fines, and victim/community restitution are among the numerous alternatives proved to be effective short-term and long-term solutions. Steelman (1984) comprehensively described specific strategies to ease jail crowding, and among those already mentioned she points out the importance of pretrial services, bail reform, and postconviction alternatives. By introducing "rational population management," Steelman carefully identifies the financial advantages to implementing these programs that make the alternatives to jail difficult to discount. As an ongoing problem, these recommended policies and remedies have been routinely proposed over the past two decades, yet they have been consistently underutilized.

The lack of progress in jail reform is intimately connected to larger social forces (Rottman and Kimberly, 1975). The chronic underutilization of these programs now has contributed to the crowding crisis by becoming a systemic problem. Therefore, it is reasonable to support and revitalize existing programs and strategies. By considering these suggestions, the unbridled misuse of primary jails can be corrected. Moreover, as public policy facilitates the sensible use of primary jails, the development of makeshift jails should not have to be considered.

Conclusions

Although makeshift jails have gained recent popularity, it should be noted that the secondary use of structures has historical precedence. In 1931, H. H. Hart completed the first national survey on jails and lockups in the United States. Hart reported that these facilities were "antiquated buildings unfit for the purpose" of detaining persons. To avoid future use of inappropriate makeshift jails, Hart recommended that jails be "intelligently planned by competent architects" (Moynahan and Stewart, 1978: 47).

Here jail crowding has been discussed as it relates to developing and implementing policy. A major issue is the use of makeshift jails with special reference to New York City's jail barge. By using the jail barge example, one might conclude that this is only a New York City problem; however, almost every city has to contend with jail crowding. The purpose of discussing the jail barge as a makeshift jail is that nearly all major cities are located on or near a large body of water. Therefore, it is safe to speculate that other cities might consider employing similar jail barges to ease jail crowding. In fact, William Bennett, the federal drug czar, recently has suggested that jail barges be placed in the Potomac River as part of the war on drugs.

The main reason why policymakers must consider the use of makeshift jails is that primary jails remain crowded. And the reason primary jails are crowded is because they lack explicit policies to guide their proper use. As a result, jails hold many people who do not belong there. These problems are deeply entrenched in the systemic conflicts that plague the correctional system. Policymakers, as part of the larger bureaucratic system, have not taken full advantage of bail reform and the numerous alternatives to incarceration.

Similar to other social problems, jail crowding is presented as a temporary crisis that can be managed easily by simple, short-term solutions. The fact is, jail crowding has been considered a crisis since detention became a routine method of social control. By proposing short-term solutions, little effort is required to convince the public that this is a serious problem. In the case of New York City's crowding crisis, officials were so confident that the problem was temporary that they began making additional plans for the barges. That is, when crowding was "under control" the barges would be used as homeless shelters. Interestingly enough, both jail crowding and homelessness were viewed from a public policy perspective as temporary social problems that could be confronted by employing floating jails and shelters. The plan to transform the jail into a homeless shelter was quickly suppressed to avoid further social service reactions, however. Nonetheless, this demonstrates how policymakers routinely place jails and homeless shelters under the same social welfare system umbrella.

Presenting makeshift jails as a temporary solution while additional jails are constructed also raises the issue of whether more jails should be built. Steelman (1984: 3) argues against more building: "the overcrowding problem cannot be solved solely through massive new construction ... experience has shown repeatedly that government cannot build its way out of these crises." Newman (1983: 85) reminds us that jails and prisons "do not deter, rehabilitate, or effectively incapacitate offenders." Historically, jails and makeshift jails were used not to protect society but simply to warehouse those considered offensive. Relying on public policy that advocates additional jail/prison construction—including makeshift jails—is inherently problematic. It should be mentioned that in light of the privatization movement, makeshift jails might become more popular as correctional companies learn of the potential, although misleading, cost incentives.

Due to the chronic misuse of primary jails and the lengthy process of new jail construction, policymakers have had to face the crowding crisis by turning to makeshift jails. These jails are taken seriously by policymakers because of their convenience and false sense of cost reduction. Decisionmakers exploit public opinion about the so-called benefits of makeshift jails, and the result is that these jails become the correctional system's "motels" because they are convenient and modest alternatives to expensive jails. Contrary to these misconceptions about costs and convenience, Steelman (1984) argues that the more feasible policy is to revitalize bail reform and existing community programs. In sum, it is unreasonable to use makeshift jails because there are better alternatives for low-risk, low-security detainees and misdemeanants.

CHAPTER 10

Changing Jail Organization and Management: Toward Improved Employee Utilization

ERIC D. POOLE AND MARK R. POGREBIN

During the past decade, local governments have been faced with two countervailing pressures. One has been to function with reduced revenues; the other, to maintain or expand types and levels of services. County jails are one set of agencies that have experimented with alternative service delivery modes in their attempt to remain responsive and viable. Some jail administrators now view traditional organizational structure and management strategies as no longer meeting increasingly complex service needs. The search is for more flexible ways of utilizing both financial and human resources toward improving ways in which to organize and manage jail operations.

Jail administration studies consistently have indicated that many of the problems facing contemporary jails involve personnel matters (Kerle and Ford, 1982). Guynes (1988) reports that jail managers rank staff shortages as the second most serious problem in their jails, just behind crowding. In accounting for these shortages, the managers most frequently cite the "poor image of jail work" and "inadequate career incentives" as problems for staff recruitment and retention, respectively. While recruitment and retention have been widely recognized as critical in local jails, the system response typically has focused on upgrading personnel (e.g., greater educational requirements and preservice and inservice training), increasing salaries, and encouraging professional career development in corrections. As Bittick (1984: iv) points out:

> The position of jail officer has assumed an importance that was not recognized even ten years ago. In the next decade you will see the training requirements and courses for study for those who aspire to a career in corrections equal in length to the training and study for other people in law enforcement. . . . For the professional jailer this fact means a continued life-long career of study and continuous training.

A neglected concern that is integral in addressing both recruitment and retention issues involves personnel utilization. It is necessary to examine ways of maximizing the use of employee talents, skills, and abilities, thus enhancing both staff and program development. For example, what in jail work might be changed so that utilization of a wider range of personnel is enhanced? What in jail work encourages greater commitment to organizational goals, objective setting, and job performance? What management strategies are best suited to address changes in staffing needs and demands of jail work?

Barriers of Formal Organization

The phrase *maximizing personnel utilization* represents a complex network of organizational structures and processes. On those rare occasions where calls for more effective use of jail personnel are advanced, there is an even rarer exploration of the implied staffing possibilities. All too often such discussions only involve assessments of generic organizational needs to fill positions (e.g., supply and demand), to the exclusion of the personal work considerations of current or prospective employees (e.g., skills and abilities, work motivation, career goals). Sheriffs and jail managers tend to couch their personnel problems in terms of shortages (e.g., understaffed shifts and posts, high staff-inmate ratios, dearth of qualified minority employees or applicants). Few have attempted to address their staffing problems in terms of effective and efficient employee utilization. If jail administrators fail to determine how well they are using their personnel, they may be wasting employees' skills and efforts through misuse, underuse or both (Lombardo, 1986).

Insights into improved personnel utilization often are derived from what may be called organizational dysfunctions. That is, we get clues to what might be effective utilization by recognizing practices and policies that seem to produce disjunctures between organizational goals and institutional means—thwarting motivation, reducing commitment, and diminishing performance of staff. To understand the context of these problems, we first need to consider briefly the characteristics of traditional administrative arrangements. As a formal organization, the jail fits Weber's classic postulation of a bureaucracy (1947). This organizational model is based on a central hierarchy with strong emphasis on authority in the superior-subordinate relationship, specialized division of labor, and standardization of rules and procedures. It explicitly promotes a management orientation stressing job task routinization, coupled with decision making based on the needs of the organization to the exclusion of personal considerations.

To maintain this traditional organizational structure, both superior and subordinate also must subscribe to certain bureaucratic dogma: (1) unity of command, (2) restricted span of control, (3) authority from top down, (4) communication through channels, and (5) work group stratification by function or goal. Adherence to these tenets reinforces the view and use of the employee as a narrowly defined relational position rather than as a resource who could be utilized flexibly. Jail administration has been carried out within this framework because there have been few incentives and little impetus to change. Studies of jails reveal them to be self-maintaining and self-reinforcing systems of communication and control (Briar, 1983; Goldfarb, 1975; Irwin, 1985). They are constituted to maintain a "steady state," to go on being just what they are and doing very much what they have been doing. Such structural perpetuation may be seen as a function of the following conditions:

1. The energy and work required simply to maintain the status quo usually exhaust initiative in an organization; in the interest of economy of effort, actual resistance to change often follows.
2. Everyday activities are the most effective teacher and, hence, practices tend to perpetuate themselves and train others who use them to continue in the same mode. Closely related are structured sets of tasks that also reduce opportunities to learn other ways.
3. The jail's goals and objectives are diverse and sometimes contradictory, with programs and activities operated at cross-purposes. For example, the delivery of treatment services and maintenance of custodial control for a highly transient pop-

ulation under what often are crowded conditions require constant monitoring of tension management (i.e., just keeping a lid on things).

4. There also are persistent ideological conflicts with external interest groups, concerning the jail's role, that must be managed: treatment versus punishment, judicial activism versus administrative autonomy, local criminal justice resource allocations versus jail expenditures.

5. With any organizational change, there is a cost to some; and those adversely affected, in either a real or imagined sense, can be expected to resist. While all organizations must learn to adapt and live with changes over time, it is clearly evident that they do not always readily respond to them or live well with them.

Directions for Change

In any organization there is a critical difference between recognizing the need for change and actually accomplishing it. This especially has been true for local jails (Mattick, 1974). Although in the past jail administration frequently has criticized itself and has been criticized, it has a meager history of planned development and change. Local jails, instead, have grown haphazardly and reactively into a segmented service organization with contradictory goals and divergent public expectations (Moynahan and Stewart, 1980). Change has been regarded as somewhat unmanageable and inevitable. When accommodations and modifications have been implemented, the primary change strategy has been incrementalism, a short-term tactic emphasizing limited variations from past policies and practices. Such attempts to influence change usually have been piecemeal and unconnected. The disadvantages of this approach have been aptly described by Etzioni (1967: 387): "While an accumulation of small steps could lead to significant change, there is nothing in this approach to guide the accumulation; the steps may be circular—leading back to where they started, or dispersed—leading in many directions at once but leading nowhere."

A more dynamic approach toward organizational change must be considered by jail administrators. They no longer can afford to wait for time and collective incrementalism to produce needed change. What is needed is a concerted effort to transform the organization through strategic personnel utilization and staff development. Greiner (1967: 119–28) identifies six organizational principles as essential to this change strategy's success:

1. The organization, and especially top management, experiences considerable pressure from both inside and outside for improvement long before an explicit organizational change is contemplated.
2. Leadership at the top allows an objective organizational appraisal and facilitates a reorientation of the power structure toward its own internal problems.
3. Total staff becomes involved in a reexamination of past practices, assumptions, and current problems within the organization. Collaborative fact-finding and problem-solving skills and activities are emphasized. Involvement of others gradually moves down through the organizational hierarchy, often using joint meetings of people from multiple organizational levels as the vehicle.
4. Total staff involvement and collaboration reduce the restraining forces impinging on individuals within the organization and support the use of newly learned problem-solving skills.
5. Solutions and decisions made in a previous stage are tested on a small scale before large-scale changes are attempted.
6. The change effort spreads, with each successful experience serving both as a reinforcer and multiplier of change. The total pattern of self-renewal is gradually absorbed into the organization's way of life.

While these principles are pertinent to affecting local jail change processes, the caveat is that their application is still dependent on the jail's organization and management nature. First, constructive response according to these principles requires the participation of both superiors and subordinates in organizational self-appraisal. Such participation has been difficult to attain in local jails because their paramilitary rank structure has centered authority and initiative at the top of the organizational hierarchy, with decisions handed down from that level. Second, many of the nation's largest jails are segmented into discrete and semiautonomous units. This characteristic is both an advantage and a disadvantage for a planned change program. At least theoretically, innovation could be stimulated through the seeding of innovation and testing locations throughout the organization. The only two prerequisites would be an interested jail administrator and the availability of competent resource help. But two factors in local jail organization may act as restraints. In the first place, the jail has been so fragmented that successes in one unit have not been communicated to similar units. Knowledge of success is a powerful and essential ingredient in sustained change. In the second place, a commitment to innovation must be present throughout the organization. A positive attitude toward research/experimentation often is lacking in jails (Gottfredson, 1982), especially because of the tradition that new ideas are the monopoly of central administration. Third, the management practices prevalent throughout many jails represent a variation of what McGregor (1960) has called *Theory X*. Under Theory X, a manager assumes that employees (1) avoid work whenever possible; (2) need supervision, control, and frequently coercion in the performance of work; and (3) are motivated by a desire for security. This set of assumptions leads to a unilateral or delegated management and change strategy. It is thus unlikely that subordinates will see the need for change or be willing to accept the risks that accomplishment of change entails. If one assumes that the organization's real problems are due to the ineptness of those at the lower levels of the organizational hierarchy, then a more astute top management should be able to prescribe solutions; however, because these assumptions influence managers' attitudes toward subordinates, they often react in ways that justify the assumptions. In this way a self-fulfilling prophecy or cycle of failure is maintained.

Managing an Open System

Though administration and management are essential elements in any complex organization, their relative size and importance to the agency often are blown out of all realism—blown up because they embrace all sorts of processes and details of little operational value or because a given administrative/managerial system simply fails to perform as such. Part of the problem lies in the view of administration/management for administration/management's sake. Social organizations, such as jails, are open systems (Rottman and Kimberly, 1975), and the open system is not easily mastered. The administrator must strive constantly to deal with variables that are to some degree unknown, unpredictable, and uncontrollable. The less competent and imaginative administrator will attempt to control this kind of system with a plethora of detailed rules and regulations. Such control brings about an atmosphere most employees find oppressive—one in which they are likely to become highly inefficient by using up energy to compensate for a cumbersome management system.

On the one hand, the proliferation of written rules controlling job performance indicates a degree of insensitivity on the part of management to the employees' work orientation. On the other hand, the lack of rules, or their nonenforcement, can lead to arbitrary treatment of workers and the reign of favoritism. To be sure, the rationale of rule making seems governed by a paradox: the lack of rules may lead to favored treatment and injustice to individuals, whereas the proliferation of written regulations may cause the magnification of an impersonal legalism, which may hinder the attainment of justice in those instances where flexibility is called for. This is one area where management practice must be both an art and a science; that is, managers must develop and adapt a rule-making approach that will balance the need for certainty with the need to exercise discretion in individual cases.

Fortunately, the organizational literature does give us some initial guidance in this area (e.g., Katz and Kahn, 1966). The guideposts may be seen as a set of assumptions that managers can adopt and test:

1. Most workers possess widely distributed creative talents.
2. Most workers have potential that is neither completely recognized nor fully utilized in the organization.
3. Most workers accept and seek responsibility.
4. Most workers use self-direction and control when committed to objectives.

This open systems approach to managing with less structural control (i.e., fewer regulations and less routinization) allows greater latitude in employees' organizational behavior, thus reinforcing an affirmative view of the worker's role.

Because reliance on standard operations manuals may be misplaced or inappropriate in times of change, each worker must have great intellectual flexibility and personal initiative. Management systems must be designed to recognize and reward both enterprise and objective scrutiny of one's own work. This is important since the management system not only reflects the organization's values but also the value the organization in turn places on its employees. The collective influence of dominant values in an organization is often referred to as its *climate*. And like climates that envelop geographical regions, organizational climates have considerable impact on the daily lives of local inhabitants. In an assessment of the effects of organizational climate on the "quality of work life," Herrick (1975: 203) posits that the greater "the degree to which workers experience security, equity, individuation and participation," the greater their job satisfaction and work performance. Selznick (1968: viii) similarly observes that "Nothing contributes more to these feelings [of self-worth and responsibility] than a social environment whose constitutive principle is justice, with its corollaries of participating, giving reasons, and protecting personal dignity."

This is the crux of the personnel utilization problem. We should be asking what the organization means to the worker instead of what the worker means to the organization. The thrust toward improved personnel utilization initially rests on a determination of the degree to which workers and their work fit. This would be facilitated by incorporating greater flexibility in job assignments to meet changing organizational demands. New organizational role systems must be created in order to mobilize new kinds of employee groups to develop and implement new work strategies.

What does all this mean in terms of jail operations? It suggests that the traditional hierarchical model for organizing staff (with its successive levels of superior and subordinate) is not required. The long line of command to the top tends to have little or no meaning. Immediate supervision represents the person one answers to because he or she happens to be boss. The cliché often is "I don't like him/her, but I respect the position he/she holds." This assessment should not be construed as pejorative; rather, it should be viewed as a plea for freeing jail management from some of the traditional ties that bind.

The organizational imperative is the flattening of the management hierarchy. As jails currently are managed, there is tremendous potential for disjuncture between policy goals and implementation practices. Policy is made at all organizational levels and does not necessarily follow down an orderly chain of command; moreover, decisions are made at all levels in accordance with the "definitions of the situation" (Thomas and Thomas, 1928). And situations defined as real have real consequences regardless of who makes the decisions. By formally recognizing the importance of individual discretionary decision making, organizations in effect serve to institutionalize the values of personal accountability and responsibility.

Line staff should have closer linkages and more direct access to jail management so that (1) the supervisory levels have less need to filter and interpret information and to issue directives and memoranda and (2) there is less interference or "noise" in the communication process. In flattening the hierarchy, one of the prescriptions is to limit the ubiquitous one-over-one bottlenecks. Another is the attempt to integrate, where functionally appropriate, line and management duties. Indeed, corrections officers always have been responsible for managing inmates (Cressey, 1977). These managerial skills must be developed and extended to other jail operations areas. Organizational support and rewards for managerial responsibilities among line staff will encourage creative problem solving and heighten stakes in organizational goals, which in turn are critical in promoting a professional orientation to corrections work. Brodsky (1982: 139–40) further notes the importance of this management perspective in proposing an occupational "bill of rights" for jail guards, "who should have a 'piece of the action'":

> The list [of occupational rights] includes the right to have a sense of personal and professional growth in one's work in order to look back and see and know that some vocational growth has occurred. It includes the right to make a difference, so that one's life and work offer a genuine contribution. It includes the right to look forward to continued recognition and improvement in one's work.

The general direction organizational change must take is toward less rigidly structured relationships both within the work unit and between superior and subordinate. Jail administration must move toward a results-oriented, as opposed to the present activity-orientated, stance. This means that jail management must shift from a reliance on task and job descriptions within structurally discrete work units to an organizational form more related to the needs of jail inmates and service delivery. Such an orientation represents a more proactive jail management approach in that it might point the direction for a changing jail environment, in part because it will lead to more freedom for employees to apply their talents and skills toward specific results-oriented objectives and away from management practices that emphasize the methodic control of hour-by-hour behavior.

According to Guenther and Guenther (1976: 532), many corrections officers apparently thrive on the nonrepetitive, unsystematic features of their work: "These officers look forward to quarterly job changes, the introduction of new treatment programs, new regulations affecting inmate conduct and a fluid, upwardly mobile staff. . . . Their distinctive preference, though, is for a job in which initiative, challenge and ingenuity are required. . . . ." Under a management system that facilitates and accommodates employee initiatives, it is conceivable that multiple service and program hierarchies can be continually articulated in adjusting to different inmate populations—thus providing timely and meaningful objectives, which become both the guides for direction of effort and the coordinating forces for the complementary use of employees' skills.

Change Management

In all people-processing organizations, the management of change is a constant process, driven by the dynamics of societal changes. Organizational change strategies largely will determine the degree of functional integration and vitality of jail operations. Each employee plays a crucial role in keeping the organization aware of and responsive to changes in the environment; moreover, each employee serves as a change agent when the deliberate purpose is to reorient fundamentally the work of the organization. What is problematic is the acquisition of new concepts and abilities that enable employees to modify and create programs and modes of interaction in order to reduce the gap between what is seen as desirable and what actually exists in jail operations. For example, Brodsky (1982: 140) argues that "jail guards . . . [must] be able to increase their options for constructive action. Rather than having limited and overly defined roles, such increased options can come from a variety of planning conferences, and the complementing of naturally occurring community change mechanisms from the courts, from community officials, and public interest groups."

In short, employees should be proficient in those skills needed for managing change rather than simply those required for maintaining the system. Change management know-how differs from traditional organizational rote learning of standard operating procedures. Employees need to develop an "unprogrammed" acumen—honing faculties for strategic planning, tactical objective setting, and qualitative process evaluation.

In this interactive context two social capacities must become increasingly characteristic of workers: collaboration and a willingness to confront and resolve conflict. In most organizations workers receive very little encouragement in developing collaborative skills; competitive skills receive considerably more emphasis. Collaboration differs from what usually is defined as cooperation; that is, a collaborative relationship involves not only cooperation but also sensitivity to the needs of others. As proportionately less and less work is accomplished through the efforts of individuals and more is achieved through the efforts of groups, collaborative skills become more important. Linking up with and utilizing a fuller range of resources require collaborative skills. Collaborative efforts are fundamental to jail operations. The goals of custodial control and treatment of inmates demand highly developed collaborative abilities among a wide range of jail personnel; consequently, jail administration must lead the way in building a collaborative network devoted to collective objective setting, task analysis, and problem solving.

Few organizations are required to serve so many ends with means so seemingly incompatible than are local jails; consequently, few threads are woven into the jail's organizational fabric as conspicuously as conflict. Community attitudes are often diametrically opposed to correctional aims. Jail personnel disagree on the relative importance assigned treatment and custody duties. One organizational work group's perception of itself (e.g., its role, status, duties, and such) differs from the way other work groups perceive it. The endless oratory over contradictory organizational goals arises from persistent uncertainty about conflict resolution. Merely to deplore conflict is not to end it. The reconciliation of competing demands requires a clear conceptualization of the interrelatedness of organizational functions and concomitant responsibilities of each employee.

Several conflict-coping options are available. First, workers may be blind to conflict because of low-level awareness or substantial distortion. Once they are aware of conflict, they may choose to (1) ignore it by withdrawal activities or disowning any role in resolving it or (2) resolve it by smoothing over differences or trying to reach a tentative compromise. Second, workers may confront the conflict with a win-lose strategy, using all of their respective resources to gain a favored solution through defeating their opponents. Third, workers may choose to confront the conflict openly, trying to understand viewpoints other than their own, so that areas of disagreement clearly can be defined and joint resolutions pursued. This latter option is the one most consistent with the type of organizational behavior required in successful change strategies described previously (Cyert and March, 1963).

Organizational change requires orientation to new tasks, new contexts for familiar tasks, and new divisions of labor. Because of the relative imprecision of organizational change technology, employees tend to be less confident about the success of efforts involving the development of alternative work groups and organizational networks. A move toward raising this confidence should involve designing systems and developing organizational environments that stimulate and reinforce risk taking. All change involves some degree of uncertainty and risk; thus, the capacity to experiment (to explore and test a variety of policy, operational, and programmatic options) allows employees themselves to determine what works. And these successes in turn foster a climate of confidence. Toch and Grant (1982: 14) assert that this process increases the resources and skills of not only the individual worker but the entire organization:

> We are hard put to separate "organization change" and "person change." We know that . . . people in organizations . . . learn to grow and fulfill themselves as they become involved. Often, the product of focused involvement is change. To put it differently, when persons become concerned with efforts to improve their environments—the inhabitants and their environments are liable to benefit.

Organizational development must come to grips with these creative manifestations of the human spirit, because management organizations are human organizations—a truism that is sometimes equally profound and trite.

Guiding Organizational Principles

Having assessed a range of salient concerns involving jail personnel utilization, we now focus attention on the formulation of some basic principles underlying organizational measures to implement our recommendations.

Administrative Responsibility

If there is any single major point to be emphasized in considering the suggestions we have offered, it is that there must be an explicit and unreserved assumption of responsibility by jail administrators for active participation in all aspects of the measures designed to deal with personnel issues. It is our contention that government agencies have an immense responsibility to strive constantly for improvement in the quality and effectiveness of the programs and services they administer. Assumption of such responsibility implies additional obligations:

- to initiate activity rather than passively accept conditions that block reform and innovation
- to support a certain level of risk taking
- to stress development of collaborative efforts as opposed to competition
- to make obligatory a continuing examination and evaluation

of the organization's aims and conduct, including its philosophy, policies, objectives, and programs
- to promote the unity of purpose

An essential first step to promote more effective personnel usage is to improve the managerial system's effectiveness. Although this step seems an obvious one, it is frequently bypassed or ignored by jail administrators who too often continue to use outdated approaches and procedures and fail to organize themselves so that they can think and act on a scale equal to the organizational problems they face. The need for stronger overall organization ties in with the simple need for a greater degree of strength and competence to overcome entropy. In addition, there must be a number of deliberately incorporated correctives and stimulants to counteract the natural tendency for any agency to deteriorate. Measures that may be instituted along these lines can result in an organizational structure that will necessitate interaction and collaboration among various work groups.

Planning

It is pointed out frequently that personnel problems cannot be dealt with outside the context of consideration of overall organizational goals and the means used to achieve them. No jail can fulfill all its aspirations at the same time. Competing claims must be balanced and conscious choices made. Jail work's increasing complexity has resulted in serious problems in discretionary decision making and prioritizing service delivery. Although these problems are widely acknowledged, too few jails have tried to develop their ability to deal with them. While the prevailing management philosophy in many local jails might be said to be in keeping with Carlyle's familiar dictum, "Our main business is not to see what lies dimly at a distance, but to do what lies clearly at hand," there is clear recognition of the necessity for a mechanism that can help ensure a continuing and comprehensive understanding of how critical decisions relate to existing policies and programs and to all present and probable future developments. In short, there must be an unqualified commitment to planning as an ongoing agency responsibility.

While the term *planning* has become familiar and popular in many jails, the process often consists of not much more than an exercise that has little chance of succeeding because it is unrelated to the reality of the situation, is based on insufficient or inaccurate data, or is carried out in isolation from the personnel affected and the setting in which problems exist or issues may be resolved. Since the resolution of many of the issues in personnel utilization undoubtedly will require changes in the ways jail services are provided, as well as the manner in which employees function, serious consideration must be given to the relationship between planning efforts and desired changes. The inevitability of changes necessitates continuity of planning, so that adjustments to it become part of the process; moreover, planning itself must be viewed as an agent for change, so that a serious commitment to planning must also carry with it a readiness to anticipate change and an understanding that it can also facilitate change.

Communications

Communication problems have been blamed for failures and inefficiency in all jail operations areas. Much has been written and said about communications breakdowns and how they can be prevented. While we are concerned with the improvement and strengthening of policies and methods involving information sharing, our major concern is with a broader concept of communication that includes all the processes by which employees influence one another. Communication in this sense has as its main objective the promotion of mutual understanding and does not refer solely to message transmittal. Our approach to the development of a systematic two-way information flow requires that equal attention be given to both the seeking out of information and its dissemination.

It is of vital importance to disseminate, both within and beyond the boundaries of the jail's network of services, a steady information flow concerning policies and developments directly or indirectly related to a broad range of personnel matters. Important as it is, however, we see information transmittal as only one aspect of the communication process. The successful implementation of staffing policies and the resolution of issues that have a bearing on them require the cultivation of independent critics who will react to what is done or proposed. It is essential that the information flow outward be countered by an input of ideas, suggestions, and criticisms from employee groups, professional associations, and the general public. This means that decentralized operations must be planned, not only to carry out activities with maximum effectiveness but also to provide jail administration with a sensory mechanism.

For the jail's goals and objectives to be understood clearly, it follows that there must be a strengthening of the activities through which the administration attempts to gain public understanding of the issues involved. This means that the public must be made aware of the consequences of carrying out certain programs and also the cost to it if a program is not carried out. In the public relations effort required, administrators must be prepared to be scrupulously honest rather than studiously polemic. In this connection, systematic observation and evaluation are essential in providing an accurate basis for reporting to the public. Finally, it should be noted that this approach also helps to make experimentation more comfortable—an important consideration as jail administrators deliberately plan for experimentation and in fact require it.

Conclusions

"In the old days, before the discovery of eruptions, the lava had to be carried by hand down the mountain and thrown on the sleeping villagers. This took a lot of time" (Clarence Brown, as quoted in Brodsky, 1982: 146). The irony of this tongue-in-cheek statement aptly reflects the legacy of organizational change efforts in local jails. The reliance on short-term, incremental strategies has proved to be the functional equivalent (in terms of difficulty and time consumption) of carrying lava down a mountain; moreover, many jail administrators seem content, or resigned, to wait for some chance organizational discovery that would make change efforts more palatable. But, as Louis Pasteur's famous dictum reminds us, "Chance favors only the prepared mind." It is hoped that our present efforts will set the groundwork for the stimulation and preparation of administrative minds to develop and implement more enterprising plans of action.

We have stressed the need for reconceptualization of the local jail's organization and management as they relate to improved personnel utilization. A long step is taken in creating such an environment when a more flexible organizational form is adopted; however, that form, in which there is less room for bossing and direct overseeing, must be enhanced with improved managerial practices. Organizational concepts based purely on routinization of employee tasks and activities are giving way to the realization that management systems are composed of people as well as tasks and that the talents and abilities of people modify tasks. The improvement mainly will be characterized by a shift to an emphasis on the results indicated in the organization's goals and objectives.

Much less emphasis will be placed on monitoring the employees' daily work logs. In the final analysis, staff strength and, in turn, agency effectiveness grow out of the assumption of responsibility for purposeful activity rather than out of specific techniques and possession of technical skills. Planned, deliberate efforts for open acknowledgment of this concept should be included in the formulation of all jail policies and programs.

In general, we have stressed organizational measures that are largely decentralized in role and function, though not completely. And we have tried to present them in a way that reflects a more ambitious and affirmative viewpoint, a way of thinking and acting in respect to personnel utilization issues that we believe must permeate jail administration. In proposing certain strategies, we are very much aware that they do not always solve the basic underlying problems jails face, but only restructure and redirect approaches to their solution. Finally, we have tried to emphasize the human element in organizational development—the individual workers and their problems, needs, and aspirations—for any administrative inability to develop this most precious resource is ipso facto a symptom of greater administrative inability.

There is no doubt that attempts to improve personnel utilization will require a willingness to bear some major start-up costs, such as organizational resistance, professional backlash, and political fallout. Conservative inertia always bears a hefty price tag for removal. Thus, we are not naively suggesting that all, or any, of our proposals and strategies can be acted on quickly and easily. First, history confirms that institutional change is slow, even if it is inevitable. Second, we have not intended to provide a final blueprint that, if followed, will ensure solving all the organizational problems we have identified. Positive prescription is difficult; complex problems do not lend themselves to simple solutions. None of the potential solutions is sufficient in itself, and none can be viewed in isolation from the others. Many are complementary but interdependent. It is unlikely that jail administrators will be able to substitute *in toto* a new organizational model for the various fragments of models now in operation in confusing array. Still, we feel that the old models will be afforded the impetus to change through the impact of strategic modifications in the use of personnel.

Many jail administrators still cling to the belief that they must exert a strong hold over their employees to ensure job commitment. To these paragons of bureaucratic tradition, our next statement is an indication of tremendous conceit: the local jail's survival could well rest on its ability to better use its human resources. Progressive jail administrators must work out the how-to-do-it of alternative organizational models. Here we have felt it important first to address the broader issues that can give government officials and top policymakers reason to consider the new directions and start asking that new models of organization be sought and adopted. For organizational changes in personnel utilization may have much more to offer than we have thus far dared to imagine.

CHAPTER 11

The New Generation Jail: An Overview

LINDA L. ZUPAN AND BEN A. MENKE

Many reasons have been offered to explain the disgraceful state of American jails. Most scholars suggest that the jail's unique organizational and environmental factors produce these conditions (see, e.g., Flynn, 1973; Mattick, 1974; Miller, 1978). They argue that mismanagement, lack of fiscal support, heterogeneous inmate populations, overuse and misuse of detention, overemphasis on custodial goals, and political and public apathy contribute to the jail's inhumanity. Others, however, view jail problems from a broader perspective. These scholars argue that jails, like other total institutions, are besieged by numerous structural defects that make incarceration a brutalizing experience for both inmates and staff. The organization's punitive goals, the alienated relationship of the inmate client to the organization, the deprivations experienced by inmates, the reliance on coercion to attain organizational goals, the lack of inmate recognition of the legitimacy of the organization's authority, and pressure on the custodial staff to circumvent the facility's rules are cited as structural defects that make safe and humane incarceration problematic whether it be in a prison, a mental institution, a prisoner of war camp, or a jail (Blau and Scott, 1962; Cloward, 1968; Etzioni, 1961; Goffman, 1961; Schrag, 1961; Sykes, 1958).

The main point that distinguishes these two perceptions is

the amenability of jail problems to solution. Those who argue that jail problems are the product of organizational and environmental factors suggest that through appropriate reforms, particularly the infusion of monies for jail construction and operation, these problems can be alleviated. Those who argue that jail problems are the result of structural defects question whether any reform effort will alleviate the deficiencies inherent to coercive institutions.

Within the last two decades a third perspective has emerged: namely, the "new generation" correctional philosophy. A primary assumption of the new generation philosophy is that deficiencies in traditional jail architecture and inmate supervision styles impede formal and legitimate institutional control of inmate behavior and actually may encourage inmates to engage in violent and destructive behavior. The new generation philosophy prescribes an innovative podular architectural design and direct inmate supervision that alleviates many of the deficiencies of traditional architecture and inmate management and provides a safer and more humane environment for inmates and staff.

Deficiencies of Traditional Jail Architecture and Inmate Management

Most jails in the United States have been built in a linear design that dates back to the eighteenth century. In a typical linear jail, multiple-occupancy cells or dormitories are aligned along corridors or hallways; the corridors are arranged at acute angles to form a spokelike effect. The facility's physical design by and large determines the inmate supervision style. In the linear jail, inmate supervision is intermittent; staff must continuously patrol the corridors in order to observe inmates. Hardware such as bars, metal doors, sally ports, electronic surveillance, and eavesdropping equipment augment staff supervision and control of inmates.

A number of assumptions inform traditional jail design (Nagel, 1973). One assumption concerns the nature of the individuals incarcerated in jails. It is assumed that jails house violent and destructive individuals who will assault staff, destroy jail property, and try to escape, given the chance. Therefore, the facility is designed to prevent these types of inmate behaviors. Inmate assaults against staff are deterred by the use of heavy metal bars to separate inmates from staff. Property destruction is minimized by furnishing living units and cells with reinforced metal or stainless steel accoutrements that are bolted to the ground or walls. Escapes are discouraged by the inclusion of bars, grills, and reinforced concrete inside the facility and fences and razor wire around the perimeter.

A second assumption is that staff are incapable of controlling inmate behavior. Less than adequate personnel standards, deficiencies in personnel recruitment and selection, lack of training, and above-average turnover rates have contributed to the widely shared perception that staff cannot be trusted to prevent inmate assaults, destruction, or escapes. It is assumed that the same architectural features that control inmate behavior also can compensate for staff deficiencies.

A third assumption pertains to the need for cost efficiency in the jail's initial construction and future operation. The reinforced concrete, metal bars, and steel furnishings that make the facility secure and destruction-proof are expensive. To keep initial building costs low, sacrifices must be made in other parts of the construction. Multiple-occupancy cells or dormitories, for example, are cheaper to build than single cells, even though research shows they are more dangerous for inmates and staff (Nagel, 1973). Cost efficiency also is essential in the facility's long-term operation. Expensive concrete, metal and steel are used in place of less durable and less expensive construction and furnishing materials because it is believed that they resist inmate destruction and, in the long run, reduce repair and replacement costs. Expensive electronic eavesdropping and surveillance devices are installed because it is believed they make it possible to supervise large numbers of inmates more cheaply than personnel can.

In principle, the architecture, furnishings, and staff surveillance are designed to maximize institutional control over inmate behavior. In practice, however, the linear architecture, institutional furnishings, and intermittent supervision style of most modern jails impede institutional control of inmates and influence violent and destructive inmate behavior in three ways. First, the architectural design and intermittent supervision style interfere with the ability of staff to enforce facility rules and detect inmate violations, and provide inmates with ample opportunities to engage in misbehavior. Because officers in a linear design facility cannot see inside all cells or dormitories in a living unit from any one location, they must continuously patrol the hallways and corridors. The frequency of these patrols is formally determined by local jail administrators but is influenced by organizational factors, such as understaffing, and by the preferences of individual correctional officers. Even in states where legislatures have imposed fairly high standards on local detention facilities, officers may be required to check on inmates only once or twice every hour. In the intervals between patrols, inmates are not under staff observation.

The brevity and infrequency of these visual checks provide few opportunities for staff to detect inmate misbehavior and enforce facility rules. Furthermore, unless inmates are engaged in flagrant misbehavior, the officer patrolling the corridors may not observe inmates long enough to discern more subtle forms of misbehavior, such as extortion and gambling.

In many modern jails, sophisticated electronic equipment has been installed to improve visual surveillance of inmates. However, because these devices are expensive and prone to vandalism by inmates, they are used sparingly. Typically they are installed to ensure perimeter security or to monitor areas deemed high-risk for inmate escapes (Nagel, 1973). Other areas of the facility, particularly cells and dormitories where staff surveillance is minimal, usually are not electronically monitored.

In theory, inmates are subjected to a formal social control system dominated by institutional rules and regulations and rigorously enforced by the facility's staff. In reality, rule enforcement and violation detection in a linear design jail are highly probabilistic, based almost solely on an officer's chance observation and recognition of rule-violating behavior. Consequently, inmates are provided numerous opportunities and locations to engage in rule-violating behavior with little risk of staff detection.

A second deficiency of the linear architectural design and intermittent inmate supervision style is that the institution alone cannot prevent or deter inmates from victimizing other inmates. In large measure, inmates must depend on their own abilities to survive victimization. However, the means available are severely limited. In most cases only two options are available: flight or fight (Toch, 1977).

In jails where multiple-occupancy cells and dormitories are the primary housing arrangement, inmates have few available means to escape victimization—particularly when the victimizer shares a cell or dormitory with the victim. To remove themselves physically from victimization by others, inmates must request transfer to segregation; however, the costs associated with such a request are quite severe. In making the request, inmates must admit to themselves that they are too weak to prevent victimization. The cost to self-esteem and self-concept may be too great to make such a request (Toch, 1977). To flee victimization also requires that the facility have available segregation space and that the staff be willing to cooperate by removing the inmate from the general population. Fear that staff may ridicule or ignore the request may deter some inmates from asking to be placed in segregation. In some cases, staff actually may advise the inmate to stand up to threatening inmates and counter the threats with violence (Toch, 1977).

Given the lack of opportunities for and costs associated with flight, fighting back may be the only means of self-protection readily available to inmates. To fight against victimization, inmates may engage in preemptive violence, make contraband weapons, "buy" protection from other inmates, or join gangs. While these alternatives provide some measure of protection, they also add to overall levels of violence and disorder in the facility, thereby reinforcing the need for self-protection.

The final deficiency of traditional jail architecture and its institutionalized furnishings is that they create physical and psychological stress among inmates that can neither be controlled nor reduced through legitimate means. Empirical research has demonstrated a relationship between environmental conditions and human behavior. This research has found that environmental "stressors" such as noise and crowding can produce arousal, frustration, annoyance, irritability, discomfort, stimulus overload, and perceived loss of control (Mueller, 1983). In turn, any of these states may provoke outbursts of aggressive or destructive behavior.

Common sources of environmentally induced stress found in traditional jails are lack of privacy, territory, and "defensible" space; crowding; excessive noise; institutionalized accoutrements; and stimuli deprivation. These stressors are, in large part, a product of the jail's architectural and interior design. Multiple-occupancy cells and dormitories, the most popular housing arrangements in jails, deprive inmates of privacy and territory and add to inmate perceptions of social and physical crowding. Cells, showers, and other physical locations where staff supervision is blocked by design features such as grillwork and walls, deprive inmates of safe and protected space. Dayrooms too small for the number of inmates they serve add to inmate perceptions of crowding. Metal doors, bars, and furnishings create excessive noise, while concrete walls and floors intensify it. Lack of windows, barren walls, and dull and uninspiring interior colors create an environment that is monotonous and boring, one that deprives inmates of any visual stimulation. The metal and steel furnishings provide little comfort, resist all efforts to personalize them, and are continuous reminders that inmates cannot be trusted with jail property.

In the jail, the stress experienced from these environmental irritants is intensified. Inmates are neither free to escape from sources of environmental stress nor are they substantially possessed of the means to control the sources of discomfort in their environment. Finally, usual strategies for coping with physical and psychological stress, such as physical exercise, alcohol and drugs, or withdrawal from the sources of stress, may not be readily and legitimately available to inmates (Toch, 1975).

Between 1973 and 1983, one thousand new jails were built in the United States (National Institute of Corrections, 1983). Most of these facilities were constructed to improve antiquated and decrepit jail conditions and to forestall court intervention. Despite claims that the newly constructed facilities were "state-of-the-art" and "on the cutting edge," most were designed as traditional linear facilities and featured many of the same deficiencies of their predecessors. A small number of jurisdictions, however, opted to construct "new generation," podular/direct supervision facilities, a design in correctional institution architecture and inmate management developed and successfully implemented in the federal Metropolitan Correctional Centers (MCCs).

History of the New Generation Philosophy

During the mid-1960s, the U.S. Bureau of Prisons undertook the construction of the first federally operated detention facilities in Chicago, San Diego, and New York City. The construction was part of a presidential directive to improve the federal correctional system (Nelson, 1988). Under a mandate from Congress, the Bureau of Prisons sought to build "humane institutions whose environment would respect the legal and moral rights of individuals" (Wener and Olsen, 1978: 1).

Three of the country's top architectural firms, commissioned independently by the bureau, were given freedom in designing the new facilities, with the stipulation that they must include singles cells for inmates, direct staff supervision, and "functional inmate living units." The concept of functional units places all "sleeping, food, and hygiene facilities, as well as some recreational equipment, in one self-contained, multi-level space" (Wener and Olsen, 1978: 4). A correctional officer is assigned to each unit to ensure direct and continuous inmate supervision.

Functional units originated in the mid- and late-1950s in federal juvenile drug treatment programs and were later implemented in federal drug treatment programs and other federal correctional facilities. A number of advantages have been found with the use of functional units. Inmates divided into smaller groups are more easily managed by staff. Functional units also increase the frequency and improve the quality of contacts between inmates and staff, increase staff involvement in decision making, ensure that decision making is done by staff who are closest to the situation, and provide flexibility in dealing with the needs of different inmates (Lansing et al., 1977).

In 1975, the Metropolitan Correctional Centers opened in Chicago, San Diego, and New York City. Although several minor design problems were found in all three facilities, for the most part they met the goals established by the bureau. According to Gettinger (1984: 11), "there was little violence, tension, or vandalism; staff requirements were not excessive; and officers seemed more satisfied with their jobs."

While the Bureau of Prisons hoped that the design and operations established in the MCCs would be models for duplication by local facilities, the concepts were not immediately accepted in other jurisdictions contemplating new jail facility construction. Even though the centers were demonstrably successful in achieving their goals of safe and humane incarceration, many local jail administrators argued that the prisoners detained in the MCCs were "softer" than the violent and destructive inmates with whom they regularly dealt.

The first local facility designed in the new style opened in Contra Costa County, California, in the 1970s. Although it was designed originally as a 642-bed, traditional high-rise facility, community opposition forced county officials to reexamine the facility's design and size. A committee appointed by the county executive to study the jail issue toured a number of facilities with different designs and recommended to county officials the design concept of the Chicago MCC.

When the 386-bed Contra Costa County Jail opened, it became a "showplace." Not only did it prove cost effective to build, but early reports indicated that it was safer for inmates and staff. Furthermore, the success dispelled the notion that the new design would not work with more serious criminals. In Contra Costa, "almost no misdemeanants are booked into the jail; the majority of inmates have been charged with burglary, armed robbery, murder, narcotics, or escape" (Gettinger, 1984: 13).

The new design's popularity quickly spread to other jurisdictions. Today, direct supervision detention facilities are in operation in Miami, New York City (the "Tombs"), Las Vegas, Portland, and Reno. By late 1988, direct supervision facilities were either in operation or being planned in forty-one local jurisdictions (Nelson,

1988). In addition, two new federal direct supervision MCCs were constructed in Tucson and Miami, and one is being planned for Los Angeles.

New Generation Architecture and Inmate Management

The new generation architectural philosophy is designed to reduce the many forms of disorder that characterize traditional jails and to promote both a safe and humane incarceration environment for inmates as well as staff. However, the architecture is only a facilitator, as it must be linked with a particular philosophy and inmate supervision style. Both the architecture and inmate management style address five assumptions about the causes of unsafe and often inhumane conditions existing in many traditional jails (Gettinger, 1984: 14).

The first of these assumptions, the *fear-hate syndrome*, argues that a traditional jail environment produces inmates who are afraid of each other and of staff, and a staff that is fearful of inmates. This leads inmates to arm themselves, associate with gangs, buy and sell protection, and continuously challenge authority. Staff who are afraid of inmates will abuse them psychologically or physically and avoid duties that bring them into contact with inmates.

The second assumption, *unprotected space*, suggests that where architectural design and/or operational procedures preclude the continuous and active supervision of inmate activities, opportunities for predation increase. The third assumption pertains to the common situation where the absence of continuous and positive legitimate leadership by correctional officers produces a *leadership vacuum*. The vacuum oftentimes is filled by the strongest, meanest, and wiliest inmates whose leadership may be far from fair and just.

The fourth assumption, *isolation*, refers to the "anything goes" mentality that develops when individuals are removed from the constraints imposed on their behavior by their ties to the outside world or to an orderly system within the jail environment. Freed from the informal social control mechanisms that directed their behavior outside the jail, and given the lack of adequate legitimate controls within the jail environment, inmate behavior is relatively unrestrained. The final assumption, *negative expectations*, posits that to the extent a facility sends messages that it expects both inmates and staff alike to behave in an unprincipled and uncivilized manner, it is likely to evoke that type of behavior.

The contrast between the traditional linear architecture and the podular architectural design of new generation facilities is indeed dramatic. The new generation facility design is based on a number of principles about the effect of architecture on human behavior. First, inmates are broken into groups of sixteen to forty-six and housed in living areas called *modules* or *pods*. Second, the modules are staffed twenty-four hours a day by specially trained corrections officers. Third, the modules are self-contained with built-in visiting, programming and recreation areas to reduce inmate movement and opportunities for breaches of security. Fourth, the modules are designed to enhance the correctional officer's interaction with and observation of inmates. Fifth, soft furnishings and accoutrements within the module function to reduce inmate stress associated with crowding, excessive noise, lack of privacy, and isolation from the outside world. Sixth, bars and metal doors are noticeably absent, reducing noise and the dehumanization associated with hard design jails.

The modules usually have two floors with individual rooms on the first floor surrounding a common dayroom and staircases leading to the mezzanine area where additional inmate rooms are situated. The layout is designed to accomplish three goals: to eliminate blind spots or those areas where inmates can congregate unobserved by correctional officers and can engage in aberrant behavior without detection; to encourage correctional officer movement among and interaction with inmates; and to reduce inmate perceptions of overcrowding.

The accommodations, fixtures, and accoutrements within the modules are designed to alleviate environmentally induced stress. Typically, each inmate room contains porcelain toilet and sink fixtures, a wooden or plastic desk and chair, an outside window, and a bed. The room is enclosed by a secure door made of wood or metal, rather than bars. Individual rooms fulfill inmate privacy and territory needs. They also provide inmates with a protected area to which they can retreat if threatened or fearful. The inclusion of porcelain and wood fixtures, and the absence of bars, fulfill a number of goals. First, they are cheaper than metal and steel and are believed to promote inmate care rather than invite destruction. Second, they reduce extraneous noise within the living unit and promote the feeling of a noninstitutional environment. Placement of a window in the rooms ensures adequate lighting and reduces feelings of isolation from the outside world.

The furnishings throughout the modules usually are crafted of wood and are upholstered. The multipurpose dayroom is designed to accommodate inmate movement and often is carpeted. Carpeting and upholstered furnishings help to reduce noise levels. The dayrooms also are furnished with several television sets and telephones to reduce fights over their use. Finally, a variety of textures and colors are used to reduce the institutional "feel" of the environment and to enhance the perception of openness.

In some facilities, the modules contain areas for programming, visitation, and indoor and outdoor recreation. By providing these spaces in the modules, inmate movement within the facility is limited, as are opportunities for escapes. Also, their presence assists in reducing inmate idleness and feelings of isolation from family and friends outside the jail.

In summary, the new generation architectural philosophy is designed to enhance facility supervision and inmate control and to reduce environmental sources of stress that can lead to expressive inmate violence and destruction. However, without appropriate inmate supervision by staff, the architecture alone cannot guarantee a safe and humane environment within the modules. The new generation philosophy recommends a direct inmate supervision style; inmates are supervised twenty-four hours a day by specially trained correctional officers.

Like the architectural design, the inmate management style seeks to reduce inmate stress and victimization and to increase institutional control over inmate behavior. The National Institute of Corrections (1983) and Gettinger (1984) identify six objectives of direct inmate supervision: (1) staff, rather than inmates, will control the facility; (2) inmates will be directly and continuously supervised; (3) rewards and punishments will be structured to ensure compliant inmate behavior; (4) open communications will be maintained between staff and inmates, and among staff; (5) inmates will be advised of the facility's expectations and rules; and (6) inmates will be treated in a manner consistent with constitutional and court standards, and they will be treated justly and fairly regardless of personal characteristics. While these goals have been used to develop direct supervision operations, until recently little was known about the actual day-to-day implementation of these values by direct supervision correctional officers.

Recent research (Zupan et al., 1986) has documented elements of an effective direct supervision inmate management style. In this research the critical incident technique, a method of job analysis, was used to identify correctional officer behaviors required for effective direct supervision in new generation facilities. The results described seven performance dimensions and specific behaviors that are required to produce a safe, humane and orderly environment. These dimensions are (1) managing the module to ensure a safe and humane environment (emphasizes proactive observation and communication skills to identify and react to situations before they escalate into serious problems); (2) handling inmate discipline (emphasizes progressive discipline that is fair and consistent); (3) responding to inmate requests (emphasizes appropriate ways to deal with inmate requests); (4) supervising in a clear, well-organized and attention-getting manner (emphasizes clear communication of orders, equitable task assignment, motivation, feedback, and follow-up); (5) building positive rapport and personal credibility with inmates (emphasizes strategies to create an environment of mutual respect between staff and inmates); (6) resolving inmate problems and conflicts (emphasizes managing and resolving confrontations between inmates); and (7) maintaining effective administrative and staff relations (emphasizes coordination and communication between staff and administrators).

While many of the behaviors for the seven dimensions may be practiced in traditional jails, the architectural design of these facilities limits their full and effective use. The fundamental element for the success of direct supervision is immediate and continuous contact between officers and inmates. Traditional jails' linear designs make this type of contact structurally and fiscally impossible. To achieve the difficult goal of humane and safe incarceration, both the architecture and the inmate management style must conform to the dictates of the new generation philosophy.

Effectiveness of the New Generation Philosophy

Despite the growing popularity of the new generation design concept and the increasing number of jurisdictions throughout the country that are investing millions of dollars in the construction of these facilities, a comprehensive and rigorous evaluation of the effectiveness of the design has yet to be conducted. A number of other studies either focus on a specific facility or attempt to compare a limited number of new generation facilities with traditional facilities. Although these studies will be cited in the following discussion, because of their methodological flaws caution should be taken in using them to conclude direct supervision a success or failure.

The new generation philosophy's primary goal is to create an incarceration environment that is safe and humane for inmates and staff alike. Early observations by the National Institute of Corrections (1983: 1) and others (Wener et al., 1985; Wener and Olsen, 1980) indicate that: "New Generation [direct supervision] jails [are] at least as secure as traditional linear jails and provid[e] a higher level of safety for both staff and inmates." Staff and administrators at five direct supervision facilities claim that the move from a traditional to a direct supervision facility produced a dramatic reduction in the number of assaults among inmates and between inmates and staff, the amount of vandalism and property destruction, the number of suicides by inmates, and the number of civil lawsuits filed by prisoners (Zupan, 1987). According to Wener et al. (1987), violent incidents in the federal MCCs and other direct supervision facilities were reduced by 30 percent to 90 percent, and homosexual activity virtually disappeared. Vandalism and property destruction also were reduced significantly. In one facility, the number of damaged mattresses dropped from one hundred fifty per year in the traditional jail to none during the first two years of occupancy in the direct supervision facility; telephone repairs dropped from two per week to two in two years; the number of destroyed sets of inmate clothing dropped from approximately ninety-nine sets per week to fifteen sets in two years (Wener et al., 1987: 42).

Researchers at the National Institute of Corrections (1983) compared incidents of aggravated assaults among inmates and between inmates and staff, homicides, suicides, escapes, and escape attempts in five podular/direct supervision facilities and six traditional linear facilities of comparable size. Four of the five direct supervision facilities were Metropolitan Correctional Centers. According to the National Institute of Corrections (1983: 31) the traditional facilities were located in "urban counties felt to be roughly comparable to the MCC's and Contra Costa and all [were] considering 'new generation' concepts for their new jails."

A perusal of these findings shows that there are important differences between both facilities as to the number of inmate incidents, with direct supervision facilities having fewer inmate homicides, suicides, escapes and escape attempts. The difference in numbers of aggravated inmate assaults are the greatest: the podular/direct supervision facilities averaged 10.4 inmate assaults in 1981 and 8.7 in 1982. In contrast, traditional facilities averaged 154.3 inmate assaults in 1981 and 141.5 in 1982.

Sigurdson (1985) found that in the first full year of operation, the Manhattan House of Detention (the "Tombs") had no homicides, sexual assaults, aggravated assaults, suicides, inmate disturbances, escapes, lawsuits, or adverse judgments. In addition, there were only four reports of contraband weapons (fashioned from plastic razor blades). In a different study, Sigurdson (1987a) found that in a two and one-half year period, the Pima County, Arizona Detention Facility had no homicides, suicides, sexual assaults, aggravated assaults, disturbances, or court-ordered judgments. During the study period, only one contraband item (a broken mop handle) was reported found in the possession of inmates. In a third study conducted in Larimer County, Colorado, Sigurdson (1987b) found similar results. In a three and one-half year period, there were no inmate homicides, suicides, sexual assaults, disturbances or court-ordered judgments against the jail. There were, however, four aggravated assaults and five contraband weapons (two fashioned from broken mop handles and three from small plastic utensils) found.

A number of other studies address whether the direct supervision design improves the "quality of life" experienced by inmates and staff. One study (Zupan and Stohr-Gillmore, 1987) found that inmates in direct supervision facilities were significantly more positive in their evaluations of the jail climate, the physical environment, and correctional officers than were inmates in traditional jails. Direct supervision inmates also experienced less psychological and physical stress than their traditional jail counterparts. Another study (Zupan and Menke, 1987) compared levels of job satisfaction and evaluations of organizational climate and job environment between correctional officers in new generation and traditional jails. It was found that correctional officers in direct supervision facilities were more satisfied with their jobs, evaluated the organization's climate more positively, and experienced more job enrichment than did officers in traditional jails.

In summary, the scant research lends support to the claims of new generation proponents. Although these studies can be faulted for a number of methodological problems, they nevertheless suggest that podular/direct supervision facilities are safer and provide a more positive incarcerative and work environment for inmates and staff than do traditional jails.

Policy Implications

The development of the new generation facility presents many challenges to correctional professionals and scholars. The first challenge concerns human resources management in correctional institutions. Innovations in correctional human resources management, particularly in jails and prisons, has been woefully inadequate. Past research (Zupan et al., 1986) suggests that the success or failure of the new generation correctional institution is dependent on at last three factors: the facility's architecture; the staff's characteristics; and the link between philosophy, architecture, and operations. First and foremost, since the development of a safe and humane facility depends in large measure on the complex and important managerial skills of correctional officers, more attention must be devoted to the recruitment, selection, and retention of appropriate personnel. This process must draw on individuals with new and traditionally neglected skills from diverse backgrounds and heretofore ignored groups of people. Often overlooked is the fact that the recruitment and selection process sends important messages about the facility's philosophy and standards of excellence. Of equal importance is basic and inservice training content. To manage inmates effectively in the new generation jail, correctional officers must use a number of sophisticated human relations skills, ranging from conflict management to problem solving to interpersonal community. Training that emphasizes traditional custodial skills, such as physical control techniques and firearms, or training that is merely superficial, will not prepare officers adequately to supervise inmates continuously and directly.

Corresponding to the demand for improved personnel processes is the need for developing a correctional officer career orientation. The new generation movement, with its strong link between theory and practice, offers the opportunity to redefine custodial work as a career. However, before this goal can be realized, several organizational matters must be resolved. First, the enriched nature of the direct supervision officer's job requires new styles and skills among first-line supervisors. It is highly unlikely that the traditional command-obey supervisory style will have a positive impact on this new type of employee. Second, the issue of appropriate compensation and reward is critical for the development of a career-oriented professional. Given increased responsibilities, direct supervision employees require commensurate salaries and benefits and an appropriate performance-reward link. In summary, these new facilities demand an entirely new management philosophy, a tall order for an occupation traditionally mired in outmoded strategies.

The direct supervision facility also offers new challenges and opportunities within the penal community. Some have suggested that the new generation/direct supervision model is applicable to prisons. Our research leads to speculation that this approach may be crucial to program delivery, even rehabilitation, in the institutional setting. It may be the case that institutional program effectiveness is dependent on ensuring inmate and officer safety through the creation of order within the institution. While there are prisons that use some of the new generation model's principles, its application to long-term confinement remains an intriguing, unanswered question.

Finally, the research agenda about new generation facilities is indeed an exciting and potentially important one to correctional scholars. While we have borrowed from our own work and that of others to draw conclusions that seem to indicate the success of this model, the data require caution. There is a pressing need for a single evaluation study comparing these facilities with traditional ones and with each other. In addition, the research agenda offers the opportunity to investigate more thoroughly the link between human behavior and architecture, managerial strategies applied to developing professionals, the brutalization hypothesis with released inmates, and the effects of more personal, consistent, safe, and humane incarceration on inmate attitudes and behaviors. Finally, as we have argued, the success of these facilities seems to be tied to the explicit link among philosophy, architecture, and operations, a research problem that leads to a consideration of organizational culture dynamics as a key to the success of innovations.

UNFINISHED AND EMERGING ISSUES CONFRONTING THE AMERICAN JAIL

As we look to the 1990s and beyond, several issues remain on the agenda for American jails. Inmate litigation is a relatively new phenomenon in relation to other problems. For many years the courts had a "hands off" policy regarding intervention in local corrections issues. In the early 1970s the courts began to look more sympathetically on many of the issues raised in inmate claims. In chapter 12, Dean Champion notes this trend has continued and, as a result, judicial intervention has increased dramatically. Champion believes that litigation will continue to increase, but not with the same rate of success. Although the number of jails under court order has increased significantly as a result of litigation, Champion sees some positive aspects: litigation has exerted pressure on local administrators and policymakers to improve the conditions of confinement. He recommends that jails establish internal grievance procedures to solve problems locally and reduce frivolous lawsuits.

Another unfinished issue is the continued confinement of juveniles in adult facilities. Ira Schwartz notes that despite federal, state, and in some cases local, attempts, juveniles still occupy ap-

proximately seventeen hundred jail beds per day. He is especially
critical of federal efforts and blames the lack of progress on several
factors: turmoil in the Office of Juvenile Justice and Delinquency
Prevention during the Reagan administration, substantial cuts in
the agency's budget, and an overall de-emphasis on this issue as a
national priority. On a positive note, Schwartz finds evidence that
state legislation has been effective. He recommends that legislation be enacted to eliminate the jailing of juveniles under any cir-
cumstance and that communities explore community-based alternatives to this practice.

Jail construction/renovation and operating costs are a significant portion of local governmental budgets. Federal cutbacks and
inelastic property tax revenues have pushed local tax efforts to the
maximum. Yet, local government officials are confronted with
pressures to maintain and/or increase a variety of services, even
unpopular ones like the local jail. As a result of these pressures and
demands, local officials have begun to look at alternative arrangements for the delivery of services. More and more they have looked
to the private sector. Norman Cox and William Osterhoff share reservations concerning privatization of local facilities. However,
they note that contracting for services has been used in many policy areas and at all levels of government. Many jails contract for a
variety of services—food and medical care, for example. The authors advocate a "partnership" approach, where private sector involvement is viewed as a "continuum of opportunities" for public/
private cooperation and mutual benefit. Like many other contributors to this volume, they see the need for a new climate of ideas
and approaches to solve the corrections crisis.

In any volume on jails the list of potential unfinished and
emerging issues is limitless. An entire book on such issues is possible and, in fact, a series of books would not exhaust the possibilities. However, these particular issues have been chosen because of
their persistence and/or their potential for impacting the greatest
number of jails—both small and large—in the United States.

CHAPTER 12

Jail Inmate Litigation in the 1990s

DEAN J. CHAMPION

On any given day, 3,400 jails in the United States house more than 234,000 detainees (Bostick, 1988: 6). In 1986 there were 16.6 million jail admissions and releases (Bureau of Justice Statistics [BJS], 1987: 1). One condition that typifies many of these jails is overcrowding. The overcrowding problem in the Los Angeles County jail system typifies many of the nation's larger jails. On March 1, 1986, for example, the Los Angeles County jail system's inmate count reached 20,056. This was regarded by the sheriff's department as "incredible," since the system was rated to accommodate 12,512 inmates (Waldie, 1988: 64). The following year, new records were achieved: the population grew to 21,509 inmates, 62 percent over the system's rated capacity. It has been estimated that between 1978 and 1986, the national jail population grew more than 73 percent, while the rated capacity of jails increased only 16 percent (Bureau of Justice Statistics [BJS], 1988: 1).

Judicial intervention in easing jail overcrowding has increased dramatically, resulting in court orders against particular jails found to be in violation of statutory or constitutional protections. In 1986, 612 jails in jurisdictions with large populations were examined to determine the extent of their compliance with constitutional safeguards and safety standards for inmates (BJS, 1987: 4). Of those studied, 166 jails were under court order to remedy one or more inmate confinement conditions. Court-ordered inmate population reduction was applicable to 123 (20 percent) of the 612 jails investigated. Among the subjects of other court-ordered improvements were recreational facilities, medical services, visitation practices, disciplinary procedures and policies, staffing patterns, grievance procedures, education or training programs, fire hazards, and counseling programs (BJS, 1987: 4). The entire jail overcrowding problem has been exacerbated by old facilities, underpaid and too few staff, and a populace that cares little about jail conditions (Huggins, 1986: 116).

Sources of Jail Overcrowding

Customarily, jails are intended as short-term detention facilities. They are designed to hold less serious offenders for less than one year and to accommodate pretrial detainees and trial witnesses. In most jurisdictions (except Alaska, Connecticut, Delaware, Hawaii, Rhode Island, and Vermont), jails are locally operated, often by counties or cities (BJS, 1988: 3). Beyond these functions, jails serve as "way stations" for suspects apprehended by law enforcement officers. A portion of the jail inmate population consists of juveniles, although their jail stays are short. Once their status has been determined, juveniles are turned over to officers who decide their disposition. Runaways or joyriders may be released to parents shortly after apprehension; those caught hitching rides on interstate highways may be arrested and temporarily detained for investigation. Those arrested for public drunkenness may be placed in drunk tanks and released the following morning after posting bail or paying fines. Thus, jails are regarded as the criminal justice system's gateway. They are people-processing stations where decisions are made by law enforcement officers about future actions to be taken against those arrested and/or detained.

Adding to these diverse functions performed by jails, many states and the federal government have contracted with local jail officials to house some of their prisoner overflow. Prisons are overcrowded and, like jails, many prisons are under court order to reduce their inmate populations. In some jurisdictions, jail officials and other local authorities calculate the financial benefits accruing as the result of accepting certain numbers of state and federal prisoners. State and federal prisons may pay local governments $30 or more per prisoner per day for maintenance costs. In contrast, maintenance costs for short-term jail inmates may be $15–$20 per day. Thus, it is financially advantageous for local facilities to accommodate state and federal prisoners. However, much of this money is allocated for expenditures unrelated to jails, such as community improvements. Regardless of how cities and counties use these funds, the important fact is that a more permanent state and federal inmate aggregate is placed in already overcrowded jail facilities.

Because the composition of jail inmates is diverse—ranging from unconvicted offenders and government witnesses to more serious convicted felons from local, state, and federal jurisdictions—inmates are segregated into designated jail areas where available space permits (Huggins, 1986). In many of the smaller jails, housing fifty or fewer inmates, segregation is a luxury and cannot be accomplished effectively because of space limitations and construction typical of small jails (Mays and Thompson, 1988; Moyer, 1988; Saxton, 1988: 16). Approximately five hundred counties nationwide have constructed new jails with fifty or fewer beds since 1974. These facilities comprise 75 percent of the nation's jails and detain about one-fourth of the nation's jail population (Saxton, 1988: 16). Thus, recommendations and proposals for providing special jail areas for those who are mentally ill, addicted to drugs or alcohol, or who are in other respects emotionally disturbed are noble but unrealistic aims. Furthermore, county jail authorities are not under any constitutional obligation to separate inmates according to age, prior record, or type of offense, provided there is an absence of evidence of assault, fights, sexual abuse, or other inmate harm (*Hutchings v. Corum*, 501 F. Supp. 1276 (1980)).

Some Bases for Inmate Litigation

It is important to recognize that inmates do not forfeit all of their constitutional rights as a result of incarceration (*Cook v. City of New York*, 578 F. Supp. 179 (1984)). However, jail authorities may limit the exercise of certain inmate rights to the extent made necessary by legitimate and reasonable institutional needs and exigencies (*U.S. v. Lewis*, 400 F. Supp. 1046 (1975)). Thus, jail officials may adopt restrictive policies that infringe on certain inmate rights, if these policies are necessary for security or rehabilitative purposes (*James v. Wallace*, 382 F. Supp. 1177 (1974)). In short, inmates' rights are limited by jail necessities and cannot be equated with the rights of noninmates (*Lawrence v. Davis*, 401 F. Supp. 1203 (1975)). Traditionally, federal courts have not intervened in state prison or jail operations and administration, unless there has been a clear finding, showing, and basis for concluding that substantial infringements of inmate constitutional rights have occurred (*Grubbs v. Bradley*, 552 F. Supp. 1052 (1982)).

Furthermore, jail inmates have no constitutional right to rehabilitation, vocational training, or education while incarcerated either in prisons or jails (*Dawson v. Kendrick*, 527 F. Supp. 1252 (1981); *French v. Owens*, 777 F. 2d 1250 (1985); *Inmates, Washington County Jail v. England*, 516 F. Supp. 132 (1980)), although inmates are protected from physically, mentally, and socially degenerative jail environments (*Ramos v. Lamm*, 485 F. Supp. 122 (1979); *Dawson v. Kendrick*, 527 F. Supp. 1252 (1981)). Jailers also have considerable latitude in enforcing state and federal rules, and their failure merely to comply with state or federal regulations is not a constitutional violation per se (*Roberts v. City of Troy*, 773 F. 2d 720 (1985)).

It is also significant to note that the Eighth Amendment "cruel and unusual" punishment provisions do not require counties and states to house their inmates in a manner most pleasing to inmates or considered by most knowledgeable penal authorities as likely to avoid confrontations and psychological depression (*Atiyeh v. Capps*, 449 U.S. 1312 (1981)). In other words, jails do not have to be comfortable. However, under certain circumstances jail confinement conditions may be considered cruel and unusual (*Inmates, D.C. Jail v. Jackson*, 416 F. Supp. 119 (1976)). The conventional standard applied by the courts in determining whether cruel and unusual punishment conditions exist in jails is the "totality of circumstances" test (*Stewart v. Winter*, 669 F. 2d 328 (1982); *Barnes v. Government of Virgin Islands*, 415 F. Supp. 1218 (1976)). Thus, confinement conditions do not exist in isolation, and as a consequence each condition's effect must be considered with other conditions' effects in evaluating confinement facilities' adequacy (*Stickney v. List*, 519 F. Supp. 617 (1981)). However, this test may be widely interpreted and therefore rests on the standards of individual judges as to what conditions are cruel and unusual. Coupled with the totality of circumstances test is the "shock the conscience" test (*Palmigiano v. Garrahy*, 443 F. Supp. 956 (1977)). If jail conditions are so deplorable as to "shock the conscience," then they may be deemed cruel and unusual punishment (Robbins, 1987: 7–5).

Generally, state and federal inmates have no right to be placed in a particular prison or jail (*U.S. v. Bergman*, 416 F. Supp. 496 (1976); *Patterson v. Walters*, 363 F. Supp. 486 (1973); *Taylor v. Strickland*, 411 F. Supp. 1390 (1976)). Prisoner transfers from one jail to another, due to administrative sanction or logistical convenience, are clearly within jail authorities' purview (*Smith v. Hal-*

ford, 570 F. Supp. 1187 (1983)). Inmates have no rights relating to these transfers, nor must they be apprised of the reasons for such transfers (*Miller v. Landon*, 545 F. Supp. 81 (1982); *Lyons v. Papantoniou*, 558 F. Supp. 4 (1982)). However, in some states inmates are statutorily entitled to a transfer hearing.

One result of an inmate transfer from one facility to another is that conditions at the second location may be less favorable (as well as more favorable) than those at the original location. Transfers for whatever reason (e.g., relieving overcrowding, invoking disciplinary measures, reclassifications, institutional security) may cause state or federal inmates to be housed in jails. Since jails are short-term facilities, it is likely that they provide fewer amenities and services than found in state or federal institutions. Under some circumstances, state prisoners may be obligated to serve large portions of their original sentences in jail facilities. The Knox County Jail (Tennessee) held in excess of two hundred state prisoners in 1989, and many of these inmates had been confined in the jail for three or more years. Since 1983, the Tennessee prison system has been under court order to limit its inmate population to zero population growth. Thus, for every new prisoner entering Tennessee prisons, another prisoner must be freed or transferred to other accommodations. In 1984, the parolee population in Tennessee increased by 84 percent, the largest growth in the United States at that time. Since then, many state prisoners have been housed in jails through contractual arrangements with local authorities. Thus, these exigent circumstances have legitimated using Tennessee jails for court-approved, long-term state prisoner confinement. However, federal prisoners housed in Tennessee county jails are mostly pretrial detainees and remain confined in these institutions for periods of six months or less.

Traditionally, courts have viewed unfavorably petitions from inmates who have been denied equal protection under the law resulting from their transfers among institutions (*Miller v. Landon*, 545 F. Supp. 81 (1982)). In fact, even in those cases where the new institution was fraught with more burdensome and undesirable conditions than the originating institution, no prisoner's liberty interests or constitutional rights have been found to be infringed as the result of such transfers (*Smith v. Halford*, 570 F. Supp. 1187 (1983); *Hudson v. Johnson*, 619 F. Supp. 1539 (1985)). If there is a rational basis for such transfers, they generally have been condoned by the courts (*McGinnis v. Royster*, 410 U.S. 263 (1973)).

These transfers also may involve changes in administrative authority (e.g., a transfer from a state or federal prison to county jail, a transfer from a county jail to a state or federal prison, a transfer from a state to a federal prison, a transfer from a federal to a state prison or to an institution within the same system but with a different security designation). These transfers also do not violate inmates' constitutional rights (*Dawson v. Kendrick*, 527 F. Supp. 1252 (1981)). However, in one jurisdiction at least, a federal district court found in favor of state inmates who had been "backed up" in county jails because of overcrowding and who experienced "less favorable" conditions in these jails compared with inmates who continued to be housed in state prisons (*Hill v. Hutto*, 537 F. Supp. 1185 (1982)). In view of the general unsuccessfulness of similar litigation among state prisoners in other states who have undergone such transfers to less hospitable facilities in county jails, the finding in the *Hill* case is the exception rather than the rule.

Provided jail visitation policies (or a lack of them) meet legitimate penological objectives, convicted offenders have no absolute constitutional right to visitation (*Evans v. Johnson*, 808 F. 2d 1427 (1987); *Johnson v. Galli*, 596 F. Supp. 135 (1984)). Of course, jails must provide inmates with access to the courts and visitation with attorneys or comparable alternatives (*Penland v. Warren County Jail*, 797 F. 2d 332 (1986)). Jail officials are also under a duty to exercise reasonable care in inmates' medical treatment. Those with contagious or highly communicable diseases such as AIDS must be provided adequate medical treatment and separation from uninfected inmates (*Smith v. Sullivan*, 553 F. 2d 373 (1977)). In the event that administrators or correctional officers act with "deliberate indifference" to inmates' serious medical needs, these actions may constitute cruel and unusual punishment (*Inmates of Allegheny County Jail v. Pierce*, 612 F. 2d 754 (1979)). However, jail inmates find it difficult to prove "deliberate indifference" on the part of jailers and their staffs in court (*Farinaro v. Coughlin*, 642 F. Supp. 276 (1986); *Goff v. Bechtold*, 632 F. Supp. 697 (1986); *Harding v. Kuhlmann*, 588 F. Supp. 1315 (1984)).

Perhaps the most important stimulus prompting numerous lawsuits against jail administrators is overcrowding. Despite definite proclamations by the various circuit courts of appeals about the minimal cell square footage provided jail inmates, no nationally accepted cell size standards or square footage minimums exist. In 1976, a Mississippi case established a minimum of 50 square feet of cell space per inmate (*Gates v. Collier*, 423 F. Supp. 732 (1976)). However, other jurisdictions have declared 38.25 square feet (*Shelby County Jail Inmates v. Westlake*, 798 F. 2d 1085 (1986)),

10 to 17 square feet (*Delgado v. Cady,* 576 F. Supp. 1446 (1983)), and 35- to 40-square-foot "cubbyholes" for inmates (*Battle v. Anderson,* 447 F. Supp. 516 (1977)) to be constitutionally acceptable.

The landmark case of *Rhodes v. Chapman,* 452 U.S. 337 (1981) gave the U.S. Supreme Court's seal of approval to "double-bunking," or placing more than one inmate in a cell designed to accommodate only one. This case involved allegations of serious overcrowding at the Southern Ohio Correctional Facility in Lucasville, Ohio. Even "triple-celling" has been declared constitutional, provided this is a temporary response to an emergency jail overcrowding situation (*Delgado v. Cady,* 576 F. Supp. 1446 (1983)). In dormitorylike confinement, square footage calculations for all inmate inhabitants are subject to diverse interpretations. In any event, the opinion delivered in the *Rhodes* case was significant because it acknowledged that in the "*abstract* prison overcrowding . . . generally results in serious harm to inmates . . . but cases are not decided in the abstract . . . a court is under obligation to examine the *actual effect* of challenged conditions on the well-being of the prisoners . . . (and that in the Southern Ohio Correctional Facility) this case was unable to identify any actual signs that the double celling at the (facility) has seriously harmed the inmates there" (452 U.S. 337 at 368, 369, emphasis added).

Another landmark case involving jail overcrowding was *Bell v. Wolfish,* 441 U.S. 520 (1979). This case was significant because it attacked the double-bunking policies of a relatively new jail in New York City designed primarily to house pretrial detainees. The Metropolitan Correctional Center (MCC) is a federally operated, short-term custodial facility that opened in August 1975 with a planned capacity of 449 inmates. There were 389 rooms originally intended for single occupancy. However, an unprecedented rise in pretrial detainees occurred. The Bureau of Prisons attempted to deal with these exigencies, but sentenced and unsentenced inmates ultimately were forced to double-bunk in these single-occupancy accommodations. In fact, some detainees and sentenced prisoners had to sleep on cots in common areas for brief periods until space became available in different rooms. The *Bell* suit was filed November 28, 1975, less than four months after the MCC opened.

The *Bell* class-action suit alleged various statutory and constitutional rights violations beyond overcrowded conditions. Undue length of confinement; improper searches including body cavity inspections; inadequate employment, recreational, and educational opportunities; and objectionable restrictions on the pur-

chase and receipt of personal items and books were among the allegations included in the suit. However, the Supreme Court
rejected all allegations as not violating any constitutional right.
The restrictions by MCC officials on the receipt of goods from the
outside as well as strip searches (including body cavity inspections) were justified as necessary security precautions to prevent
the intrusion of contraband and dangerous materials. Furthermore, inmate due process rights were not infringed, nor was
double-bunking deemed as punishment, particularly where nearly
all pretrial detainees were released within sixty days. Despite these
rulings, which were clearly adverse to inmates and the rights they
sought to establish, the jail inmate litigation flood has not abated.

Avenues for Inmate Litigation

Jail inmates may initiate lawsuits against jailers, sheriffs, correctional officers, and even other inmates, although inmate/adminis-
trator lawsuits are most frequent. Several litigation avenues are
available to inmates. They may sue jail officials on various constitutional bases: freedom of speech, religion, and the press under
the First Amendment are frequent litigation issues. The Fourth
Amendment provisions against unreasonable search and seizure
do not apply to jail inmates in an absolute sense, although correctional officers are cautioned to exercise care while searching inmate cells and personal effects. Ordinarily, prisoners do not enjoy
the same reasonable expectation of privacy in their cells that non-
incarcerated citizens enjoy in their homes. Warrants to enter jail
cells to search for and seize illegal contraband are not required.

The Eighth and Fourteenth amendments protect inmates
from conditions of cruel and unusual punishment and provide
them with due process and equal protection of the laws. These
rights are not relinquished whenever inmates are incarcerated. Because of the vagueness of *cruel and unusual punishment* and the
numerous circumstances under which it can be cited, considerable
litigation occurs alleging cruel and unusual punishment or correctional officer/administrator actions. However, the Eighth Amendment's touchstone is the effect upon the imprisoned [*Laaman v.
Helgemoe*, 437 F. Supp. 269 (1977)]. Thus gross, intentional neglect
by administrators or wanton infliction of pain unwarranted by jus-
tifiable penological goals supports allegations of cruel and unusual
punishment in view of the *Laaman* standard. Under the Fourteenth
Amendment, all inmates are entitled to equal protection under the
law. Thus the stage is set for allegations of discrimination on the

basis of race, ethnicity, gender, and other variables. If one inmate is permitted to subscribe to a religious magazine while another inmate is not, grounds may exist for a Fourteenth Amendment violation.

However, in recent years, administrative grievance procedures have been placed into operation in many prisons and jails. Furthermore, jail inmates in certain jurisdictions may form councils to resolve disputes among other inmates. The establishment of these internal procedures for addressing and settling grievances has done much to head off a great deal of potential jail inmate litigation. Judges shudder to think of the massive number of inmate lawsuits that would be filed if these grievance procedures did not exist. Ordinarily, if such procedures exist in a jail, inmates are obligated to exhaust these internal remedies before seeking redress formally in court. All prisons have administrative grievance procedures, and some jails have similar mechanisms for resolving inmate disputes. Not all of these incarcerative facilities have inmate councils, and in spite of the existence of these internal remedies, much litigation occurs and is directed by inmates against jail officials. Much of this litigation is inmate-generated on a *pro se* basis, where the inmate prepares the filing personally or has another inmate, a jailhouse lawyer, prepare these documents (unless other reasonable alternatives to legal services are provided and made available to inmates) (*Johnson v. Avery*, 393 U.S. 483 (1969); *Wolff v. McDonnell*, 418 U.S. 539 (1974); *Graham v. State Dept. of Corrections*, 392 F. Supp. 1262 (1975)). Since jailhouse lawyers usually are not as legally literate as full-fledged attorneys, their filings frequently are defective in one respect or another and rejected outright by the courts.

For jail inmates, there are three major avenues for filing lawsuits: (1) civil rights violations, (2) habeas corpus petitions, and (3) mandamus actions. Civil rights violations are alleged under 42 U.S.C. 1983, and these suits involve a wide array of inmate complaints. Some of these complaints include administrators and/or correctional officers negligence (e.g., under the doctrine of *respondeat superior*, jailers, sheriffs, entire department, or the county-at-large may be responsible for subordinates' actions while those personnel are acting in a negligent fashion within the scope of their employment); negligent hiring, training, entrustment, or retention; excessive force used by officers; unreasonable cell searches; damage to personal property during cell shakedowns; objections to male prisoners being guarded by female officers; administrative slothfulness in responding to inmate grievances and complaints;

and the unjustified infliction of bodily harm. Among jail inmates, civil rights suits are the most popular and prevalent litigation mechanisms.

Habeas corpus lawsuits challenge (a) the original decision to confine inmates in jail or, simply, the fact of confinement, and (b) the conditions under which inmates are housed (28 U.S.C. 2254; *Coffin v. Reichard*, 143 F. 2d 443 (1944)). Thus, habeas corpus petitions challenge both confinement and the conditions of confinement. The *Coffin* case reasoned that inmates are entitled to habeas corpus relief despite their lawful custody, provided they are deprived of some right to which they are entitled, even while confined, the deprivation of which makes their confinement more burdensome than the law allows (Palmer, 1985: 223). This extension of habeas corpus to "conditions of confinement" challenges was upheld by the Supreme Court in *Jones v. Cunningham*, 371 U.S. 236 (1963). Habeas corpus suits rank second in all jail inmate suits filed and represent about one-third of all jail inmate filings.

The third category, mandamus actions, represents attempts by inmates to compel their keepers to perform their administrative responsibilities. Sometimes, jailers will refuse to comply with a new governmental directive about jail operations. Knowing that jailers are not complying with directives from higher-ups and that this noncompliance is causing some or all of the inmates' physical discomforts, psychological stress, or other problems, inmates may file suits to compel officials to do their jobs. A duty is owed the inmates by administrators, and administrators are not fulfilling that duty. Mandamus actions are drastic solutions and are seldom used by inmates against jailers, sheriffs, and others.

Some Pitfalls for Jail Inmates

Lawsuits filed by or on behalf of inmates, either on a *pro se* or class-action basis, often are regarded by the courts as "frivolous" and "lacking in merit" (Anderson, 1986). During the 1970s, an inmate, Green, filed between 600–700 lawsuits on behalf of himself and/or other inmates (*In re Green*, 669 F. 2d 779 (1981); Knight and Early, 1986). The courts consistently found his suits to be frivolous, irresponsible, and unmeritorious; one court even suggested that Green hoped to force his own release by deluging the courts with these frivolous suits (Knight and Early, 1986: 15). Suit frivolity aside, state and federal district and appellate courts have been inclined to grant jail administrators the benefit of the doubt in many cases.

Particularly disadvantageous to jail inmates is the presumption of correctness relative to decisions rendered by lower courts and/or by jail administrators in the governance of their institutions and the general conduct of their correctional staffs. With few exceptions, courts presume earlier jail decision making to be correct or meritorious concerning penological objectives including jail security and inmate safety.

Jail inmates may file their suits either in federal or state courts, but preference for the federal court forum is precedented on 42 U.S.C. 1983 and 28 U.S.C. 1331(a), 1334(3). If suits seek habeas corpus relief, there is the rather stringent requirement (with exceptions) that inmates first must exhaust all state administrative and judicial remedies before seeking habeas corpus relief in federal courts (*Roba v. United States*, 604 F. 2d 215 (1979); *Harris v. MacDonald*, 555 F. Supp. 137 (1982)). Otherwise, federal district judges will remand these cases to state courts for appropriate action. Thus, habeas corpus actions filed in federal courts by state prisoners or jail inmates in recent years have not been as voluminous as civil rights filings.

State prisoner and jail inmate habeas corpus actions have been accepted on their merits in large numbers by federal district judges. However, most of these cases have been rejected outright later. Some logical reasons for this will be noted below, reasons that have nothing to do with the meritoriousness of the complaint or whether all state remedies were initially exhausted. For 42 U.S.C. 1983 civil rights actions, however, either state or federal courts may entertain such litigation. Robbins (1987: 17–11) suggests a rule of thumb that might be appropriate for deciding the forum: state actions ought to be filed in state courts, whereas constitutionally based actions ought to be filed in federal courts. For cases filed under state laws, the following seven-point checklist must be considered. State courts usually:

1. impose burdensome pleading requirements;
2. apply unfairly short statutes of limitations requirements;
3. restrict the availability of class actions;
4. fail to afford broad discovery;
5. impose archaic notions of immunity, especially executive immunity;
6. apply technical evidentiary rules in civil cases; and
7. fail to provide for an award of attorney's fees in appropriate circumstances (Robbins, 1987: 17–11).

Curiously, federal courts have accepted numerous state and local inmate suits in past years, especially those seeking habeas corpus relief. However, it is significant that many of these suits have been dismissed outright or remanded to state courts for adjudication because all state remedies were not exhausted or because of technical irregularities in petitions. Since many suits are filed by prisoners on a *pro se* basis, it has been suggested that federal district judges in some jurisdictions at least accept such suits as a means of manipulating their docket volume (Palmer, 1989). Thus, many *pro se* cases might be accepted by federal judges on their merits, and the large number of cases appearing on their court dockets makes their figures look good in order to justify larger court staffs. However, most of these cases are dismissed summarily by judges. Therefore, it may be argued that some federal judges have created an "industry" in *pro se* inmate complaints and that they are able to make their court statistics and caseloads show exactly what they want them to show (Palmer, 1989). It is possible that state courts emulate federal district courts in this regard as well, and that inmates have "lost" before they have even commenced their litigation.

One important problem posed for inmates who select federal instead of state courts for their filings, whether habeas corpus or civil rights under Section 1983, is that stringent statute of limitations requirements exist under state laws for inmates to litigate their claims. The timeliness of a filing in federal court will affect adversely the timeliness of a subsequent state court filing. Sometimes, prisoners have difficulty obtaining transcripts of previous court cases. Lacking these and other materials or experiencing delays in obtaining them may cause their cases to lapse beyond the statute of limitations for filings.

There are many pros and cons relative to which court should function as the jail inmate litigation forum. Arguably, one of the stronger reasons for filing habeas corpus petitions in federal courts where constitutional issues are involved is the federal court's greater familiarity with these constitutional issues compared with that of state courts (Robbins, 1987: 17–8,9). However, a strong reason not to file such suits in federal courts is the tremendous likelihood that these suits will be rejected outright without a hearing. Some statistics are in order: by mid-1985, 8,534 habeas corpus petitions had been filed by local jail and state prison inmates in federal district courts (Administrative Office of the U.S. Courts, 1985). Of these, only 114 cases proceeded to hearings, where 102 of these hearings lasted one day or less (Robbins, 1987: 13–84). The remaining 8,420 cases were dismissed outright or remanded to state courts so that state remedies could be exhausted.

The best route for jail inmates to follow is to file suits under 42 U.S.C. 1983 and allege civil rights violations including insufficiency or absence of due process and/or equal protection under the law. These suits may be heard by either federal or state courts. Furthermore, federal district judges are prevented from remanding such cases back to state courts, since the "exhaustion of state remedies" requirement associated with habeas corpus petitions is not applicable to Section 1983 actions, with some rare exceptions. Consistent with this notion, jail inmates today are filing increasing numbers of Section 1983 actions and proportionately fewer habeas corpus petitions. Mays and Bernat (1988) have noted this trend, and they further have indicated that one important reason for this changing situation is that jail inmates seem to be accepting the fact of their confinement with greater frequency compared with past years. However, these inmates have not and are not accepting the confinement *conditions* and *policies* to which they are subjected (Mays and Bernat, 1988; Thomas et al., 1986). This observation may be true, but in view of the unsuccessfulness of habeas corpus petitions filed in federal courts in recent years and the fact that district judges may indeed use these cases to adjust their docket statistics more favorably for the benefit of outsiders, policymakers, and Congressional purse-string holders, it is debatable that jail inmates have changed their acceptance of jail confinement appreciably during the past decade or so.

Some Recent Jail Inmate Litigation Trends in Selected Jurisdictions

Empirical research is useful for shedding light on current jail inmate litigation trends, even if such research is on a comparatively small scale contrasted with federal district court filing statistics. However, a preliminary examination of federal filing statistics is useful for understanding the annual profile of state court habeas corpus or civil rights filings by jail inmates. Thomas (1988) has examined federal court civil rights and habeas corpus filings among state and federal prisoners between 1962 and 1987. He noted, in summary, that federal inmates are far more litigious than state inmates and that they file two to three times as many suits per 100 inmates compared with their state counterparts. Although the filing rate per 100 federal inmates deviates somewhat between 1962 and 1987, their filings generally have increased during these years.

In 1962, federal inmates filed 6.25 suits per 100 inmates, reaching a high of 19.25 suits per 100 inmates in 1972, and then dropping to 9.48 suits per 100 inmates in 1987.

State inmate filing figures reflect systematic increases in filing volume in federal district courts between 1962 and 1987. Furthermore, state inmates' habeas corpus filings accounted for 97 percent of all state inmate suits in federal courts in 1962, about 4.73 per 100 inmates. By 1987, however, although habeas corpus petition volume had increased slightly for state prisoners, these cases accounted for only 29 percent of all state prisoner filings in 1987 (about 1.88 per 100 state inmates). Accordingly, civil rights suits filed in federal courts by state prisoners rose from .5 per 100 inmates in 1967 to 4.39 per 100 inmates in 1987 (Thomas, 1988: 125). Increased federal court filings have been attributable to the corresponding growth of state and federal prisoner populations (Doyle and Thomas, 1987).

The picture seems clear, at least for state and federal prisoners considered apart from jail inmates. State prisoners filed proportionately fewer habeas corpus petitions and proportionately more civil rights suits per 100 inmates during the 1980s. However, are these trends similar to jail inmate litigation trends, especially for random years during the 1980s and in selected jurisdictions? A summary report of some preliminary findings provides a tentative answer to this question. A random sample of 105 county or city jails was obtained from six states (Tennessee, North Carolina, South Carolina, Alabama, Georgia, and Kentucky), chosen because each was contiguous to Tennessee and minimized travel to and from central locations that maintained filing records for jail inmates and others. Years 1981 through 1985 were chosen for examination through the content analysis method. Available information was obtained in mid-1987 from courthouses in the jurisdictions where these jails were located. Because of record-keeping inconsistencies, unofficial prohibitions against disclosures of available court documents to researchers, or a general reluctance from some clerks in various counties to make space and time available to investigators for records examination, the original 105 jails scheduled for examination declined to 71. Despite this reduction in the original number of jails selected, the aggregate average annual number of inmates in these jails for the period 1981–84 was 13,209.

Inspection of jail inmates lawsuits filed during 1981–1985 disclosed a total of 826 filings on diverse grounds. A breakdown of these 826 filings is shown in table 12.1. An additional feature of

TABLE 12.1

Jain Inmate Filings for Seventy-One Jails in Six States, 1981–85, by Type of Filing and Destination of Filing

	Court (Proportions in Parentheses)						
	Federal		Type of Suit		State		
Year	CR*	HC**	O***	CR	HC	O	Total
1981	29(.28)	15(.15)	3(.03)	41(.40)	9(.09)	6(.06)	103
1982	36(.30)	12(.10)	5(.04)	46(.38)	19(.16)	3(.02)	121
1983	48(.37)	10(.08)	6(.05)	42(.33)	15(.12)	8(.06)	129
1984	109(.49)	22(.10)	14(.06)	62(.28)	15(.07)	0(.00)	222
1985	128(.51)	10(.04)	21(.08)	61(.24)	17(.06)	14(.06)	251
T =	350(.42)	69(.08)	49(.06)	252(.31)	75(.09)	31(.04)	826

   * Civil rights petitions
  ** *Habeas corpus* petitions
*** Other (e.g., mandamus, tort actions, etc.)

table 12.1 is the distribution of filings according to state or federal jurisdictions and whether the filings involved Section 1983 civil rights complaints, habeas corpus petitions, or "other" (e.g., tort actions against correctional officers and/or administrators, mandamus actions, etc.).

Table 12.1 discloses some interesting information. First, civil rights lawsuits among the jail inmates investigated here make up 73 percent of all filings. Proportionately, more civil rights petitions are filed in federal courts (42 percent) compared with state courts (31 percent). The "other" category is erratic and cannot be meaningfully interpreted consistently. Of course, this may be due to the randomness and selectivity of the jurisdictions examined. Of interest is the fact that the proportionate number of civil rights lawsuits filed in federal courts has increased systematically during 1981–85, from .28 to .51. However, these petitions have declined proportionately for the same time period in state courts (e.g., .40 to .24 between 1981–85).

At the same time, habeas corpus filings declined, with one exception between 1981 and 1985, rising from 9 percent to 16 percent between 1981–82 but eventually declining to 6 percent in 1985. A larger proportion of these petitions by jail inmates in federal courts was observed, again with exceptions, although there appeared to be a general proportionate decline in these petitions as well. The sudden change in 1984–85 compared with the figures of the two preceding years may have been influenced by a substantial drop in Tennessee jail inmate lawsuits during that period, which coincided with a court-ordered reduction in the state prison population. As was noted before, an 84 percent increase in Tennessee's parolee population occurred between 1983–84. While no attempt was made to provide a state-by-state breakdown of filings and the issues involved in lawsuits, Tennessee jail inmate lawsuits comprised about one-third of all inmate lawsuits among the six states for all years except 1984–85. That year, Tennessee jail inmate lawsuits accounted for about 20 percent of all suits filed among the jurisdictions sampled. Thus, the overall habeas corpus petition decrease during 1984–85 may have been due, in part, to Tennessee's penological changes.

Clearly, civil rights Section 1983 filings are dominant among the jail inmate lawsuits examined here. Habeas corpus filings in federal courts, with few exceptions, have declined between 1981 and 1985, while the petitions filed in state courts have been proportionately higher (in some years by more than 50 percent). The inverse proportionate relation between jail inmates' civil rights filings in federal and state courts suggests that, at least for the inmate petitions investigated here, proportionately more jail inmates are using federal rather than state courts for resolution of their civil rights-related lawsuits. As Thomas (1988) has suggested, this may be explained by local jail inmates preferring to take their chances in federal courts with Section 1983 petitions where district judges are more aware of constitutional issues and violations than are state trial judges. This may be termed "plausible speculation" for the present study.

At least one interesting contrast may be made between Thomas's (1988) report and the present research. Thomas noted a gradual increase in state prisoner civil rights filings in federal district courts. This trend also has been observed here for the jail inmate litigation investigated. By the same token, jail inmates' habeas corpus petitions have declined proportionately for both state and federal courts. However, the present study shows a significant decline in civil rights Section 1983 filings among jail inmates in state courts, tapering off systematically from .40 in 1981 to .24 in 1985. While only 252 civil rights cases were filed in state courts among these inmates for the five-year period, this suggests that a larger proportion of inmates who file lawsuits are bypassing state courts and opting for federal district courts as forums for their Section 1983 petitions.

One explanation for this apparent trend already has been suggested by Robbins (1987). He has observed that for Section 1983 petitions, jail inmates and others are not bound to exhaust state remedies before filing their petitions with federal district courts. Furthermore, if injunctive relief is sought, although both state and federal courts may issue injunctions against local jails, federal judges may be more impartial arbiters. Since injunctive relief sought in either state or federal courts is not subject to trial by a jury, judges decide inmate claims. Thus, federal district judges' decisions may be less affected by local politics, whereas state and local judges may be inclined to rule favorably for their political associates and constituencies.

Furthermore, certain defenses ordinarily used by jailers and jail staff (qualified immunity or "good faith," statute of limitations, and notice of claims) cannot be used in injunctive actions. Thus, if jail inmates wish to make their lives less oppressive and local jails more fit for human habitation, they may have service initiated against local sheriffs or chief executives personally and subsequent court orders are binding on their staffs (Robbins, 1987: 17–13; *Johnson v. Teasdale*, 456 F. Supp. 1083 (1978); *Shakman v. Democratic Org. of Cook County*, 533 F. 2d 344 (1976); *Mary and Crystal v. Ramsden*, 635 F. 2d 590 (1980); *Rhodes v. Robinson*, 612 F. 2d 766 (1979); *Baskin v. Parker*, 602 F. 2d 1205 (1979)).

The success rate for inmates who filed these 826 lawsuits included 81 suits heard (slightly less than 10 percent), five favorable rulings for jail inmates (.06 percent), and nine favorable rulings for jailers and jail staff (11 percent). The remaining 67 suits were summarily dismissed after brief hearings. Over 90 percent of the other suits were rejected outright for various reasons, including frivolity.

Conclusion

The future of jail inmate litigation is bleak. However, this does not mean that it will decline appreciably during the 1990s; in fact, it probably will increase to record levels. What this statement means is that the success rate for favorable court rulings on jail inmate petitions probably will decrease during the next decade. But this is not necessarily unfavorable for jail inmates generally.

During the past ten to fifteen years, public awareness of jail problems has been heightened. City, county, state, and federal officials are increasingly under pressure to do something about jail conditions, and not just within their own jurisdictions. Federal and state prison overcrowding is shifting the inmate housing burden to already overcrowded jails. The hydraulic effect is evident here: when pressure is alleviated at one point in the correctional system, it is increased at another. Some of this pressure resulting from prison overcrowding is shifted to "front-end" and "back-end" correctional agencies and personnel—probation and parole officers. Community correctional programs, electronic monitoring, house arrest, and a host of other programs in various experimental stages currently are being devised as potential temporary solutions to the growing inmate population problem.

Inmate litigation in the general sense is good, regardless of how it is viewed by the courts. It exerts pressures on chief executives, sheriffs, jailers, and correctional officers to act more responsibly in their jobs. Wardens, superintendents, and correctional officers in jails and prisons are becoming more sensitive to the possibility that they may face inmate litigation. Thus, major steps are being taken to educate corrections professionals in their legal liabilities and duties. Organizations such as the American Correctional Association currently offer courses to those interested in improving their professional skills and correctional education. The general correctional executive response to allegations of negligent hiring, retention, training, and entrustment have been to fire those who do their jobs poorly, to train those who exhibit potential to improve, and to be more selective in job assignments. Standards of care are improving in many jails, either through court order or through administrative concern for jail improvements. Many jails are old and need to be demolished. In their place new jails must be constructed. Assuming there will never be enough jail space to accommodate all jail inmates, even short-term ones, citizens must bear the financial responsibility for much of this needed improvement. But separating citizens from their tax dollars is difficult. Many solutions to jail overcrowding have been proposed besides those mentioned here. Intensive supervised probation is one alternative; however, this alternative presumes that convictions have been obtained. Even plea bargaining in lieu of trial and jail terms takes time. In the meantime, bail standards might be changed so that low-risk pretrial detainees may be freed prior to trial. Thus, much valuable jail space may be made available to accommodate more dangerous inmates. Many minor cases may be resolved through alternative dispute resolution.

One solution to minimizing the volume of jail inmate litigation is to establish internal administrative grievance procedures. Some jail systems have these grievance procedures, and some large jails have inmate councils to hear and resolve disputes between inmates that might otherwise lead to civil rights suits. Obviously, a balance needs to be struck between jail security needs and administrative authority to accomplish effective management of jail operations *and* inmates' rights to be housed under humane conditions and have court access when desired. As we have seen, inmates are not entitled as a matter of right to visitation privileges, with exceptions. They must be permitted to consult with their attorneys for appeals, for ongoing cases, and for lodging legitimate grievances pertaining to rights violations by correctional officers and others. Many of the smaller, older jails are unable or unwilling to initiate policies and procedures that will achieve such a balance. Staffing problems create security problems. Jail overcrowding, a chronic and prevalent condition, especially of larger jails, aggravates almost all other inmate problems. If jail overcrowding were eliminated instantly through some miraculous confinement or adjudicatory alternative, this would not eliminate many of the problems that are the bases of contemporary jail inmate litigation under both Section 1983 and habeas corpus. Of course, it would be a start. But realistically, drastically diminishing overcrowding in any penal facility, especially jails, is unlikely. Even jails that have been ordered by courts to reduce their inmate populations continue to exceed their rated capacities.

Architectural designers are hard at work drafting and experimenting with more economic jail construction plans. One by one, jail inmate complaints and grievances are being resolved, either through courts or administrative actions. By the year 2000, there will still be jail problems and inmate litigation. At the same time, many of the older jails will have been replaced by newer more sanitary ones. Because of jail space limitations and other exigencies, public policy shifts toward alternatives to confinement will have occurred. It is impossible presently to forecast what these policy shifts will be, but unless major action is undertaken politically and legally, citizens of the future may be accommodating certain low-risk jail inmates for short terms in their spare bedrooms as a form of tax-deductible public service.

CHAPTER 13

Removing Juveniles from Adult Jails: The Unfinished Agenda

IRA M. SCHWARTZ

America's jails are in a state of crisis. Three-quarters of the more than 8 million persons admitted to jails in 1986 were incarcerated in overcrowded facilities. Twenty-three percent of the jails with an average daily population of one hundred or more inmates "were under court order to reduce their inmate populations" (Bureau of Justice Statistics [BJS], 1988c: 2). In 1984, it was reported that only about 11 percent of the 3,343 jails in the United States were under court order to improve conditions (Advisory Commission of Intergovernmental Relations [ACIR], 1984: 232). By 1986, "27 percent were under court order to improve one or more conditions of confinement (of this, 86 percent were cited for crowded living units, 51 percent for inadequate recreational facilities, and 41 percent for deficient medical facilities and services)" (BJS, 1988c: 2).

The overcrowding problem is so severe that jail administrators in some jurisdictions are releasing inmates early in order "to cope with the crowding and comply with court ordered reductions" (BJS, 1988: 10). This is a practice that threatens to compromise public safety and "calls into question the integrity of the administration of justice" (BJS, 1988: 10).

Interestingly, while there is a critical shortage of jail space for adult offenders, approximately 100,000 juveniles are incarcerated in adult jails each year (BJS, 1987: 2). Juveniles are confined in adult jails despite the mandate in the federal Juvenile Justice and Delinquency Prevention Act calling for a ban on the jailing of juveniles, and despite evidence suggesting that the overwhelming majority of the youth incarcerated in jails are not serious offenders.

Removing Children from Adult Correctional Facilities: A Brief History

Social reformers in the United States have been calling for removing juveniles from adult correctional facilities for nearly two centuries. The Houses of Refuge that sprang up during the early and mid-1800s represented one of the first attempts by reformers to try and separate juveniles from adult offenders. The Houses of Refuge were "full-time residence(s) for dependent, delinquent, and neglected youth" (Schlossman, 1977: 23). With respect to delinquent youth, they served as an alternative to sentencing or committing juveniles to serve time in adult jails and prisons (Schlossman, 1977: 24).

It was not until around 1899, during the creation of the juvenile court, that active interest developed in removing juveniles from adult jails, where they were confined pending their appearance in court. Children awaiting their trials or court appearances routinely were incarcerated in antiquated jails with unsanitary conditions amid adult offenders (Schlossman, 1977: 59). The juvenile court's advocates felt that all children who needed to be institutionalized should be kept separate from adults and that they should be housed in facilities that were designed especially for them, particularly those who needed to be confined or "protected" from being harmed by themselves or others pending their court appearance. This led to the development of a network of physically secure juvenile detention centers (Schlossman, 1977: 59).

The Federal Government's Role in Removing Juveniles from Adult Jails and Lockups

The juvenile court's advent and the construction of juvenile detention centers did not bring an end to jailing children. For example, the Children's Defense Fund (CDF) conducted an in-depth study of the jailing of juveniles in the states of Florida, Georgia, Indiana, Maryland, New Jersey, Ohio, South Carolina, Texas, and Virginia in the mid-1970s. The CDF researchers found that while the incidence varied, juveniles were confined in adult jails in each of the jurisdictions they visited. They found that:

> . . . the overwhelming majority [of the youth] . . . were not detained
> for violent crimes and could not be considered a threat to themselves
> or to the community. Only 11.7 percent were charged with serious
> offenses against persons. The rest—88.3 percent—were charged with
> property or minor offenses. (Children's Defense Fund, 1976: 3–4)

Moreover, nearly 18 percent of the youth were charged only as status offenders (youth accused of minor and petty crimes, probation
and parole violators, and youth who failed to appear in court for
their hearing) and, more alarming, more than 4 percent were not
charged with any offense at all.

This study also was important because it documented the deplorable conditions to which juveniles in adult jails were subjected. The CDF researchers reported that:

> . . . the conditions of most of the jails in which we found children are
> abysmal, subjecting them to cruel and unusual punishment through
> physical neglect and abuse. Most jails are old and dirty, with insuffi-
> cient sanitary, food or medical facilities. Only 9.8 percent of the jails
> in our study states had any educational facilities; only 12.4 percent
> reported any recreational facilities. With insufficient, poorly trained
> and poorly supervised staff, there is often no one suitable to deal
> with children to assess their needs. Often adult inmates serving as
> trustees are in control of jailed children. Often, too, the physical lay-
> out and size of the jail makes it impossible to separate children from
> adult inmates, although such separation is required by most state
> laws. Children regularly come into total, or visual or aural contact
> with adult prisoners. Even if a jailer is careful about obeying the law
> requiring separation of children from adults, the result can be
> equally terrifying. Solitary confinement or confinement in a dank
> basement or closet-like enclosure for the sole child in an adult jail
> removes him or her from other inmates, but also from the attention
> of caretakers and can have severe traumatic effects on an already
> troubled or frightened youngster. (Children's Defense Fund, 1976: 4)

In addition to being confined in old prisonlike institutions—
with inadequate educational, counseling, health care, and recreational services—juveniles in adult jails were subjected to psychological and physical abuse and were committing suicide at an
alarming rate. For example, juveniles confined in adult jails were
committing suicide at a rate more than four and one-half times
greater than the rate in the general population (Community Research Center, 1983: 2). The plight of children in adult jails eventually captured the attention of the U.S. Senate Subcommittee to
Investigate Juvenile Delinquency. One of the first witnesses to tes-

tify before the subcommittee was Professor Rosemary Sarri from the University of Michigan. Sarri, one of the country's leading juvenile justice experts, delivered a compelling and sobering account of what was known about the problem at the time. Sarri informed the subcommittee that "an accurate portrait of the extent of juvenile jailing in the United States does not exist" (U.S. Congress, Senate, Subcommittee to Investigate Juvenile Delinquency, 1973: 23; cited hereafter as Senate Subcommittee). She indicated that it would be "difficult to develop one because of the lack of reliable and comparable information from the cities, counties, states and federal government" (Senate Subcommittee, 1973: 23). Sarri told the subcommittee that her research indicated that "the jailing of juveniles occurs in both rural areas where available alternatives for custody of children are limited, and (even) in larger metropolitan communities" where both alternatives to preadjudication confinement and secure detention facilities may be accessible (Senate Subcommittee, 1973: 23).

Sarri reported that:

> . . . most jails were more than fifty years old, dilapidated, and designed to service only the most dangerous offenders. Almost none have been constructed to permit humane segregation of juveniles from adults or of unsentenced from sentenced offenders. Sanitary conditions, food, exercise facilities, fire control and so forth almost never met basic minimal public health requirements. (Senate Subcommittee, 1973: 26)

Also, Sarri indicated that "despite frequent and tragic stories of suicide, rape, and abuse of youth, the placement of juveniles in jail has not abated" (Senate Subcommittee, 1973: 23). Sarri concluded her testimony by stating that she doubted that significant progress could be made on this issue unless laws were enacted in every state that prohibit the incarceration of juveniles in adult jails "under any circumstances" (Senate Subcommittee, 1973: 34).

After completing their inquiry, the subcommittee developed the Juvenile Justice and Delinquency Prevention Act of 1973. This bill included a provision that would have prohibited the confinement of juveniles in institutions where adults were incarcerated (Senate Subcommittee, 1973: 343). The 1973 bill ran into stiff opposition from key Republican senators, particularly the section of the bill banning the incarceration of juveniles in adult jails. This opposition, coupled with their fear that they would not have enough votes to override a presidential veto (because President Ford was threatening to veto any new block grant program for the states) caused the authors to negotiate a watered-down version (Schwartz, 1988: 70). The bill that eventually passed, the Juvenile Justice and Delinquency Prevention Act of 1974, included the provision that juveniles "shall not be detained or confined in any institution in which they have regular contact with adult persons incarcerated because they have been convicted of a crime or are awaiting trial on criminal charges" (U.S. Dept. of Justice, Office of Justice Assistance, Research, and Statistics, 1980: 400). This was interpreted to mean that state and local officials could incarcerate juveniles in adult jails as long as they kept them completely separate from adult offenders.

In 1980, the Juvenile Justice and Delinquency Prevention Act was amended. One of the important changes was a mandate requiring states participating in the federal juvenile justice program to eliminate the practice of confining juveniles in adult jails and local lockups within a five-year time period (Committee on Education and Labor, House of Representatives, 1980: 21). The time period subsequently was extended for another few years to give jurisdictions additional time in which to comply.

The Jailing of Juveniles: A Persistent Problem

The best available evidence suggests that there has been virtually no progress toward removing juveniles from adult jails nationally. According to the Bureau of Justice Statistics (BJS) (1986: 1), there were 1,611 juveniles confined in adult jails on February 15, 1978. On June 30, 1986, there were 1,708 juveniles incarcerated in such facilities (BJS, 1986: 2).

The lack of progress in this area is disappointing but not entirely surprising. There are many who will argue that this is primarily due to the lack of available community-based alternatives and secure detention facilities for youth needing to be confined while awaiting their court appearance. This is certainly true for some jurisdictions—but not for all. For example, more than 99,000 juveniles were admitted to county jails and local lockups in California in 1982, some of whom were dependent and neglected children (National Council on Crime and Delinquency, 1985: 2–3). There were 6,502 juveniles admitted to adult jails in Florida in 1986 (Florida Center for Children and Youth, undated: 126). California and Florida have an abundance of juvenile detention centers and a wide variety of community-based services.

Another, and perhaps more important, reason for the lack of progress is that while the Juvenile Justice and Delinquency Prevention Act enjoyed broad bipartisan support in the Congress and had the support of the national juvenile justice and child welfare communities, the support from many of the groups and individuals who ultimately would be responsible for implementing this mandate at the state and local levels was "soft" at best. Such influential groups as the National Association of Counties, the American Bar Association, the National Council on Crime and Delinquency, the Children's Defense Fund, the American Correctional Association, and the National Coalition for Jail Reform were strong advocates for removing children from adult jails. However, the National Coalition of State Juvenile Justice Advisory Groups, the state advisory groups created by the Juvenile Justice and Delinquency Prevention Act, articulated the view that removing children from jails "was not initiated by the States as an urgent item for the national agenda" (National Coalition of State Juvenile Justice Advisory Groups, 1986: 29). Many of these state advisory groups already were having trouble implementing the federal juvenile justice programs mandate calling for removing status offenders from secure facilities and felt they could not respond effectively to another requirement. In addition, the membership of these state advisory groups typically included representatives from law enforcement, the judiciary, youth correctional programs, prosecutors, and local and state elected public officials. Many of these officials did not feel that the jailing of juveniles was a significant problem. Some actually endorsed the practice and believed that jailing juveniles "teaches children a lesson" and has some deterrent value (Schwartz, 1988: 79, 82; Schwartz et al., 1988: 145). Also, it is not uncommon for probation and parole officers, particularly in rural areas, to put a youth in jail for a night or two to "get the youth's attention" or to "prevent" further delinquent behavior. They feel that this practice provides them with a mechanism for holding youth accountable; that it is an important tool and that their effectiveness would be diminished if it were taken away from them.

Also, the politically potent National Council of Juvenile and Family Court Judges was somewhat ambivalent on this issue. The council, while endorsing the amendment to the federal act calling for removing children from adult jails, publicly questioned how much progress could be realized because the council felt that "most of these situations involve serious juvenile crime" (National Council of Juvenile and Family Court Judges, undated: 6). They cautioned that some states might lower their age of juvenile court jurisdiction or transfer more juveniles to the adult courts rather than fully implement this new mandate (National Council of Juvenile and Family Court Judges, undated: 5). The council expressed these views despite the evidence indicating that the overwhelming number of juveniles incarcerated in adult jails were status offenders. For example, a recent study in Minnesota revealed that 3,941 juveniles were incarcerated in adult jails and lockups in 1986. Eight hundred eighty-one of the admissions were females and 3,060 were males. Of the females who were confined, two-thirds were incarcerated for Part II crimes, status offenses, public order offenses, and relatively minor probation and parole violations. Slightly more than 60 percent of males were confined for similar offenses (Schwartz et al., 1988: 138). The study also revealed that juveniles who were charged with Part I violent offenses were incarcerated for shorter time periods than were those who were held for minor and petty offenses, status offenses, and other relatively nonserious forms of misbehavior (Schwartz et al., 1988: 142).

The reality is that many judges condone the practice of jailing juveniles. Judges are key actors in the juvenile justice system and exert tremendous influence over youth policy development. Without the judges' support it would be virtually impossible to make any significant progress on this issue.

Another important factor was that a change in the federal administration shortly after the amendment calling for an end to the practice of jailing juveniles was added to the Juvenile Justice and Delinquency Prevention Act. This change in administration had a significant impact on impeding progress toward removing juveniles from adult jails. The amendment was added to the Juvenile Justice and Delinquency Prevention Act during the last year of the Carter administration. At the time, the budget for the Office of Juvenile Justice and Delinquency Prevention (OJJDP) was $100 million. The Carter administration approved a 34 percent increase in the OJJDP's FY 1981–82 budget so that additional resources could be made available to assist states in complying with this important new mandate (Schwartz, 1988: 83).

When the Reagan administration took office, they proposed to eliminate the OJJDP and to "zero out" the office's budget. Congress managed to save the federal juvenile justice program, but at a substantially reduced funding level. This, in turn, significantly reduced the amount of federal funds available to the states to implement this mandate. Moreover, the Reagan administration claimed that removing juveniles from adult jails was not an appropriate national priority because it was essentially a state and local problem (Schwartz, 1988: 83–84).

Discussion

The jailing of juveniles is a complex and troublesome issue that must be addressed by juvenile and criminal justice professionals, elected public officials, child advocates and public interest groups. Juveniles are occupying space in jails and lockups that is desperately needed for adult offenders. Moreover, jurisdictions where juveniles are being incarcerated in adult facilities are at great litigation risk because of unconstitutional confinement conditions, abusive practices, and inability to provide youth with adequate supervision and programming. The various strategies that have been developed to try and resolve this problem have met with limited success. Despite this, the strategies help to provide some insights with respect to the policy options that are likely to be promising in the future.

There is some merit to the argument that so little progress has been made to remove juveniles from adult jails because of inadequate involvement and commitment of key state and local juvenile justice actors and elected public officials. However, there are some other factors that appear to have been even more significant. The turmoil that characterized the OJJDP during the Reagan years, the fact that the OJJDP's budget was cut by 50 percent, and the fact that removing children from adult jails and lockups was de-emphasized as a national priority had a major adverse impact. Moreover, the experiences in other juvenile justice policy areas where there was less than a consensus suggest that considerable progress can be made in spite of the opposition. For example, the deinstitutionalization of status offenders was one of the most successful juvenile justice policy initiatives implemented under the Juvenile Justice and Delinquency Prevention Act (Krisberg and Schwartz, 1983: 357). This policy thrust was successful despite opposition from many juvenile court judges, probation workers, and law enforcement officials throughout the country.

In addition, while the national data on removing children from adult jails is discouraging, a somewhat different picture emerges when one looks at the states individually. Between 1978 and 1983, officials in thirty states reduced the numbers of juveniles incarcerated in adult jails on a given day, while officials in twenty states increased their numbers (Community Research Associates, undated: 2). In general, the most significant reductions occurred in states where legislation was enacted that banned or significantly curtailed the incidence of juvenile jailing, where state and local juvenile justice professionals, elected public officials, child advocates, and public interest groups exercised leadership on the issue, or where litigation has occurred. For example, officials in the state of Pennsylvania moved to eliminate the jailing of juveniles several years before the juvenile jail removal amendment to the Juvenile Justice and Delinquency Prevention Act was enacted in 1980. "A key to the State's success was early passage of jail removal legislation. In 1977 the Pennsylvania legislature passed a law which prohibited the holding of juveniles in an adult jail or lockup. The law was a valuable tool for those who wanted to convince local officials that the State was sincere about removal" (Community Research Associates, undated: 7).

The Colorado Sheriffs' Association and the Colorado Division of Youth Services joined forces to try and eliminate the jailing of juveniles along that state's western slope. There were approximately six thousand juveniles jailed in Colorado in 1981. One year later, the number dropped to nearly 3,200 (Community Research Associates, undated: 1). Colorado officials claim that the reduction was due, in large part, to the collaborative effort between these organizations.

Michigan's Upper Peninsula is a rural and isolated part of the state. In 1980, there were 396 juveniles confined in adult jails in that area. By 1985, the number jailed had been reduced to 71 (Community Research Associates, undated: 8). Reduction in the jailing of juveniles was the result of the leadership provided by the Michigan Department of Social Services in the development of small "holdover" facilities, home detention programs and shelter care (Community Research Associates, undated: 2).

Between the mid-1970s and the mid-1980s, litigation was initiated against jails in Puerto Rico, Missouri, Indiana, Ohio, California, Texas, Oregon, Iowa, Utah, New Mexico, Idaho, Colorado, Maine, and Wisconsin (Soler, 1988: 196–97). In virtually each case, the litigation resulted in a ban or severe curtailment of juvenile jailing. In Oregon, a lawsuit filed against the adult jail in Columbia County resulted in a federal court order banning the jailing of juveniles statewide (Soler, 1988: 197). The potential for litigation is an issue that should be of particular concern to elected public officials and juvenile and criminal justice professionals who have some responsibility (e.g., administration, financing, and so forth) for adult jails and lockups where juveniles are being incarcerated. Few, if any, adult jails and lockups meet generally accepted professional standards and federal requirements for the detention of juveniles. Also, as mentioned previously, juveniles confined in adult jails are at great risk for suicide and for being physically or sexually abused. The fact that "children injured in adult jails could sue the county as well as the sheriff for damages, and the county would, in effect be strictly liable" should be reason enough for officials to bring an end to this practice as soon as possible (Soler, 1988: 199–200).

Summary and Recommendations

Overcrowding in the nation's jails is one of the most pressing problems confronting our criminal justice system. The problem is so severe that adult inmates are being released early in some jurisdictions to make room for new inmates and to comply with court-ordered limits on institutional capacities. This is a dangerous practice and one that threatens to compromise public safety. Ironically, while there is a critical shortage of jail space for adult offenders, approximately seventeen hundred jail beds are occupied on any day by juveniles—juveniles who, by and large, are not serious law violators. They are youth who could be released without significantly increasing the risk to the community if objective detention intake criteria were used and if appropriate community-based alternatives were available. Moreover, juvenile jailing could be eliminated completely if these options were coupled with the development of secure detention facilities for those youth who really needed to be confined because they present a clear and substantial threat to the community.

In light of this, juvenile justice professionals, elected public officials, child advocates, and public interest groups interested in addressing the problem of juvenile jailing should consider the following:

1. The most effective way to eliminate the jailing of juveniles is to enact legislation prohibiting the practice under any circumstances. Such legislation, as was the case in Pennsylvania, should include a grace period so that the deed could be accomplished within a reasonable time period.
2. Experience has shown that there are a variety of policies and community-based alternatives to jailing that can be implemented without significantly increasing the risk to the community. Also, many of these options can be implemented at relatively low cost. For example, one of the most effective strategies for limiting juvenile jailing would be to develop and utilize objective detention intake criteria, particularly

those recommended by the National Juvenile Justice Advisory Committee. In addition, such programs as home detention, family-operated shelter care, report centers, and staff-operated shelter care have proved to be effective options.

3. There are some juveniles who need to be detained pending their court appearance. Experience has demonstrated that the numbers of youth who fall into this category are relatively small. Because of this, and because secure detention facilities are costly to build and operate, a careful and comprehensive needs assessment should be completed to determine how many secure beds may be needed in a particular jurisdiction or jurisdictions, and how those needs can be met best.

CHAPTER 14

Managing the Crisis in Local Corrections: A Public-Private Partnership Approach

NORMAN R. COX, JR., AND
WILLIAM E. OSTERHOFF

Local corrections in the United States is in a state of crisis. In spite of new institutions, increased funding, and growing professionalism, correctional administrators continue to be faced with crowding, insufficient programs, inadequate staffing, and litigation. A record average daily population of more than 300,000 inmates is being held in local detention facilities. Overall jail occupancy in the United States was 98 percent of the rated capacity of the nation's jails in 1987 (Bureau of Justice Statistics [BJS], 1988b). During the same year, there were more than 17 million admissions and releases from city and county jails (BJS, 1988b). No reversal of this trend is anticipated in the immediate future.

To keep pace with the current population growth, jail capacities need to be increased by more than four hundred additional beds each week. An even greater increase is required to relieve the current inmate backlog in facilities that already are overcrowded. Annual jail expenditures have increased dramatically over the past twenty years (BJS, 1986c) and are expected to continue to increase as county and city governments attempt to cope with local correctional problems.

A number of factors have contributed to the dramatic increase in the nation's jail population. Among these factors are perceived increases in crime rates; heightened fears of being victimized; increased arrests for drug offenses, domestic abuse, and sex offenses; a shift from an emphasis on rehabilitation and reintegration to a renewed emphasis on punishment; higher bail bonds, more stringent criminal codes; and, mandatory sentences for offenses such as driving under the influence (DUI) and driving while license suspended (DWLS). Compounding the problems faced by local government is a public that is less than enthusiastic about increased taxes to pay for the corrections facilities that are required, and state governments that have failed to manage correctional crowding in state prisons, thereby creating a state prisoner backup in local jails. Of the nearly 27,000 inmates held in local jails for other jurisdictions in 1987, over 11,000 were being held principally because of state prison overcrowding (BJS, 1988b).

To resolve the crisis, responsible jail management must review current policies and trends and seek additional solutions within the existing framework of corrections theory and practice. A more enlightened jail management, however, also must examine alternative approaches to resolve the increasingly complex problems faced by corrections and society, other than continued reliance on the public sector alone. Cooperative public and private sector involvement can result in a more effective and efficient response to the nation's jail problems than can be provided by the public sector alone. Cooperative ventures between the public and private sectors have been useful toward resolving society's problems in fields as diverse as public health, rapid transit, wastewater treatment, and aerospace. In addition, all levels of government have contracted for professional services from the private sector to augment public resources in architecture, engineering, finance, and other professions. Contracting with the private sector also has occurred for planning, management, and legal services. Private services currently are being utilized to some degree in the nation's jails in the areas of medical and mental health care, food service, community-based inmate programs, jail work programs, architectural services, facility financing, and facility construction. In a few jails, the private sector is being used for total facility management.

Historical Development

Private sector involvement in corrections has a long history. Unfortunately, inmate exploitation by the private sector also has a long history. In early American jails, fees collected from inmates or their families contributed to the sheriff's and jailer's incomes and varied with the number of inmates and their lengths of incarceration. Fees were paid to the jailer for better food, improved accommodations, visiting rights, and other marginal conveniences. To minimize expenses, poor food and inadequate inmate care often resulted. Combined with a lack of concern for the inmates' well-being on the part of the public, facilities frequently were unsanitary, poorly heated and ventilated, vermin infested, and overcrowded. Inmate classification often was nonexistent, resulting in men, women, and even children sometimes being housed together.

Other forms of private sector corrections involvement included the participation of private industry, generally in the forms of leased labor, contract labor, and public account systems (Sexton, Farrow, and Auerbach, 1985). The use of contract or leased inmate labor temporarily reduced inmate idleness and overcrowding while resulting in additional income to operate the jails and prisons or the private gain of corrections officials. Because industry's primary concern was to maximize profits, exploitation of adult and juvenile offenders was not uncommon. Under the contract or leased labor systems, inmates generally received no compensation while working long hours under poor conditions. Under the public account system, similar conditions prevailed, except that prison industries were operated by the correctional agencies, which sold the products on the open market in direct competition with private industry.

Opposition to the contract labor, leased labor, and public account systems developed rapidly. By 1900, a number of states had passed legislation restricting the use of inmate labor by private firms and the sale of prison-made goods on the open market through "state use" laws. Legislation also was passed by the federal government restricting interstate commerce of prison-made products and the use of inmate labor on federally funded projects. As a result, private sector involvement in correctional industries was substantially reduced. Recently, however, there has been a renewed interest in prison industry programs by both the public and private sectors (Sexton, Farrow, and Auerbach, 1985).

The private sector has played a significant role in the development of community-based corrections as alternatives for jail inmates. Concerned citizens and religious groups established the first halfway houses and group homes for adult offenders. Probation was started by John Augustus in Boston, Massachusetts, as an alternative to jail for alcoholic and minor offenders in 1841. The continued development of adult probation was marked by a shift from local volunteer efforts to publicly funded local, state, and federal agencies to which interested individuals could volunteer their services. More recent trends reflect an increased interest in contracting for services with community and private service providers.

During the late 1960s and throughout the 1970s, as the focus of corrections shifted from a rehabilitation philosophy to an emphasis on reintegration, numerous local community-based correctional programs were developed. Many of these programs were implemented through contracts with private for-profit and nonprofit agencies from public correctional agencies, state criminal justice planning agencies, the Law Enforcement Assistance Administration (LEAA), and other governmental organizations. Cooperation between private sector community-based corrections programs and public sector agencies generally has been favorable, although evaluation data indicate mixed results when costs and effectiveness of private and public sector programs are compared (Legislative Research Council, 1986).

The juvenile justice field also is heavily indebted to the early efforts of individuals and private organizations whose concern for the welfare of delinquents, status offenders, and dependent and neglected youth contributed to the development of the current juvenile justice system. Unfortunately, as had happened in adult corrections, there were examples of abuse, neglect, and exploitation of youth by both private and public sectors. The change in focus from rehabilitation to reintegration in adult corrections was paralleled by a movement to deinstitutionalize troubled youths who were being held in juvenile institutions, juvenile detention facilities, and jails. Massachusetts led the movement by closing its juvenile institutions and allocating 60 percent of the Division of Youth Services' 1983 budget for the purchase of services from private, nonprofit organizations (Mullen, Chabotar, and Carrow, 1985).

The private sector also played an important role in the development of frontier America. Many public buildings, including courthouses and jails, were financed and constructed by the railroads to encourage settlers to locate near rail depots. The Pauley Jail Building and Manufacturing Company of St. Louis, Missouri, privately financed many of the jails it built around the turn of the century. A renewed interest in jail and prison financing and construction has been shown by large investment firms and by corporations that have been formed specifically for the purpose of correctional facility financing, construction, and management.

Current Trends

A historical perspective of the private sector's role in corrections indicates that much of modern corrections is based on private initiatives of the past. After initial enthusiasm, however, the involvement of the private sector in corrections waned, only to be followed by a strong resurgence in recent years. In 1981, the Attorney General's Task Force on Violent Crime recommended that federal and state governments explore private correctional facility operations. Shortly thereafter, a number of private corporations emerged, organized along the lines of private hospital corporations, to finance, own, and operate private prisons and jails. This position was reiterated in 1988 by the President's Commission on Privatization, but has failed to gain support from a number of other sources. Nevertheless, private sector correctional services and programs have gained support, as has the concept of private sector correctional facility financing.

Correctional Services and Programs

Currently, many communities are using private contracts to provide various forms of correctional services and programs for local jails, including food, medical, and mental health services; pretrial release programs; pretrial diversion; halfway houses; restitution centers; alcohol and drug offender treatment centers; and facilities and programs specifically for DUI offenders. Some of the services and programs are being provided by small, local, for-profit or nonprofit agencies eager to contract with multiple jurisdictions (local, state, and federal). Other services and programs are being provided by larger organizations, which are able to offer reduced costs because of savings that result from their mass purchasing powers.

In general, private contracting for correctional services and programs has presented more advantages to local, state, and federal correctional agencies than disadvantages. Acceptance of private sector services and programs by public sector employees and professional organizations generally has been favorable.

Correctional Facility Financing

The building boom fostered by the jail population explosion, coupled with the inability of local and state governments to raise sufficient revenues to finance the needed new construction through additional bond issues or higher taxes, has encouraged private investment firms' entry into the area of local correctional facility financing. In recent years, major investment and brokerage firms have been attracted by the growing investment opportunities in the corrections field while simultaneously looking for new areas to expand their services in an increasingly competitive and aggressive financial marketplace.

While there is ample historical precedence for the lease/purchase of buildings and other large-cost items by state and local governments, only recently has the lease/purchase concept become an important option in the corrections field. It is likely that local and state governments will use the lease/purchase option more frequently as current indebtedness approaches legal limits and as the public becomes less willing to pass additional bond issues. Resentment expressed by the public toward tax increases and the passage of tax limitation legislation also make private funding arrangements increasingly more attractive and acceptable to local government officials.

Correctional Facility Management and Operations

Since 1980, the private sector has shown increased interest in the management, operation, and ownership of correctional facilities (Attorney General's Task Force, 1981). While several firms have been incorporated specifically for correctional facility management and operation, it is in these areas where the greatest resistance to private sector corrections involvement has been exhibited. Concerns have been expressed by sheriffs, local corrections employees and administrators, professional groups, legislators, and inmate advocate organizations.

Concerns expressed by local correctional employees have centered on anticipated loss of careers, job security, and benefits. Sheriffs and local correctional administrators have expressed reservations about liability issues and about the potential loss of control over jail facilities, jail staff, and inmate populations. Professional associations, including the National Sheriffs' Association and the American Jail Association, officially have expressed opposition to correctional privatization for similar reasons. The appropriateness of delegating intrinsic government responsibilities, such as inmate incarceration and punishment, to private enterprise has been questioned by various parties. Public officials also are concerned about the potential political leverage that will be gained by the private sector from its involvement in functions and responsibilities traditionally under public control. In addition, liability issues, inmate classification, security, and the use of force (particularly deadly force) have not been adequately resolved and remain of primary concern to elected and appointed officials. These concerns also have been expressed by the American Bar Association, the American Civil Liberties Union, and other prisoner advocate organizations, which fear that cost and profit motives will ultimately outweigh inmate welfare and public safety considerations, as has happened in the past. Reservations about prison and jail privatization are reflected in the following resolution formally adopted by the American Bar Association:

> Be It Resolved, That the American Bar Association urges that jurisdictions that are considering the privatization of prisons and jails not proceed to so contract until the complex constitutional, statutory, and contractual issues are satisfactorily developed and resolved. "Privatization" refers to contracting for total operational responsibility for a prison or jail; it does not encompass construction or leasing physical facilities or contracting for institutional services, such as food preparation, medical care, and vocational training, in full security institutions or for operation of non-secure facilities such as half-way houses. (Robbins, 1988: iv)

Resolutions adopted by the National Sheriffs' Association and the American Jail Association reflect similar concerns and reservations.

Private jail management and operation issues raise other problems for local public officials, including determination of the actual short-, medium-, and long-term costs of private jail management. Minimum standards and performance criteria, contractor monitoring and evaluation, and provisions for terminating contract services, if necessary, also need to be more fully developed. As a result of these and other concerns, the interest that is being expressed by the private sector toward local correctional facility management, operation, and ownership has been met with substantial resistance. Consequently, most state contracts have been limited to juvenile offender institutions and nonsecure community-based facilities for adult offenders. In 1983, nearly two-thirds of the three thousand juvenile detention and correctional institutions in the United States were private facilities. Contracts for the nonsecure community-based facilities for adult offenders reportedly were being used in thirty-two states. There has been modest contracted facility usage, primarily for illegal aliens, by the Immigration and Naturalization Service, the U.S. Marshals Service, and the Federal Bureau of Prisons (Mullen, Chabotar, and Carrow, 1985).

In contrast, only 1 percent of the nation's jail and prison bed capacity was under private contract, as of early 1988. At that time, approximately three thousand beds in various jails, prisons, reformatories, and detention facilities in nine states were being privately managed and operated (President's Commission on Privatization, 1988). Whether the reluctance to contract for the management and operation of confinement facilities for adult offenders will continue, remains to be seen. While the National Sheriffs' Association, the American Jail Association, and the American Bar Association have expressed reservations about jail and prison privatization, the President's Commission on Privatization recommended a far less cautious approach, as has the American Correctional Association. The President's Commission (1988: 149) recommended that "Contracting should be regarded as an effective and appropriate form for the administration of prisons and jails at the federal, state, and local levels of government." The commission further recommended that the "problems of liability and accountability should not be seen as posing insurmountable obstacles to contracting for the operation of confinement facilities. Constitutional and legal requirements apply, and contracted facilities may also be required to meet American Correctional Association standards" (President's Commission on Privatization, 1988: 153). Additional experimentation, research, and evaluation of privately operated confinement institutions also were recommended by the commission (President's Commission on Privatization, 1988).

In summary, while there has been general acceptance of private sector involvement in correctional services, programs, and correctional facility financing, the renewed interest in private sector correctional facility management, operation, and ownership thus far has led to an adversarial relationship with public correctional agencies, employee unions, professional associations, and prisoner advocate groups. The long-range consequences are likely to result in mistrust, employee subversion, and a lack of cooperation between public and private correctional agencies and officials.

A Public-Private Partnership

Privatization, when defined as the practice of contracting with the private sector for the provision of products and services traditionally supplied by the public sector, may offer limited advantages for government. As defined, however, privatization suggests supplanting public products or services with private products or services. Because of the magnitude and complexity of the problems faced by local corrections, the emerging concept of a public-private partnership may hold more promise for county and city governments than the concept of privatization. Instead of *supplanting* public products or services by the private sector, the public-private partnership concept suggests *supplementing* the provision of public products or services by the private sector.

The concept of a public-private partnership has been articulated by the Research and Policy Committee, a nonprofit organization of two hundred business and professional leaders, educators, and public officials. It is the committee's position that it is in the best interests of both the public and the private sectors to form a cooperative relationship to solve state and local governments' complex problems (Research and Policy Committee, 1982).

The public and private sectors are both principal components of a modern economy. Government policies and activities affect citizen welfare through public service functions and through laws, regulations, taxes, and financial policies, all of which impact on private sector activity. The private sector is composed of a rich mosaic of for-profit and nonprofit organizations engaged in a wide variety of enterprises with diverse objectives. The private sector's activities, likewise, have an important public dimension. As corporate citizens of the community, private organizations have a stake in the community's well-being and future, just as individuals do in their capacity as citizens (Research and Policy Committee, 1982). A public-private partnership implies mutually beneficial cooperation between individuals and organizations in the public and private sectors. The objective of a public-private partnership is to pursue mutual goals in such a way that the participants contribute to the benefit of the broader community while pursuing their own organizational goals and objectives (Research and Policy Committee, 1982).

The basic premise on which the concept of a public-private partnership is formulated assumes that the long-run economic success, survival, and health of the private sector depend on the well-being of the communities in which corporations operate and on the endurance and well-being of the society in which they exist. Since the private sector mutually benefits from and affects society, corporations should take a leadership role in the public sector's response to social issues and problems. In addition, utilization of relevant expertise in politics, government, economic development, and community action can increase the likelihood of success in solving society's problems (Research and Policy Committee, 1982).

Historical developments and current trends suggest that neither the public sector nor the private sector, when acting alone, has the capacity or the resources to solve the present local corrections crisis. Fear of crime, reported crimes, victimization data, and recidivism rates clearly indicate that government has not been able to provide the protection from criminal activity that citizens have the right to expect. Protection of life and property is not exclusively a government concern or responsibility (Research and Policy Committee, 1982). The criminal justice system is dependent on private citizens for reporting crime, assisting in the prosecution of offenders, aiding in offenders' reintegration into the community, and funding local, state, and federal criminal justice system agencies.

The following policy statement of the American Correctional Association reflects public and private sector interdependence and the need for mutual cooperation to solve current corrections problems:

> Serious and difficult problems currently facing the nation's correctional systems require that concerted efforts be made by both public and private correctional agencies to work together to insure that constitutional and effective programs and services are delivered to persons assigned to correctional care. The American Correctional Association urges all correctional workers, as well as legislators, elected officials, and other policy makers, to strengthen their efforts to enhance collaboration between public and private correctional agencies. (American Correctional Association, 1984: 4)

The public-private partnership concept can be visualized as a continuum with exclusively public sector responsibilities at one end and exclusively private sector involvement at the other. Other responsibilities would fall along the continuum depending on their respective public and private involvement. At the end of the continuum where private sector involvement is more acceptable are jail services and programs, including medical and mental health care, food service, and alcohol and drug treatment programs. At the end of the continuum where public control is more acceptable are jail management, operation, and facility ownership. Toward the center of the continuum are community-based correctional facilities and programs, jail industries, and selected special-purpose facilities and programs that can be operated jointly by the public and private sectors.

Mullen (1985) suggests that private sector participation may be particularly advantageous for corrections when rapid mobilization, experimentation, decentralization, specialization, and regionalization are desired. When there is a need for rapid mobilization of additional facilities and staff, it may be advantageous to contract for the provision of needed facilities and services. Because of the flexibility and capability to rapidly construct, renovate, or acquire additional facilities and provide staff, private sector contracting may facilitate the accommodation of short-term population shifts resulting from court-ordered compliance deadlines or changes in legislation. Planning for permanent facility expansion can then proceed on a more gradual basis.

Private sector contracting also may allow for experimentation with innovative programs and new service delivery methods without making permanent commitments to staffing the programs until adequate evaluations have been completed. Considerable program flexibility can be achieved by governmental agencies if traditional bureaucratic constraints to innovation can be minimized (Mullen, 1985).

Decentralization of correctional facilities and services to provide greater geographic and programmatic diversity may be possible by contracting with private agencies. Agreements with local contractors who employ community residents and have local public officials' confidence may circumvent opposition to programs and services that are under a centralized agency's direct control (Mullen, 1985).

Another potential advantage of private sector involvement includes the ability to achieve greater correctional institution and program specialization. Offenders with special needs are difficult to manage in the best of systems. Contracting with the private sector for institutions and programs for special-needs offenders may offer significant benefits over generalized facilities and correctional programs for the criminally insane, sex offenders, offenders with alcohol and drug related problems, geriatric and infirmed offenders, and DUI offenders. Work release and prerelease centers also could be financed, constructed, and operated by the private sector.

For many years, facility and program regionalization has been advocated by correctional professionals and by state and national advisory committees. Regionalization's potential largely has been untapped, however, because of the political and jurisdictional disputes that emerge when regional planning activities begin. The private sector, not being bound by jurisdictional politics, may be able to foster the development of shared facilities among states or among counties within a state (Mullen, 1985). This may have particular potential for local governments in attempting to deal with the increasingly high costs associated with local corrections.

Each of these suggested areas of private sector involvement is concerned with supplemental services required by government. Private sector firms willing to assume a supplemental role should be able to market successfully their specialized services to government without the adversarial relationship that has dominated recent privatization attempts. Therefore, opportunities should be sought to create public-private forums where partnership opportunities may be explored, where resources can be combined, and where activities can be focused on the local corrections crisis.

Conclusion

A review of historical and contemporary private sector corrections involvement reveals three key factors that are pertinent to any discussion of local corrections privatization. It can be concluded that, historically, private sector involvement has produced both significant advances and flagrant abuses in corrections; local governments have been, and continue to be, resistant to institutional corrections privatization, while accepting private sector provision of specialized and community-based correctional facilities and correctional programs and services; and the private sector has demonstrated neither superior performance nor sufficient safeguards to convince critics that privatization is appropriate for corrections.

Based on these factors, it may be anticipated that a continued push toward privatization will meet with increased local resistance, which is already showing signs of growing strength and solidarity. Privatization, by definition, requires government to surrender traditional services to the private sector; therefore, confrontation is inherent in the process. Such an adversarial climate militates against open and rational discussion, which is necessary to explore and refine the private sector corrections concept. Instead, a continued climate of emotionalism and mistrust can be expected with slogans like "cheaper and better" from private sector interests and allegations of "profit-mongering" from public sector representatives, which characterize the polarized debate.

However, if private sector involvement is viewed as a continuum with opportunities for public-private cooperation and mutual benefit at various points along that continuum, confrontation may be diminished and a deliberate exploration of options may take place. For such exploration to occur, each side must be willing to retreat from its extreme polar position and examine the middle ground. A new climate must be created in which to solve the current local corrections crisis. The debate should be refocused with less of a unidimensional emphasis on privatization and more of a multidimensional emphasis on public-private partnerships. The focus should combine each sector's strengths and proficiencies to create viable solutions to the complex problems facing local corrections in today's society.

The public-private partnership concept is a preferred vehicle for developing solutions for local corrections because its philosophy is inherently different from the privatization philosophy. The public-private partnership philosophy encourages continued governmental involvement, limits private sector involvement to mutually acceptable services and programs, and provides government with implementation options that, acting alone, it does not have. The philosophy is based on alliance rather than surrender, mutuality instead of unilateral actions, and cooperation in lieu of preemption.

The public-private partnership concept, however, is not without its critics. Davis (1986) points out that a public-private partnership may diffuse responsibility with neither sector accepting its share and, in the event of failure, each blaming the other. Furthermore, long-standing public-private partnerships, such as the military-industrial complex, may evolve into bureaucratic entities that are inefficient and elude accountability and control.

Despite these concerns, the public-private partnership concept is consistent with the best values, as have been reflected historically, of private sector corrections involvement. Citizens and private organizations, both for-profit and nonprofit, historically have risen to challenges that have plagued government. The most dramatic results have involved public-private cooperation and joint ventures. If such an approach can be successful in complex areas such as space exploration and mass transit, the concept is well worth exploring in the corrections field.

CHAPTER 15

Paying the Piper but Changing the Tune: Policy Changes and Initiatives for the American Jail

JOEL A. THOMPSON AND G. LARRY MAYS

Several themes have been sounded in this volume: jails invariably come out on the short end of local priority and resource sticks and, as a result, they are in trouble and in need of help. The situation is severe enough that many of the contributors to this volume have used the word *crisis* with some frequency. With regard to contemporary jails, the use of the term is not inappropriate. As we stated in the opening chapter, jails did not get into this sad state overnight, and their problems will not be cured overnight; nor perhaps in the very near future. That does not mean, however, that they can or should continue to exist and operate in a crisis mode.

Jails are a crucial cog in the criminal justice system. If this system is to come to grips with the crime problem in this country, each agency at each level of government must be prepared and equipped to do its job. If there has been a central theme throughout most studies of local jails, it has been that they are ill-equipped and ill-prepared to do their job. The reasons are many and varied, but eight of them are worthy of discussion (Pogrebin, 1982a).

First, most jails and their programs rarely, if ever, have been evaluated in regard to their operational effectiveness. This means that most jails go on unquestioningly performing their traditional functions. As Jackson, Klofas, Schwartz, and others have noted, we cannot afford to utilize jails for inappropriate functions. They are *not* drunk tanks, juvenile halls, mental wards, or prisons. Further-more, to use them as places to house delinquent child supporters is a very inefficient use of taxpayers' money. *Jails should be a place for those awaiting trial or sentenced to short terms who are a threat to themselves or to society.* They need not be anything more, but they should not be anything less.

Second, jails lack the capacity to plan. Anyone who has ob-served the daily operations of a jail will understand this lack of planning. Most jail employees, including sheriffs and administra-tors, are so caught up in the frantic pace of the jail's routine that they do not have time to plan. They are part of the jail's crisis man-agement atmosphere.

Third, jails lack rational bases for allocating scarce resources. Although major investments must be made in the jail's physical plant, ongoing costs are heavily weighed in favor of personnel ex-penditures. Pogrebin (1982a: 17) stresses that jails are very "labor intensive" organizations that typically have taken little advantage of technology.

Fourth, jails have very little public support. In this is because jails are misunderstood institutions with no politically important clientele, and most citizens are not aware of the legal implications of substandard facilities. These perceptions perpetuate a tradition of underfunding at the local level that causes problems to grow and fester for far too long.

Fifth, jails operate without clearly defined missions. They are detention facilities, but given the wide variety of persons they in-carcerate, jails are called on to do more than merely detain. Tro-janowicz (1978) says that jails can both detain and treat and that they should play the central role in reintegrating offenders with the community. Part of this role definition or redefinition will have to come from jails themselves, so that they are not constrained by their most common public image of being warehouses for law vio-lators. But the larger criminal justice community, including state officials, must aid in this redefinition as well.

Sixth, jails are physically and relationally isolated. Although many criminal justice agencies influence jails, and are influenced by them, for the most part they are a "dumping ground for some of society's problems. When other institutions were either not avail-able or full, people were placed in jail because there was no other place to put them" (Moynahan and Stewart, 1980: 104). This dumping ground image is reinforced by the sights, sounds, and smells of jails and contributes to their institutional isolation.

Seventh, jails are more politically than professionally accountable. This may make adoption of jail standards and operating procedures difficult, especially if it is done by local option. Sheriffs and county commissions are attuned to actual or perceived electoral winds, and if they err it will be in the direction of conservative fiscal policies. No sheriff or county board wants to be known for having the best jail in the state or nation; usually they will settle for having the best in the county.

Finally, staff resistance is a major impediment to jail reform (Pogrebin, 1982a: 30). In their seminal study of jails, Kerle and Ford (1982: 230–31) found a number of factors associated with personnel problems in jails:

1. The ratio of inmates to corrections officers indicates that most jails employ far fewer jail personnel than recommended by groups like the National Advisory Commission on Criminal Justice Standards and Goals.
2. Salaries for jail employees are lower than for sheriffs' deputies, in a comparative sense, and incredibly low, in an absolute sense. Figures from the 1983 National Jail Census show that annual median jail salaries range from $7,200 for jails in states with no standards to $8,889 for jails in states with voluntary standards.
3. For many employees jail duty results from poor job performance on patrol, as a result of injury and confinement to limited duty, or while serving a probationary period prior to being transferred to patrol; in most jails being a jail officer is the bottom of the ladder, and there is limited promotion potential or career development (see especially, Pogrebin and Poole, 1988).
4. Where sheriffs' deputies are used as jail personnel in place of career-line corrections officers, there can be severe motivational problems; Irwin (1985: 75) says that deputies assigned to jail duty "tend to hold strongly negative attitudes toward most persons who are arrested and held in jail. These attitudes stem largely from their work with prisoners, which is in many ways more annoying than police work."
5. Jail training is poor at best and, in most places, nonexistent (ACIR, 1984: 172–73). Jail personnel training is a necessity, not a luxury. It should not be *police* training, nor should it be *corrections* training—although appropriate training will involve elements of both.

These five personnel issues have been raised to illustrate one point: jails, for the most part, recruit at the lowest level of personnel qualifications. Too often jail employees are minimally educated, untrained, and undercompensated. They are people looking for a steady, albeit small, income from a job in the community. Often they are not equipped to handle the complex people-management requirements in the jail, nor do they particularly desire to see jails reformed. If jails are improved, rank-and-file personnel and managers must be meaningful parts of the process; otherwise well-intentioned policy initiatives will founder at the implementation stage.

These problems are at the core of what Pogrebin has called the "political, organizational, and systemic obstacles" to meaningful change in jails (1982a: 16–19). Unless we as a society are willing to allow jails to operate in a crisis mode and perhaps deteriorate even more, unable to function as either a source of security, rehabilitation, or a bridge between state corrections and the local community, then we must begin to find ways to remove these obstacles. In short, we cannot afford to do nothing; something must change.

The impetus for change already may have been set in motion. The courts undoubtedly have provided the greatest incentive. The *hands on* rather than *hands off* doctrine virtually has assured us that we can no longer sing the same old refrain, "out of sight, out of mind," when it comes to local jail policies and programs. As the chorus grows louder with the addition of middle-class DWI convictees, other white-collar offenders, and those whose awareness has been raised by successful litigation, there well may be sufficient numbers within communities to support genuine reform efforts.

But change will not come without costs. The Reagan era allowed us to fantasize that there really was something akin to a free lunch in regards to governmental programs. This false promise, combined with our current emphasis on getting tough on crime (i.e. reclaiming our streets from drug pushers, locking up violent offenders), simply means that the old bills are coming due and new, larger ones are to follow. Simply put: it's time to pay the piper, but we will have to change the tune.

Given the uniqueness of the jail and its complex problems, it is unlikely that any single reform will have dramatic results. In addition, many problems transcend the jail and the community, reaching all the way to the state capital. For these reasons, recommendations must be addressed to both the local jail and its extended environment. Based on the discussions in this volume and our previous research, we offer eight recommendations that will help states and counties operate jails that are safe, humane, and likely to pass the scrutiny of the courts. The first four are addressed to the states, and the last four deal with local government responsibilities.

Recommendations

States must be willing to accept some responsibility for the jail crisis and be a willing partner in the search for solutions. A major role that states can play is in the area of financial aid, and here they are not doing enough. Although state and local governments pay 88 percent of all government costs for criminal and civil justice, states spend only about 3 percent of their budgets on average for corrections. By far the largest share of this sum is spent for state prisons and detention facilities. In most states, virtually none of this spending trickles down to local jails. By contrast, counties spend on average about 31 percent of their budget dollars for local corrections (see U.S. Department of Justice, 1988: 116). States have superior resource structures compared to local governments. Therefore:

Recommendation 1. States should provide some form of aid to local governments for jail construction and/or renovation. This could come as a direct subsidy, as is currently done in six states. Alternately, states can utilize their superior rating to sell bonds to form a capital pool from which it can lend money to local governments at low interest rates. Or, states can assist local governments in lease-purchase agreements. Jail construction or renovation is a major financial burden on many communities, especially poor ones. As a contributor to the problem, states should likewise be a contributor to the solution.

Recommendation 2. States should develop mandatory jail standards. Standards have been found to be an effective tool for local administrators (Thompson and Mays, 1988a). However, the development process must include a significant representation of local officials (sheriffs, jailers, and other county officials) so that local officials will view standards as a management resource and legal defense, not as another state-imposed burden (see, especially, National Institute of Justice, 1987). Standards should address critical issues like construction and minimum staff training and serve as a guide to local officials who need to develop satellite facilities to alleviate crowding problems caused by less serious (nonviolent) offenders and weekend detainees (May, 1978).

Recommendation 3. Where they do not exist, inspection and enforcement programs should be developed by states. States that currently have such programs should strengthen their authority. Inspections and enforcement powers should be vested in a state agency, removed from local politics, and these agencies should be given adequate staffs and resources and the authority to close jails found to be unconstitutional.

Recommendation 4. States should adopt legislation enabling local governments to engage in cooperative agreements to build regional facilities when economies of scale dictate such arrangements. Local governments should use their authority over local facilities to the fullest extent possible.

Local governments must not only share the responsibility for safe and humane facilities but be willing to assume their preeminent role in this function within the criminal justice system. Although local governments spend a large portion of their budgets for corrections, it is not enough. In addition, they have allowed jails to wallow in ruts of lowest priority. The result has been the perpetuation of a tradition of underfunding and an attitude of benign neglect of this unpopular institution. Finally, local governments have failed to educate the citizenry as to the roles, functions, and liabilities of the jail. It is time that local governments did their share.

Recommendation 5. Since local officials are hesitant to commit funds to politically unpopular causes, they should take steps to educate citizens as to the local jail's functions and conditions (Ricci, 1986). Jails are not prisons, and citizens should be made aware of the legal and financial implications of operating an unconstitutional facility. In the absence of a crisis (the local jail is shut down, a major judgment is awarded to an inmate), it is unlikely that local officials will be willing to move too far from their perceptions of local sentiment. To our knowledge, no local official has ever run a campaign on a platform of improving conditions in the jail; but it *should* be an issue in more local campaigns, and it *could* be an issue were the public more knowledgeable.

Recommendation 6. After creating greater awareness among the citizenry, local officials should develop long-term financial plans that ensure adequate funding for jail construction and/or renovation, staffing, and operation. Adequate funding is a necessity, not a luxury to be confused with notions of "coddling criminals."

Recommendation 7. Local officials should require jails to have written policies and procedures. These would serve as valuable planning and training tools and provide a form of legal defense.

Recommendation 8. Communities should explore alternatives to incarceration. Many jail detainees are not threats to society and should not occupy scarce and expensive cell space.

Jails are an integral part of America's criminal justice system. In all likelihood, their position will be enhanced as we seek alternatives to our traditional methods of confinement. But jails cannot—should not—continue to be society's dumping ground. It is time we more clearly define their roles and functions, provide them with adequate finances and personnel, and let them do their job. The challenge for the twenty-first century will be to develop, implement, and monitor jail policies that will bring about fundamental changes to the jail's organizational and operational world.

Contributors

Dean J. Champion is a professor of sociology at the University of Tennessee. His research interests include prosecutorial and judicial priorities in plea bargaining, juvenile justice and procedures, and sentencing systems. His works include books and articles on probation, parole, corrections, and the U.S. sentencing guidelines.

Norman R. Cox, Jr., is the president of N. R. Cox Associates, Inc., a firm specializing in planning and management consultation for criminal justice and corrections agencies. He has a master's degree in criminal justice from Auburn University, Alabama, and is a past president of the American Jail Association.

Patrick G. Jackson is an associate professor in the Department of Criminal Justice Administration at Sonoma State University, California. He received his Ph.D. in sociology from the University of California, Davis. He is author of *The Paradox of Control: Parole Supervision of Youthful Offenders* and numerous articles on jails, preventive detention, arson, youth gangs, methods, deviance, and other topics. He currently is conducting research on the reasons for attrition among felony offenders and the development of laws to control gangs in California.

Jeanette M. Jerrell, Ph.D., is Director of Evaluation and Research for the Santa Clara County Mental Health Bureau. She has published extensively in the field of mental health services research and is currently specializing in conducting cost-effectiveness studies, especially related to mental health services for the severely mentally ill.

Patrick T. Kinkade is currently a Ph.D. candidate in the Program in Social Ecology, University of California, Irvine. He received B.A. degrees in psychology and anthropology from the University of California, Berkeley. His research interests include the effects of drunk driving legislation on criminal justice systems in California and the implications of privatization for modern corrections.

John M. Klofas is associate professor of criminal justice at Rochester Institute of Technology, New York. He received his doctorate from the School of Criminal Justice at SUNY-Albany and has taught at Illinois State University and worked for the Massachusetts Department of Corrections. Along with Stan Stojkovic and David Kalinich he has authored *Criminal Justice Organizations: Administration and Management*, and he and Kalinich have edited a book on jails entitled *Sneaking Inmates Down the Alley*. His current research interests center on management in corrections and criminal justice and the jail as a community institution.

Richard Komisaruk, M.D., was Medical Director of the Santa Clara County Criminal Justice Mental Health Unit. He has worked extensively as a psychiatrist in adult and juvenile correctional facilities in California and Michigan. He maintains an ongoing interest in the provision of mental health care to detainees in the criminal justice system.

James E. Lawrence, a specialist in forensic medicine, is Director of the New York State Correction Medical Review Board, the health care regulatory and oversight body of the New York State Commission of Correction.

Matthew C. Leone is currently a Ph.D. candidate in the Program in Social Ecology, University of California, Irvine. He obtained his B.A. in psychology from San Diego State University and his M.A. in social ecology from the University of California, Irvine. His research interests include the effects of social, economic, and demographic factors on jail conditions.

G. Larry Mays is a professor of criminal justice at New Mexico State University and, since 1981, has been the Criminal Justice Department head. He is coauthor of a textbook entitled *Juvenile Delinquency and Juvenile Justice* (John Wiley) and has contributed to such professional journals as the *Journal of Criminal Justice, Justice Quarterly, Judicature, Justice System Journal, American Journal of Criminal Justice*, and *Policy Studies Review.* His teaching and research interests are in the areas of criminal and juvenile justice policy development, implementation, and evaluation.

Ben A. Menke is Director of the Criminal Justice Program at Washington State University. He is currently on leave at the College of Public and

Community Service, University of Massachusetts-Boston. His research interests include deterrence, corrections, and the police and public opinion.

William E. Osterhoff, Ph.D., is a professor and director of graduate studies for the Justice and Public Safety Department of Auburn University at Montgomery. He served as the first corrections and juvenile justice planner for the state of Alabama and was a charter member of the board of directors of the American Jail Association.

Mark R. Pogrebin is Director of and professor of criminal justice in the Graduate School of Public Affairs at the University of Colorado—Denver. He received his Ph.D. in social science from the University of Iowa in 1973. His current research interests include a study of crime among Korean immigrants.

Henry N. Pontell is a professor of social ecology and social science at the University of California, Irvine. He has written extensively on issues related to deviance, crime and punishment, and is author of *A Capacity to Punish* (Indiana University Press, 1984).

Eric D. Poole is a professor of criminal justice in the Graduate School of Public Affairs at the University of Colorado—Denver. He received his Ph.D. in sociology from Washington State University in 1976. His current research interests include a longitudinal study of deputy sheriffs as jail guards.

Ira M. Schwartz is a professor and Director of the Center for the Study of Youth Policy at the University of Michigan's School of Social Work, where he has been since September 1987. Between 1981 and 1986, Professor Schwartz was a senior fellow at the University of Michigan's Hubert H. Humphrey Institute of Public Affairs. He has served as the administrator of the Office of Juvenile Justice and Delinquency Prevention, U.S. Department of Justice, between 1979 and 1981. Prior to that time, he directed criminal and juvenile justice agencies in the states of Illinois and Washington and has worked extensively in both the public and private sectors. Professor Schwartz has authored numerous articles on juvenile justice and has recently completed a book entitled *(In)Justice for Juveniles: Rethinking the Best Interest of the Child* (Lexington Books).

Joel A. Thompson is a professor and Chairperson of Department of Political Science/Criminal Justice, Appalachian State University, North Carolina. His research interests are in state and local politics and administration, public policy, and evaluation. His research has been published in the *Journal of Politics, Policy Studies Review, Policy Studies Journal, Administration and Society, Justice Quarterly,* and other journals and books.

Michael Welch is assistant professor of sociology at St. John's University in Jamaica, Queens, New York. He earned his doctorate at the University of North Texas, and has correctional experience at the federal, state, and county levels. His research interests include jails, prisons, and social control.

Wayne N. Welsh is a Ph.D. candidate in the Program in Social Ecology, University of California, Irvine. He earned his M.A. in applied social psychology from the University of Saskatchewan, Canada. His research has included studies of aggression in prison inmates and, currently, the impact of court orders against county jails.

L. Thomas Winfree, Jr., is associate professor of criminal justice and coordinator of graduate studies at New Mexico State University. He is coeditor of *Expert Witnesses: Criminologists in the Courtroom* (State University of New York Press). He has published in such justice-related journals as *Justice Quarterly, Journal of Criminal Justice, Journal of Police Science and Administration, Journal of Security Administration, Juvenile and Family Court Journal,* and *Victims and Violence,* as well as *Rural Sociology, Sociological Spectrum, Youth and Society, Journal of Youth and Adolescence, International Journal of the Addictions,* and *Policy Studies Review.* His research interests include professional socialization in criminal justice, youth drug use and abuse, delinquency theory testing, and jail deaths.

John D. Wooldredge is an assistant professor of criminal justice at New Mexico State University. His most recent research involves an examination of correlates to victimization among prison inmates in New Mexico and causes of variations in criminal case disposition rates across state trial courts in the United States. He has published recently in the *Journal of Quantitative Criminology, Journal of Research in Crime and Delinquency, Justice Quarterly, Social Science Quarterly, Sociology and Social Research,* and *Journal of Marriage and the Family.* His areas of specialization include corrections, criminal case processing, criminology, and demography.

Van Zwisohn, an attorney, is an assistant counsel to the New York State Commission of Correction. He is the former executive director of the New York State Coalition for Criminal Justice, an independent advocacy organization.

Linda L. Zupan is an assistant professor in the Department of Criminal Justice, Illinois State University. She is the author of a forthcoming book on the new generation philosophy entitled *Reforming the American Jail.*

Bibliography

Abrams, Kathleen S. (1988). "Prisons as LULUs: A sequel, Part 2." *Environmental and Urban Issues* (Jan.), 24–27.

Abt Associates. (1980). *American Prisons and Jails*, Vol. 1. Washington, DC: U.S. Department of Justice.

Adelson, L.; Huntington, R.; and Reay, D. (1986). "A Prisoner Is Dead." *Police*, 13:49–58.

Administrative Office of the U.S. Courts. (1985). *Annual Report of the Director of the Administrative Office of the United States Courts, 1985.* Washington, DC: U.S. Government Printing Office.

Advisory Commission on Intergovernmental Relations. (1984). *Jails: Intergovernmental Dimensions of a Local Problem.* Washington, DC.

Allen, H. E., and Simonsen, C. E. (1986). *Corrections in America*, 4th ed. New York: Macmillan.

Allinson, Richard. (1982). "Crisis in the Jails: Overcrowding Is Now a National Epidemic." *Corrections Magazine* (Apr.), 18–24.

Alpert, Geoffrey; Crouch, Ben M.; and Huff, C. Ronald. (1984). "Prison Reform by Judicial Decree: The Unintended Consequences of *Ruiz v. Estelle.*" *Justice System Journal* 9(3):291–305.

Altman, D. (1983). "Health Care for the Poor." *Annals of the American Academy of Political and Social Science* 468:103–21.

American Bar Association Task Force on Crime. (1981). Report to the House of Delegates. Washington, DC.

American Correctional Association. (1981). *Standards for Adult Local Detention Facilities*. Rockville, MD.
———. (1983). *The American Prison: From the Beginning . . . A Pictoral History*. Rockville, MD.
———. (1984). *Policy Statements and Resolutions*. College Park, MD.
———. (1987). *Legal Responsibility and Authority of Correctional Officers*. College Park, MD.
American Justice Institute. (1984). *Measurement and Analysis of Jail Populations*. Washington, DC: National Institute of Justice.
American Medical Association. (1979). *Standards for Health in Jails*. Chicago: Project to Improve Heath Services in Correctional Institutions.
Anderson, Debra J. (1986). *Curbing the Abuses of Inmate Litigation*. College Park, MD: American Correctional Association.
Angel, Arthur; Green, E.; Kaugman, H.; and Van Loon, E. (1971). "Preventive Detention: An Empirical Analysis." *Harvard Civil Rights—Civil Liberties Law Review* 6:289–396.
Anson, R. (1983). "Inmate Ethnicity and the Suicide Connection: A Note on Aggregate Trends." *Prison Journal* 63(1):91–99.
———. (1984). "Overcrowding and Inmate Facilities." *International Journal of Comparative and Applied Criminal Justice* 8(1):93–99.
Associated Press. (1988). "Imperial County Bids for Proposed 2,200-Inmate, High-security Prison." *Orange County Register*, July 30, p.B11.
Atlas, Randall I. (1987). *Guidelines for Architects, Jail and Prison Managers; Reducing the Liability for Inmate Suicide: A Design Guide*. Miami, FL: Atlas and Associates.
Attorney General's Task Force. (1981). *Final Report of the Attorney General's Task Force on Violent Crime*. Washington, DC: U.S. Department of Justice.
Aubert, Vilhelm and Messinger, Sheldon S. (1965). "The Criminal and the Sick." In Vilhelm Aubert, ed., *The Hidden Society*. Totowa, NJ: Bedminister Press.
Austin, J., and Krisberg, B. (1982). "The Unmet Promise of Alternatives to Incarceration." *Crime and Delinquency* 28:374–409.
———. (1984). *Differential Use of Jail in California: A Study of Jail Admissions in Three Counties*. Washington, DC: National Institute of Justice.
Bail Reform Act of 1966. Public Law No. 89-465, 80 Stat. 214.
Bailey, William C., and Smith, Ronald W. (1972). "Punishment: Its Severity and Certainty." *Journal of Criminal Law, Criminology, and Police Science* 63:530–39.
Baldassare, Mark. (1984). *Orange County Annual Survey*. Irvine: University of California, Irvine.
Ball, R.; Huff, C. R.; and Lilly, J. R. (1988). *House Arrest and Correctional Policy: Doing Time at Home*. Beverly Hills, CA: Sage.
Bamonte, T. J. (1981). Eighth Amendment—A Significant Limit on Federal

Court Activism in Ameliorating State Prison Conditions." *Journal of Criminal Law and Criminology* 72(4):1345–73.

Bartollas, C. (1981). *Introduction to Corrections.* New York: Harper and Row.

Bases, Nan C., and MacDonald, William F. (1972). *Preventive Detention in the District of Columbia: The First Ten Months.* Washington, DC: Georgetown Institute of Criminal Law and Procedure.

Becker, Howard S. (1963). *Outsiders: Studies in the Sociology of Deviance.* New York: Free Press.

Beigel, A., and Russell, H. (1972). "Suicidal Behavior in Jail: Prognostic Considerations." *Hospital and Community Psychiatry* 23 (Dec.), 361–63.

Belcher, J. R. (1988). "Are Jails Replacing the Mental Health System for Homeless Mentally Ill?" *Community Mental Health Journal* 24(3):185–95.

Bennis, W. (1966). "Leadership in Human Behavior." In W. Bennis, K. Benne, and R. Chin, eds., *The Planning of Change.* New York: Holt, Rinehart, and Winston.

Berk, Richard A., and Rossi, Peter H. (1977). *Prison Reform and State Elites.* Cambridge, MA: Ballinger.

Birnbaum, M. (1960). "The Right to Treatment." *American Bar Association Journal* 46:499.

Bittick, L. C. (1984). *Jail Officer's Training Manual.* Alexandria, VA: National Sheriffs' Association.

Blackmore, John (1978). "Minnesota's Community Correction Act Takes Hold." *Corrections Magazine* (Mar.), 46–56.

———. (1986). "Community Corrections." In Kenneth C. Haas and Geoffrey P. Alpert, eds., *The Dilemmas of Punishment.* Prospect Heights, IL: Waveland.

Blau, P. M., and Scott, W. R. (1962). *Formal Organizations.* San Francisco, CA: Chandler Pub. Co.

Blumstein, Alfred. (1988). "Prison Populations: A System Out of Control?" In Michael Tonry and Norval Morris, eds., *Crime and Justice. A Review of Research,* Vol. 10. Chicago: University of Chicago Press.

Blumstein, A.; Cohen, J.; and Miller, H. (1980). "Demographically Disaggregated Projections of Prison Populations." *Journal of Criminal Justice* 8:1–26.

Blumstein, A.; Cohen, J.; and Gooding, W. (1983). "The Influence of Capacity on Prison Population: A Critical Review and Some New Evidence." *Crime and Delinquency* 29:1–51.

Bolduc, A. (1985). "Jail Crowding." *Annals of the American Academy of Political and Social Science* 478:47–57.

Bonovitz, J., and Guy, E. (1979). "Impact of Restrictive Civil Commitment Procedures on Prison Psychiatric Service." *American Journal of Psychiatry* 136:1045–48.

Bonta, R.; Cormier, R.; Peter, R. D.; Gendreau, P.; and Marquis, H. (1983). "Psychological Services in Jails." *Canadian Psychology* 24(2):135–39.

Bostick, Barbara A. (1988). "Facing the Future: Challenges for Small Jails."
    Corrections Today 50:6.
Bowker, L. (1981). *Corrections: The Science and the Art*. New York: Macmil-
    lan.
Brakel, C., and Rock, E. (1971). *The Mentally Disabled and the Law*. Chi-
    cago: University of Chicago Press.
Briar, K. H. (1983). "Jails: Neglected Asylums." *Social Casework* 64:387–93.
Brodsky, S. L. (1977). "The Ambivalent Consultee: Consultation in Crimi-
    nal Justice." In S. Plog and P. Ahmed, eds., *The Art of Mental Health
    Consultation*. New York: Plenum.
———. (1982). "Intervention Models for Mental Health Services in Jails."
    In C. S. Dunn and H. J. Steadman, eds., *Mental Health Services in Lo-
    cal Jails*, pp.126–48. Rockville, MD: U.S. Department of Health and
    Human Services.
Bureau of Justice Statistics, U.S. Dept. of Justice. (1981). *Census of Jails,
    1978*. Vol. 1–4: Northeast, North Central, South, and West. Washing-
    ton, DC: U.S. Government Printing Office.
———. (1983a). *Jail Inmates, 1983*. Washington, DC: U.S. Government
    Printing Office.
———. (1983b). *National Jail Census*. Washington, DC: U.S. Government
    Printing Office.
———. (1983c). *Report to the Nation on Crime and Justice*. Washington, DC:
    U.S. Government Printing Office.
———. (1984). *Jail Inmates*. Washington, DC: U.S. Government Printing
    Office.
———. (1986a). *Historical Corrections Statistics in the United States, 1850–
    1984*. Washington, DC: U.S. Government Printing Office.
———. (1986b). *Jail Inmates, 1985*. Washington, DC: U.S. Government
    Printing Office.
———. (1986c). *Justice Expenditures and Employment, 1983*. Washington,
    DC: U.S. Government Printing Office.
———. (1987). *Jail Inmates, 1986*. Washington, DC: U.S. Government Print-
    ing Office.
———. (1988a). *Annual Report, Fiscal 1987*. Washington, DC: U.S. Govern-
    ment Printing Office.
———. (1988b) *Jail Inmates, 1987*. Washington, DC: U.S. Government
    Printing Office.
———. (1988c). *Our Crowded Jails: A National Plight*. Washington, DC: U.S.
    Government Printing Office.
———. (1988d). *Pretrial Release and Detention: The Bail Reform Act of 1984*.
    Washington, DC: U.S. Government Printing Office.
———. (1988e). *Report to the Nation on Crime and Justice*, 2nd ed. Washing-
    ton, DC: U.S. Government Printing Office.
Burks, D., and De Heer, N. (1985). "Jail Suicide Prevention." *Corrections
    Today* 48(1):52,73–88.
Busher, W. (1983). *Jail Overcrowding: Identifying Causes and Planning for*

Solutions. Washington, DC: Office of Justice Assistance, Research and Statistics.

California Board of Corrections. (1985). *The State of the Jails in California; Report 2: Prisoner Flow and Release.* Sacramento: State of California.

———. (1988). *Report to the Legislature. Jail Standards and Operations Division. Jail Inspections and Costs of Compliance.* Sacramento: State of California.

Casper, Jonathan D., and Brereton, David. (1984). "Evaluating Criminal Justice Reform." *Law and Society Review* 18:121–44.

Carney, Robert. (1982). "New Jersey: Overcrowding Is Blamed on the States." *Corrections Magazine* (Apr.), 24–27.

Centers for Disease Control. (1988). "Update: Universal Precautions for Prevention of Transmission of Human Immunodeficiency Virus, Hepatitis B Virus, and Other Bloodborne Pathogens in Health Care Setting." *Mortality and Morbidity Weekly Report.* 37:377–82, 387–88.

———. (1989). *HIV/AIDS Surveillance Report,* pp.1–16. Atlanta, GA.

Chan, Janet B. L., and Ericson, Richard V. (1981). *Decarceration and the Economy of Penal Reform.* Toronto: University of Toronto Centre for Criminology.

Charle, S. (1981). "Suicide in the Cellblocks." *Corrections Magazine* 7(4):6–16.

Children's Defense Fund. (1976). *Children in Adult Jails.* Washington, DC: Washington Research Project, Inc.

Clark Foundation. (1982). *Overcrowded Time: Why Our Prisons Are So Overcrowded and What Can Be Done.* New York: Edna McConnell Clark Foundation.

Clear, Todd R., and Cole, George F. (1986). *Introduction to Corrections.* Monterey, CA: Brooks/Cole.

Cloward, R. A. (1968). "Social Control in the Prison." In L. Hazelrigg, ed., *Prison Within Society.* Garden City, NY: Doubleday.

Cohen, Stanley. (1972). *Folk Devils and Moral Panics: The Creation of the Mods and Rockers.* New York: St. Martin's.

Colin, Isaac. (1984). "Perspectives on NIMBY." In Audrey Armour, ed., *Hazardous Waste Management.* Downsview, Ontario: York University Press.

Committee on Education and Labor. (1980). *Juvenile Justice Amendments of 1980.* Hearing before the Subcommittee on Human Resources of the Committee on Education and Labor, House of Representatives. Washington, DC: U.S. Congress.

Community Research Associates. (Undated). "Jail Removal in the States: Where Do We Stand?" *Profile: Juvenile Justice Prevention.* Champaign, IL.

———. (Undated). "The Michigan Holdover Network: Short-Term Supervision Strategies for Rural Counties." *Profile: Juvenile Justice Prevention.* Champaign, IL.

———. (Undated). "The Sheriff's Dilemma: Juveniles in Jail. The Jail Removal Initiative in Colorado." *Profile: Juvenile Justice Prevention.* Champaign, IL.

———. (1983). *Juvenile Suicides in Adult Jails: Findings from a National Survey of Juveniles in Secure Detention Facilities.* Urbana-Champaign: University of Illinois Press.

Cory, B., and Gettinger, S. (1984). *Time to Build? The Realities of Prison Construction.* New York: Edna McConnell Clark Foundation.

Council of State Governments. (1977). *State Subsidies to Local Corrections.* Lexington, KY.

County Administrative Office. (1986). *Systems Approach to Jail Overcrowding in Orange County.* Santa Ana, CA: County of Orange.

Cox, V.; Paulus, P.; and Mc Cain, G. (1984). "Prison Crowding Research: The Relevance for Prison Housing Standards and a General Approach to Crowding Phenomena." *American Psychologist* 39(10):1148–60.

Cressey, D. R. (1977). "Sources of Resistance to Innovation in Corrections." In R. M. Carter, D. Glaser, and L. T. Wilkins, eds., *Correctional Institutions*, 2nd ed., pp.491–511. Philadelphia, PA: J. B. Lippincott.

Cromwell, Paul F. (1975). *Jails and Justice.* Springfield, IL: Charles C. Thomas.

Crouch, Ben, ed. (1980). *The Keepers: Prison Guards in Contemporary Corrections.* Springfield, IL: Charles C. Thomas.

Cullen, Francis T.; Clark, Gregory A.; and Wozniak, John F. (1985). "Explaining the Get Tough Movement: Can the Public Be Blamed?" *Federal Probation* 49:16–24.

Cullen, Francis T., and Gilbert, Karen E. (1982). *Reaffirming Rehabilitation.* Cincinnati, OH: Anderson Pub. Co.

Cyert, R. M., and March, J. G. (1963). *A Behavioral Theory of the Firm.* Englewood Cliffs, NJ: Prentice-Hall.

Danto, B. (1971). "The Suicidal Inmate." *Police Chief* 38(8):64–71.

———. (1972). "Suicide at the Wayne County Jail 1967–1970." *Police Law Quarterly* 1:34–41.

———. (1973). *Jail House Blues: Studies of Suicidal Behavior in Jail and Prison.* Orchard Lake, MI: Epic Publications.

Davis, Dale, and Gaudino, James L. (1987). *A 1987 Report on the State of Michigan's Jails.* Lansing, MI: Michigan Sheriffs' Association Jail/Lockup Resource Center.

Davis, P. C., ed. (1986). *Public-private Partnerships: Improving Urban Life.* New York: Academy of Political Science.

Daviss, Ben. (1982). "Colorado: Grappling with a Boom in Busts." *Corrections Magazine* (Apr.), 28–30.

Dawson, Adam. (1988). "ACLU Wants OC Branch Jails Included in Court Orders." *Orange County Register,* June 7, p.B3.

Dawson, Adam, and Warner, Gary A. (1988). "Inmate-Rights Suit Against OC Jail Ends." *Orange County Register,* July 6, pp.B1,6.

Dean, C. W. (1979). "The Story of Newgate." *Federal Probation,* 43 (June), 8–14.

De Heer, N., and Schweitzer, H. (1985). "Suicide in Jail: A Comparison of

Two Groups of Suicidal Inmates to Jail Suicide Victims." *Corrective and Social Psychiatry and Journal of Behavior Technology Methods and Therapy* 31(3):71–76.

Demos, Nicholas L. (1984). "The Future Jail." *Federal Probation* 48 (Mar.), 35–39.

Dennis, R. E. (1980). "Health Beliefs and Practices of Ethnic and Religious Groups." In A. E. Johnson and E. L. Watkins, eds., *Removing Cultural and Ethnic Barriers to Health Care*, pp.12–28. Chapel Hill: University of North Carolina School of Public Health and Social Work.

Dershowitz, Alan. (1976). *Fair and Certain Punishment.* New York: Twentieth Century Fund.

Dexter, Lewis. (1970). *Elite and Specialized Interviewing.* Evanston, IL: Northwestern University Press.

Doble, John. (1987). *Crime and Punishment: The Public's View.* New York: Public Agenda Foundation.

Dougherty, F. I. (1984). "Issues in the Provision of Mental Health Care in Corrections." *Corrections Today* 69:96–97.

Downs, A. (1967). *Inside Bureaucracy.* Boston: Little, Brown.

Doyle, Daniel P., and Thomas, Jim. (1987). "Why Do Prisoners Sue? Assessing Theories of Prisoner Litigation." Paper presented at the American Society of Criminology meeting, Montreal.

Dunn, C. S., and Steadman, H. J., eds. (1982). *Mental Health Services in Local Jails.* USDHHS Publication No.(ADM) 82-1181.

Durham, A. M. (1989). "Origins of Interest in the Privatization of Punishment: The Nineteenth and Twentieth Century American Experience." *Criminology* 27(1):107–40.

Edelman, M. (1964). *The Symbolic Uses of Politics.* Champaign: University of Illinois Press.

Edwards, H. E., and Coner, A. F. (1983). "Intermediate Care Program for Mentally Ill Detainees: Development and Implementation." *Psychiatric Annals* 13(9):716–31.

Eisenstein, James, and Jacob, Herbert. (1977). *Felony Justice.* Boston: Little, Brown.

Embert, Paul S. (1969). *A Sociological-Economic Systems Analysis of Attitudes: Training and Police Community Relations.* Unpublished master's thesis, Michigan State University.

————. (1986). "Correctional Law and Jails." In David B. Kalinich and John Klofas, eds., *Sneaking Inmates Down the Alley.* Springfield, IL: Charles C. Thomas.

Empey, LaMar T. (1978). "From Optimism to Dispair: New Doctrines in Juvenile Justice." Foreword to Charles A. Murray and Louis A. Cox, Jr., *Beyond Probation: Juvenile Corrections and the Chronic Delinquent.* Beverly Hills, CA: Sage.

Esparza, R. (1973). "Attempted and Committed Suicide in County Jails." In B. Danto, ed., *Jail House Blues.* Orchard Lake, MI: Epic.

Etzioni, A. (1961). *A Comparative Analysis of Complex Organizations.* New York: Free Press of Glencoe.

———. (1967). "Mixed Scanning: A 'Third' Approach to Decision Making." *Public Administration Review* 27:385–92.

Fair, Daryl R. (1982). "Remedies Without Rights? The Legal Basis of Broad-Gauge Decrees in Prison Conditions Cases." *Policy Studies Review* 2 (Nov.), 262–70.

Fairchild, Erika S. (1984). "The Scope and Study of Prison Litigation Issues." *Justice System Journal* 9(3):325–41.

Farrington, David. (1983). "Randomized Experiments on Crime and Justice." In M. Tonry and N. Morris, eds., *Crime and Justice: An Annual Review of Research*, Vol. 4, pp.257–308. Chicago, IL: University of Chicago Press.

Fawcett, J., and Marrs, B. (1973). "Suicide at the County Jail." In B. Danto, ed., *Jail House Blues*. Orchard Lake, MI: Epic.

Feeley, Malcolm. (1979). *The Process Is the Punishment: Handling Cases in a Lower Criminal Court*. New York: Russell Sage Foundation.

———. (1983). *Court Reform on Trial: Why Simple Solutions Fail*. New York: Basic Books.

Feldman, J. J. (1982). "Health of the Disadvantaged: An Overview." In D. L. Parron, F. Solomon, and C. D. Jenkins, eds., *Behavior, Health Risks, and Social Disadvantage*, pp.13–31. Washington, DC: Institute of Medicine, National Research Council.

"First Amendment—Prisoner Rights and Immunity for Prison Officials." (1978). *Journal of Criminal Law and Criminology* 69(4): 588–604.

Fisher, Margaret; O'Brien, Edward; and Austern, David T. (1987). *Practical Law for Jail and Prison Personnel*, 2nd ed. St. Paul, MN: West.

Fishman, J. F. (1923). *Crucibles of Crime: The Shocking Story of the American Jail*. Montclair, NJ: Patterson Smith. Reprinted in 1969.

Florida Center for Children and Youth. (Undated). *Florida Juvenile Adult Project*. Tallahassee, FL.

Florida Jail Assistance Bureau. (1989). "State Funding Support for County Jails." *American Jails* 3(1):34.

Flynn, E. E. (1973). "Jails and Criminal Justice." In L. E. Ohlin, ed., *Prisoners in America*. Englewood, NJ: Prentice-Hall.

Fogel, David. (1975). *We Are the Living Proof: The Justice Model for Corrections*. Cincinnati, OH: Anderson Pub. Co.

Foucault, M. (1979). *Discipline and Punish: The Birth of the Prison*. New York: Vintage Books.

French, L., and Porter, J. (1978). "Jail Crises: Causes and Control." In W. Taylor and M. Braswell, eds., *Issues in Police and Criminal Psychology*. Lanham, MD: University Press of America.

Frug, Gerald E. (1978). "The Judicial Power of the Purse." *University of Pennsylvania Law Review* 126 (Apr.), 715–94.

Galtung, Johan. (1968). "The Social Functions of a Prison." In Lawrence Hazelrigg, ed., *Prison Within Society*, pp.27–49. Garden City, NY: Anchor/Doubleday.

Gettinger, Stephen H. (1984). *New Generation Jails: An Innovative Ap-*

proach to an Age-Old Problem. Washington, DC: U.S. Department of Justice, National Institute of Corrections.

Gibbs, J. J. (1978). "Stress and Self-Injury in Jail." Unpublished doctoral dissertation, State University of New York.

———. (1982). "The First Cut Is the Deepest: Psychological Breakdown in the Detention Setting." In Robert Johnson and Hans Toch, eds., *The Pains of Imprisonment.* Beverly Hills, CA: Sage.

———. (1982). "On 'Demons' and 'Gaols': A Summary and Review of Investigations Concerning the Psychological Problems of Jail Prisoners." In C. S. Dunn and H. J. Steadman, eds., *Mental Health Services in Local Jails.* USDHHS Publication No.(ADM) 82-1181:14–33.

Gido, R., and Slater, T. (1989). "Jail Use Patterns: An Application of the Klofas Typology to New York State Jail Overcrowding." Paper presented at the annual meeting of the Academy of Criminal Justice Sciences, Washington, DC.

Gill, H. G. (1962). "Correctional Philosophy and Architecture." *Journal of Criminal Law, Criminology, and Police Science* 53:312–22.

Glaser, D. (1970). "Some Notes on Urban Jails." In D. Glaser, ed., *Crime in the City*, pp.236–44. New York: Harper and Row.

Glasgow, P. (1979). "Differential Health Status by Culture and Class: Need for Social Concern." In A. E. Johnson and E. L. Watkins, eds., *Removing Cultural and Ethnic Barriers to Health Care*, pp.1–10. Chapel Hill: University of North Carolina School of Public Health and Social Work.

Goffman, E. (1961). *Asylums.* Garden City, NY: Anchor Books.

Goldfarb, Ronald. (1975). *Jails: The Ultimate Ghetto.* Garden City, NY: Anchor Press/Doubleday.

Goldstein, I., and Katz, R. (1973). "Abolish the Insanity Defense—Why Not?" *Yale Law Journal* 72:853.

Goode, Erica E. (1989). "When Mental Illness Hits Home." *U.S. News and World Report*, April 24, pp.54–65.

Gottfredson, D. M. (1982). "Jails and Mental Health: Suggestions Toward a Research Agenda." In C. S. Dunn and H. J. Steadman, eds., *Mental Health Services in Local Jails*, pp.174–84. Rockville, MD: U.S. Department of Health and Human Services.

Gottfredson, Stephen D., and Taylor, Ralph B. (1987). "Attitudes of Correctional Policymakers and the Public." In Stephen D. Gottfredson and Sean McConville, eds., *American Correctional Crisis: Prison Populations and Public Policy.* New York: Greenwood.

Greenfeld, Larry (1980). "Assessing Prison Environments: A Comparative Approach." Paper presented to the Environmental Design and Research Association, College Park, MD.

Greenwood, P. (1982). *Selective Incapacitation.* Santa Monica, CA: Rand.

Greiner, L. E. (1967). "Patterns of Organizational Change." *Harvard Business Review* 45:119–28.

Gross, Bertram. (1982). "Reagan's Criminal 'Anti-Crime' Fix." In Alan

Gartner, Colin Greer, and Frank Riessman, eds., *What Reagan Is Doing to Us.* New York: Harper and Row.

Guadayol, Ana Maria. (1985). "Sheriff Files Suit Over Crowded Jails." *Tampa (Florida) Tribune,* March 5, p.B1.

Guenther, A. L. and Guenther, M. Q. (1976). "'Screws' vs. 'Thugs.'" In A. L. Guenther, ed., *Criminal Behavior and Social Systems,* 2nd ed., pp.511–28. Chicago: Rand McNally.

Guy, E.; Platt, J. J.; Zwerling, I. S.; and Bullock, S. (1985). "Mental Health Status of Prisoners in an Urban Jail." *Criminal Justice and Behavior* 12(1):29–33.

Guynes, R. (1988). *Nation's Jail Managers Assess Their Problems.* Rockville, MD: National Institute of Justice.

Hair, J.; Anderson, R.; Tatham, R. and Grabowsky, B. (1979). *Multivariate Analysis.* Tulsa, OK: Petroleum Pub.

Hall, A. (1987). *Systemwide Strategies to Alleviate Jail Crowding.* Washington, DC: U.S. Government Printing Office.

Hall, Richard. (1987). *Organizations: Structures, Processes, and Outcomes,* 4th ed. Englewood Cliffs, NJ: Prentice-Hall.

Hall, Stuart; Critcher, Chas.; Jefferson, Tony; Clarke, John; and Roberts, Brian (1978). *Policing the Crisis: Mugging, the State, and Law and Order.* London: Macmillan.

Halleck, Seymour L. (1967). *Psychiatry and the Dilemmas of Crime.* Berkeley: University of California Press.

———. (1968). "American Psychiatry and the Criminal." *International Journal of Psychiatry in Medicine,* 6:185–207.

———. (1980). "Psychiatry and the Prisoner." *American Journal of Psychiatry,* 603–4.

Handberg, R. (1982). "Jails and Correctional Farms: The Neglected Half of Rural Law Enforcement." *Journal of Correctional Education* 32:20–23.

Hardy, S. L. (1984). "Dealing with the Mentally and Emotionally Disturbed." *Corrections Today* (June), pp.16–18, 126.

Hart, H. H. (1931). "Police Jails and Village Lockups." In *Report on Penal Institutions, Probation, and Parole,* No.9. Washington, DC: National Commission on Law Observance and Enforcement.

Hawes, Jerry A. (1985). *Cities with Prisons: Do They Have Higher or Lower Crime Rates?* Sacramento: Senate Office of Research, State of California.

Hayes, L. (1983). "And Darkness Closes In . . . A National Study of Jail Suicides." *Criminal Justice and Behavior* 10(4):461–84.

Healey, Jon. (1987). "Assembly Creates a System of Satellite Jails." *Winston-Salem (NC) Journal,* May 16, p.27.

Heilig, S. (1973). "Suicide in Jails: A Preliminary Study in Los Angeles County." In B. Danto, ed., *Jail House Blues.* Orchard Lake, MI: Epic.

Herrick, N. Q. (1975). "A Process for Reducing Occupational Stress." In W. H. Kroes and J. J. Hurrell, eds., *Job Stress and the Police Officer:*

Identifying Stress Reduction Techniques, pp.203–16. Cincinnati, OH: National Institute for Occupational Safety and Health.

Hicks, Jerry. (1985). "Orange County Jail Full to Overflowing." *Los Angeles Times,* Mar. 18, Part I, pp.1,16–17.

"Houston Sheriff Threatens State if Prisons Won't Accept Convicts." (1987). *Las Cruces (NM) SUN-NEWS* Jan. 11, p.3A.

House, R. J. (1967). *Management Development: Design, Evaluation and Implementation.* Ann Arbor: University of Michigan Press.

Hudson, P., and Butts, J. (1979). "Causes of Deaths in North Carolina Jails and Prisons 1972–76." *Popular Government* (Fall), pp.16–17.

Huggins, M. Wayne. (1982). "The Local Jail, Circa 1982." *The National Sheriff* (Apr.-May), pp.14,19,20,38.

———. (1986). "Urban Jails: Facing the Future." *Corrections Today* 48:114–20.

Hurley, Brian E. (1988). "An Examination of the Legal Duty to Prevent Inmate Suicides and Steps That Can Be Taken to Fulfill That Duty." Unpublished manuscript, Xavier University.

Hylton, John H. (1982). "Rhetoric and Reality: A Critical Appraisal of Community Correctional Programs." *Crime and Delinquency* 28:341–73.

Illinois Department of Corrections. (1986). *Jail and Detention Statistics and Information.* Springfield.

Institutions Etc. (1987). "Jail Suicides: Almost One a Day." *Institutions Etc.* 4(1):17–18.

Irwin, John. (1985). *The Jail: Managing the Underclass in American Society.* Berkeley: University of California Press.

Jackson, Patrick G. (1987a). "The Differential Use of Jail Confinement in Three California Counties." Paper presented at the annual meeting of the Academy of Criminal Justice Sciences, St. Louis.

———. (1987b). "The Impact of Pretrial Preventive Detention." *The Justice System Journal* 12:305–34.

———. (1988). "The Uses of Jail Confinement in Three Counties." *Policy Studies Review* 7(3):592–605.

James, F. J.; Gregory, D.; Renee, K.; Jones, M. S.; and Rundell, O. H. (1980). "Psychiatric Morbidity in Prisons." *Journal of Hospital and Community Psychiatry* 31(10):674–77.

Jenkins, Willie C. (1989). Commentary, April 21. Michigan Department of Mental Health.

Johnson, Bruce D., and Wexler, Harry K. (1986). *Projections of Jail and Prison Populations for the U.S.A. and New York State.* Chicago, IL: Commission on Behavioral and Social Sciences and Education of the National Research Council.

Johnson, R. (1976). *Culture and Crisis in Confinement.* Lexington, MA: D. C. Heath.

Johnston, N. (1973). *The Human Cage: A Brief History of Prison Architecture.* New York: Walker and Company.

Jordan, F.; Schmeckpeper, K.; and Strope, M. (1987). "Jail Suicides by Hanging: An Epidemiological Review and Recommendations for Prevention." *American Journal of Forensic Medicine and Pathology* 8(1):27–31.

Journal of the American Medical Association. (1981). "Health Care Reforms Still Needed in Nation's Prisons." *JAMA* 245(3):211–20.

Juszkiewicz, Jolanta. (1988). "Dealing Effectively with Crowded Jails: The Judge's Role." *Policy Studies Review* 7(3):581–91.

Kal, E. F. (1977). "Mental Health in Jail." *American Journal of Psychiatry* 134:463.

Kalinich, D. B., and Postill, F. J. (1981). *Principles of County Jail Administration and Management.* Springfield, IL: Charles C. Thomas.

Kalinich, David B.; Lorinskas, R.; and Banas, D. (1985). "Symbolism and Rhetoric: The Guardians of Status Quo in the Criminal Justice System." *Criminal Justice Review* 10(1):41–46.

Kalinich, David B., and Emberg, Paul S. (1987). *The Fatal Chain of Events: Suicide Prevention in Jails and Lockups, Detention Homes, and Other Secure Facilities.* East Lansing, MI: KER and Associates.

Kalinich, Dave; Embert, Paul; and Senese, Jeffrey D. (1988). "Integrating Community Mental Health Services into Local Jails: A Policy Perspective." *Policy Studies Review* 7(3):660–70.

Katz, D., and Kahn, R. L. (1966). *The Social Psychology of Organizations.* New York: Wiley.

Kaufman, E. (1973). "Can Comprehensive Mental Health Care Be Provided in an Overcrowded Prison System?" *Psychiatry and Law* (Summer), pp. 243–62.

Kelling, G. L.; Wasserman, R.; and Williams, H. (1988). "Police Accountability and Community Policing." *Perspectives on Policing,* No.7. Washington, DC: National Institute of Justice.

Kennedy, D. B. (1983). "Transition to Custody as a Factor in Suicides." *Corrections and Social Psychiatry* 30:88–91.

———. (1984). "A Theory of Suicide While in Police Custody." *Journal of Police Science and Administration* 12(2):191–98.

Kennedy, D. B., and Homant, R. J. (1988). "Predicting Custodial Suicides: Problems with the Use of Profiles." *Justice Quarterly* 5(3):441–56.

Kerle, Kenneth. (1983). "The Rural Jail: Its People, Problems and Solutions." *Human Services in the Rural Environment* 8:9–17.

Kerle, K. E., and Ford, F. R. (1982). *The State of Our Nation's Jails.* Washington, DC: National Sheriffs' Association.

Kizziah, Carol A. (1984). *The State of the Jails in California. Report #1: Overcrowding in the Jails.* Sacramento: Board of Corrections, State of California.

Klecka, W. R. (1980). *Discriminant Analysis.* Beverly Hills, CA: Sage.

Klofas, John. (1987). "Patterns of Jail Use." *Journal of Criminal Justice* 15:403–11.

———. (1988). "Measuring Jail Use: A Comparative Analysis of Local Corrections." Paper presented at the annual meeting of the American Society of Criminology, Chicago.

Knap, Chris. (1988a). "County's Jail Plan Might be Shelved." *Orange County Register,* July 29, pp.A1,18.

———. (1988b). "Two-Year Jail Delay Possible." *Orange County Register,* Aug. 3, pp.A1,18.

———. (1988c). "Initiative for Centralized Jails Earns Place on 1990 Ballot." *Orange County Register,* Sept. 1, p.B5.

Knapp, Kay A., and Hauptly, Denis J. (1989). "The U.S. Sentencing Guidelines in Perspective: A Theoretical Background and Overview." In D. Champion, ed., *The U.S. Sentencing Guidelines: Implications for Criminal Justice.* New York: Praeger.

Knight, Barbara B., and Early, Stephen T., Jr. (1986). *Prisoner's Rights in America.* Chicago, IL: Nelson-Hall.

Komarnicki, Mary, and Doble, John. (1986). *Crime and Corrections: A Review of Public Opinion Data Since 1975.* New York: Public Agenda Foundation.

Krisberg, Barry. (1988). "Public Attitudes About Criminal Sanctions." *The Criminologist* 13(2):12,16.

Krisberg, Barry, and Schwartz, Ira M. (1983). "Rethinking Juvenile Justice." *Crime and Delinquency* 29:333–64.

Lamb, H. R., and Grant, R. W. (1982). "The Mentally Ill in an Urban County Jail." *Archives of General Psychiatry* 39:17–22.

Lamb, H. R.; Schock, R.; Chen, P. W.; and Gross, B. (1984). "Psychiatric Needs in Local Jails: Emergency Issues." *American Journal of Psychiatry* 141(6):774–77.

Lansing, D.; Bogan, J. B.; and Karacki, L. (1977). "Unit Management: Implementing a Different Correctional Approach." *Federal Probation.* 41:43–49.

Legislative Research Council. (1986). *Report Relative to Prisons for Profit.* Commonwealth of Massachusetts.

Lofland, John. (1971). "Intensive Interviewing." In John Lofland, ed., *Analyzing Social Settings.* Belmont, CA: Wadsworth.

Lombardo, L. X. (1981). "Mental Health Work in Prisons and Jails: Inmate Adjustment and Indigenous Correctional Personnel." *Criminal Justice and Behavior* 12(1):17–28.

———. (1986). "Jail Officer Training: Goals, Techniques, and Evaluation Criteria." In D. B. Kalinich and J. Klofas, eds., *Sneaking Inmates Down the Alley: Problems and Prospects in Jail Management,* pp.181–92. Springfield, IL: Charles C. Thomas.

Lunden, W. A. (1959). "The Rotary Jail, or Human Squirrel Cage." *Journal of the Society of Architecture Historians* 18(4):149–57.

Majchrzak, A. (1984). *Methods for Policy Analysis.* Beverly Hills, CA: Sage.

Malcolm, B. (1975). "Today's Problem in Penology." *New York State Journal of Medicine* 75(10):1812–14.

Martinson, Robert. (1974). "What Works? Questions and Answers About Prison Reform." *Public Interest* 35:22–54.

Massachusetts Special Commission to Investigate Suicide in Municipal Detention Centers (1984). *Final Report.* Boston: Commonwealth of Massachusetts.

Mattick, Hans W. (1974). "The Contemporary Jails of the United States: An Unknown and Neglected Area of Justice." In D. Glasser, ed., *Handbook of Criminology.* Chicago: Rand McNally.

May, Edgar. (1978). "Weekend Jail: Doing Time on the Installment Plan." *Corrections Magazine* (March), pp.28–38.

Mays, G. Larry, and Bernat, Frances P. (1988). "Jail Reform Litigation: The Issue of Rights and Remedies." *American Journal of Criminal Justice* 12(2):254–73.

Mays, G. Larry, and Taggart, William A. (1985). "The Impact of Litigation on Changing New Mexico Prison Conditions." *Prison Journal* 65(Spring/Summer): 38–53.

Mays, G. Larry, and Thompson, Joel A. (1988). "Mayberry Revisited: The Characteristics and Operations of America's Small Jails." *Justice Quarterly* 5(3):421–40.

McClatchy News Service. (1988). "New Prisons a Plus, Community Leaders Say." *Orange County Register,* July 18, p.B12.

McCoy, Candace. (1982). "New Federalism, Old Remedies, and Corrections Policy-making." *Policy Studies Review* 2 (Nov.): 271–78.

McGee, Richard A. (1975). "Our Sick Jails." In Paul F. Cromwell, ed., *Jails and Justice.* Springfield, IL: Charles C. Thomas.

McGregor, D. (1960). *The Human Side of Enterprise.* New York: McGraw-Hill.

McGuire, W. J., and Sheehan, R. G. (1983). "Relationship Between Crime Rates and Incarceration Rates: Further Analysis." *Journal of Research in Crime and Delinquency* 20:73–85.

Meinhardt, K.; Tom, S.; Tse, P.; and Yu, C. Y. (1985). "Southeast Asian Refugees in the 'Silicon Valley': The Asian Health Assessment Project." *Amerasia* 12(2):43–65.

Meinhardt, K., and Vega, W. (1987). "A Method for Estimating Underutilization of Mental Health Services by Ethnic Groups." *Hospital and Community Psychiatry* 38(11):1186–90.

Merton, Robert K. (1957). *Social Theory and Social Structure.* New York: Free Press.

Michigan Mental Health Code. (1986). Lansing: Michigan Department of Mental Health.

Michigan Police Officer. (1980). *Prison Report* (Summer), p.74.

Miller, E. E. (1978). *Jail Management: Problems, Programs, and Perspectives.* Lexington, MA: Lexington Books.

Miller, R. (1986). "Prisoner Suicide: Caselaw and Standards." *Detention Reporter* 30 (April), 3–14.

Monahan, J., and Steadman, H. J. (1983). "Crime and Mental Disorder: An Epidemiological Approach." In M. Tonry and N. Morris, eds., *Crime and Justice: An Annual Review of Research*, Vol. 4, pp.145–190. Chicago: University of Chicago Press.

Morgan, C. (1981). "Developing Mental Health Services in Local Jails." *Criminal Justice and Behavior* 8:259–73.

——. (1982). "Service Delivery Models: A Summary of Examples." In C. S. Dunn and H. J. Steadman, eds., *Mental Health Services in Local Jails.* USDHHS Publication No.(ADM) 82-1181: 34–68.

Morris, J. (1968). "Psychiatry and the Dangerous Criminal." *University of Southern California Law Review* 41:514–542.

——. "'Criminality' and the Right to Treatment." *University of Chicago Law Journal* 36:748–801.

Morris, Joan. (1986). "A Big No: Sierra Voters Dump Jail Questions by 5-1 Ratio." *El Paso Times*, Jan. 22, p.1A.

Morris, Norval. (1974). *The Future of Imprisonment.* Chicago, IL: University of Chicago Press.

Morrissey, J. P.; Steadman, H. J.; and Kilburn, H. C. (1983). "Organizational Issues in the Delivery of Jail Mental Health Services." In J. Greenley, ed., *Research in Community and Mental Health,* Greenwich, CT: JAI Press.

Moyer, Frederic D. (1988). "The Crowding Problem—Architectural Response." *Corrections Today* 50:24–26.

Moynahan, J. M., and Stewart, E. K. (1978). "The Origin of the American Jail." *Federal Probation,* 42:41–50.

——. (1980). *The American Jail: Its Growth and Development.* Chicago: Nelson-Hall.

Mueller, C. W. (1983). "Environmental Stressors and Aggressive Behavior." In R. G. Green and E. I. Donnerstein, eds., *Aggression: Theoretical and Empirical Review,* Vol. 2. New York: Academic Press.

Mullen, J. (1985). *Corrections and the Private Sector.* National Institute of Justice Research in Brief. Washington, DC: U.S. Department of Justice.

Mullen, J.; Chabotar, K. J.; and Carrow, D. M. (1985). *The Privatization of Corrections. National Institute of Justice Issues and Practices.* Washington, DC: U.S. Department of Justice.

Murray, C. A., and Cox, C. A. (1975). *Beyond Probation.* Beverly Hills, CA: Sage.

Nagel, W. G. (1973). *The New Red Barn: A Critical Look at the Modern American Prison.* New York: Walker.

National Advisory Commission on Criminal Justice Standards and Goals. (1973). *Corrections.* Washington, DC: U.S. Department of Justice.

National Association of Counties. (1987). "House Panel Begins Debate on Changing Juvenile Justice Act." *Criminal Justice Newsletter* 18(19): 2–4.

National Association of Pretrial Services Agencies. (1978). *Performance Standards and Goals for Pretrial Release and Diversion.* Washington, DC: U.S. Department of Justice.

National Coalition of State Juvenile Justice Advisory Groups. (1986). *The First Report to the President, the Congress and the Administrator of the Juvenile Justice and Delinquency Prevention.* Unpublished document.

National Council on Crime and Delinquency. (1985a). *Children in California Jails*. Unpublished document.

———. (1985b). *Marin County Jail Alternatives Study, Final Report*. Prepared by James Austin, Barry Krisberg, and Shirley Melnicoe. San Francisco, CA.

———. (1988). *Draft, San Francisco Jail Needs Assessment*. San Francisco, CA.

National Council of Juvenile and Family Court Judges. (Undated). "Juvenile Justice In the 1980s." *Bench Sense*. Reno: University of Nevada.

National Institute of Corrections. (1983). *New Generation Jails*. Boulder, CO: Library Information Specialists, Inc.

———. (1986). *Small Jail Special Issues*. Washington, DC: U.S. Department of Justice.

National Institute of Justice. (1984). *Jailing Drunk Drivers: Impact on the Criminal Justice System*. Washington, DC: U.S. Department of Justice.

———. (1985). *Alleviating Jail Crowding: A Systems Perspective*. Washington, DC: U.S. Department of Justice.

———. (1986a). *Flórida Sets Examples with the Use of Concrete Modules*. Washington, DC: U.S. Department of Justice.

———. (1986b). *New Construction Methods for Correctional Facilities*. Washington, DC: U.S. Department of Justice.

———. (1987). *Maine Jails: Progress Through Partnership*. Washington, DC: U.S. Department of Justice.

———. (1988). *AIDS In Correctional Facilities: Issues and Options, Third Edition*, pp. 21–33. Washington, DC: U.S. Department of Justice.

NCCD Publications. (1983). "The Executive Suite." *Criminal Justice Newsletter*, Oct. 24.

Needham, John. (1987a). "Overseer Suggests Home Monitor System to Help Ease Jail Crowding." *Los Angeles Times*, Mar. 1, Part II, p.6.

———. (1987b). "Supervisors Flooded with Jail Opposition." *Los Angeles Times*, July 13, Part II, p.1.

Nelson, W. R. (1988). "The Origins of the Podular Direct Supervision Concept: A Personal Account." In K. Kerle, ed., *Proceedings of the 3rd Annual Symposium on Direct Supervision Jails*. Boulder, CO: National Institute of Corrections Jail Center.

Newman, Charles L. and Price, Barbara R. (1977). "Jails and Services for In-mates: A Perspective on Some Critical Issues." *Criminology* 14(Feb.), 501–12.

Newman, D. J. (1983). "A Critique of Prison Building." In L. F. Travis, M. Schwartz, and T. Clear, eds., *Corrections: An Issues Approach*, 2nd ed. Cincinnati, OH: Anderson Pub. Co.

Newman, G. (1978). "Prison Reform: Great Men and Great Failures; Review Article." *Journal of Criminal Law and Criminology* 69:133–38.

New York Codes, Rules and Regulations. Title 10, Part 63.

New York State Commission of Correction. (1988). *Acquired Immune Defi-*

ciency Syndrome: A Demographic Profile of New York State Inmate Mortalities—1981–1987. Albany, NY.

———. (1989a). *HIV Disease in New York's County Correctional Facilities.* Albany, NY.

———. (1989b). *1988 Data Compendium: AIDS in the Nation's Prisons.* Albany, NY.

New York State Department of Health. (1988a). *AIDS Surveillance Monthly Update.* Albany, NY.

———. (1988b). "Status of HIV Seroprevalence Studies." *Epidemiology Notes* 3:2.

———. (1989a). *Proceedings of the AIDS Advisory Council.* Unpublished manuscript.

———. (1989b). *AIDS Surveillance Monthly Update.* Albany, NY.

New York State Public Health Law. (1988). Section 2783.

Nielson, E. D. (1979). "Community Mental Health Services in the Community Jail." *Community Mental Health Journal* 15(1):27–32.

———. (1980). "Suicidal Behavior in Jail: A Preventive Approach." *Crisis Intervention* 2(1):19–27.

Novick, L. and Remmlinger, E. (1978). "A Study of 128 Deaths in New York City Correctional Facilities (1971–1976): Implications for Prisoner Health Care." *Medical Care* 16(2):749–56.

Office of the President of the United States. (1982). *President's Task Force on Victims of Crime: Final Report.* Washington, DC.

Orr, R. H. (1978). "The Imprisonment of Mentally Disordered Offenders." *British Journal of Psychiatry* 133:194–99.

Overall, J. E., and Gorham, D. R. (1962). "The Brief Psychiatric Rating Scale." *Psychological Reports* 10:799–812.

"Overcrowding Plagues Tarrant County Jails" (1987). *El Paso Times,* Sept. 7, p.4B.

Packer, H. (1968). *The Limits of The Criminal Sanction.* Palo Alto, CA: Stanford University Press.

Palmer, John W. (1985). *Constitutional Rights of Prisoners,* 3rd ed. Cincinnati, OH: Anderson Pub. Co.

———. (1989). "Inmate Litigation Trends and Constitutional Issues." In D. J. Champion, ed., *The U.S. Sentencing Guidelines: Implications for Criminal Justice.* New York: Praeger.

Peele, Elizabeth. (1985). *Hazardous Waste Management Outlook: Are There Ways Out of the 'Not-in-My-Backyard' Impasse?* Paper presented at the annual meeting of the New York State Sociological Association, Rochester, NY.

Perlman, Jeffrey A. (1986). "Sheriff Gets OK to Release Inmates Early to Reduce Jail Overcrowding." *Los Angeles Times,* Mar. 8, Part II, pp.1,14.

Perlstein, J. J., and Henry, D. A. (1986a). *Dealing Effectively with Overcrowded Jails—A Manual for Judges.* Rockville, MD: National Institute of Justice.

———. (1986b). *The Implications of Effective Case Processing for Crowded Jails—A Manual for Prosecutors.* Rockville, MD: National Institute of Justice.

Petersilia, Joan. (1987). *Expanding Options for Criminal Sentencing.* Santa Monica, CA: Rand.

Petrich, J. (1976). "Psychiatric Treatment in Jail: An Experiment in Health-Care Delivery." *Hospital and Community Psychiatry* 27:413–15.

Pfeiffer, M. G. (1984). "A Progressive Approach to Inmate Mental Health Care." *Corrections Today* (Aug.), 66,68.

Pinkele, Carl F. (1986). "Jails: An Invisible Political Issue." In David B. Kalinich and John Klofas, eds., *Sneaking Inmates Down the Alley.* Springfield, IL: Charles C. Thomas.

Pivan, Frances Fox, and Cloward, R. A. (1971). *Regulating the Poor: The Functions of Public Welfare.* New York: Vintage Books.

Place, M., and Sands, D. A. (1975). "Incarcerating the Innocent: Pretrial Detention in our Nation's Jails." In Paul F. Cromwell, ed., *Jails and Justice.* Springfield, IL: Charles C. Thomas.

Pogrebin, Mark. (1982a). *Managing Scarce Resources for Jails.* Washington, DC: University Press of America.

———. (1982b). "Scarce Resources and Jail Management." *International Journal of Offender Therapy and Comparative Criminology* 26(3):263–73.

Pogrebin, Mark, and Neugarten, Dail A. (1982). "Jails and Resources Scarcity." *Policy Perspectives* 2(1):443–49.

Pogrebin, Mark, and Poole, Eric D. (1988). "The Work Orientations of Jail Personnel: A Comparison of Deputy Sheriffs and Career Line Officers." *Policy Studies Review* 7(3):606–14.

Pogrebin, Mark, and Regoli, Robert M. (1985). "Mentally Disordered Persons in Jail." *Journal of Community Psychology* 13 (Oct.), 409–12.

Pontell, Henry N. (1984). *A Capacity to Punish: The Ecology of Crime and Punishment.* Bloomington: Indiana University Press.

Popper, Frank J. (1981). "Siting LULUs." *Planning* 47(4):12–15.

———. (1985). "The Environmentalist and the LULU." *Environment* 27(2):6–11,37–40.

President's Commission on Law Enforcement and Administration of Justice. (1967). *Task Force Report: Corrections.* Washington, DC: U.S. Government Printing Office.

President's Commission on Privatization. (1988). *Privatization: Toward More Effective Government.* Washington, DC: U.S. Government Printing Office.

Price, R. H., and Smith, S. S. (1985). "Two Decades of Reform in Mental Health System." In E. Seidman, ed., *Handbook of Social Intervention,* pp.408–37. Beverly Hills, CA: Sage.

Rakis, J. (1984). "Suicide Prevention Measures in Urban Detention Facilities Throughout the United States." *Journal of Prison and Jail Health* 4(2):91–95.

Research and Policy Committee. (1982). *Public-private Partnership, An Op-*

portunity for Urban Communities. New York: Committee for Economic Development.

Reyes, David. (1985). "Fear, Safety: Mixed Bag Near Main Jail." *Los Angeles Times,* Mar. 22, Part I, pp.1,16.

Reynolds, W. J., and Tonry, M. H. (1981). "Professional Mediation Services for Prisoner Complaints." *American Bar Association Journal* 67 (Mar.), 294–97.

Ricci, Kenneth. (1986). "What Can County Commissioners Do About Their Jails?" *Prison Journal* 61:14–18.

Riley, Pamela J., and Rose, Vicki M. (1980). "Public Opinion vs. Elite Opinion on Correctional Reform." *Journal of Criminal Justice* 8:345–56.

Ringel, N. B., and Segal, C. A. (1986). "A Mental Health Center's Influence in a County Jail." *Journal of Community Psychology* 14:171–82.

Robbins, Ira R. (1987). *Prisoners and the Law.* New York: Clark Boardman Co.

———. (1988). *The Legal Dimensions of Private Incarceration.* Washington, DC: American Bar Association.

Robins, L. N.; Helzer, J. E.; and Marcus, S. (1986). *The Screening DIS.* St. Louis, MO: Washington University School of Medicine.

Rogers, D. E. (1984). "Providing Medical Care to the Elderly and Poor: A Serious Problem for the Downsizing 1980's." In D. Yaggy, ed., *Health Care for the Poor and Elderly: Meeting the Challenges,* pp.6–10. Durham, NC: Duke University Press.

Ross, H. Laurence. (1967). "Law, Science and Accidents: The British Road Safety Act of 1967." *Journal of Legal Studies* 2:1–78.

Roth, Jeffrey A., and Wice, Paul B. (1978). *Pretrial Release and Misconduct in the District of Columbia.* Institute for Law and Social Research. PROMISE Report Publication No.16.

Rothman, D. (1980). *Conscience and Convenience.* Boston, MA: Little, Brown.

Rottman, D. B., and Kimberly, J. R. (1975). "The Social Context of Jails." *Sociology and Social Research* 59:344–61.

Rowan, Joseph R., and Haynes, Lindsay M. (1988). *Training Curriculum on Suicide Detection and Prevention in Jails and Lockups.* Alexandria, VA: National Center on Institutions and Alternatives.

Runck, B. (1983). "Study of 43 Jails Shows Mental Health Services and Inmate Safety are Compatible." *The Journal of Hospital and Community Psychiatry* 34(11):1007–10.

Saxton, Samuel F. (1988). "Crowding: Small Jails Cope with the Crisis." *Corrections Today* 50:16–18.

Schafer, Nancy E. (1986). "Jails and Judicial Review: Special Problems for Local Facilities." In David B. Kalinich and John Klofas, eds., *Sneaking Inmates Down the Alley.* Springfield, IL: Charles C. Thomas.

Schlossman, Steven L. (1977). *Love and the American Delinquent: The Theory and Practice of "Progressive" Juvenile Justice, 1825–1920.* Chicago, IL: The University of Chicago Press.

Schmidt, A. (1989). "Electronic Monitoring of Offenders Increases." *National Institute of Justice Reports* 212:2–5.

Schmidt, W. W. (1985). "Section 1983 and the Changing Face of Police Management." In W. A. Geller, ed., *Police Leadership in America*. New York: Praeger.

Schoen, Kenneth F. (1987). Preface. In J. Doble, *Crime and Punishment: The Public's View*. New York: Edna McConnell Clark Foundation.

Schrag, C. (1961). "Some Foundations for a Theory of Correction." In D. R. Cressey, ed., *The Prison: Studies in Institutional Organization and Change*. New York: Holt, Rinehart and Winston.

Schuckit, M.; Herrman, G.; and Schuckit, J. (1977). "The Importance of Psychiatric Illness in Newly Arrested Prisoners." *Journal of Nervous and Mental Disease* 165(2):118–25.

Schumacher, Michael. (1987). *Supervised Electronic Confinement Pilot Program. Final Report*. Santa Ana, CA: Orange County Probation Department.

Schwab, J.; Bell, R.; and Warheit, G. (1979). *Social Order and Mental Health*. New York: Bruner-Mazel.

Schwartz, Ira M. (1988). *(In)Justice for Juveniles: Rethinking the Best Interest of the Child*. Lexington, MA: Lexington Books.

Schwartz, Ira M.; Harris, Linda; and Levi, Laurie. (1988). "The Jailing of Juveniles In Minnesota: A Case Study." *Crime and Delinquency* 34(2):133–49.

Schwartz, Jeffrey A. (1989). "Promoting a Good Public Image: Effective Leadership, Sound Practices Make the Difference." *Corrections Today*, 51(1):38–42.

Scull, Andrew. (1981). "Deinstitutionalization and the Rights of Deviants." *Journal of Social Issues* 37:6–20.

———. (1984). *Decarceration: Community Treatment and the Deviant: A Radical Approach*. Englewood Cliffs, NJ: Prentice-Hall.

Sechrest, L.; White, S. D.; and Brown, E. D. (1979). *The Rehabilitation of Criminal Offenders: Problems and Prospects*. Washington, DC: National Academy Press.

Selznick, P. (1968). Foreword. In E. Studt, S. L. Messinger, and T. P. Wilson, *C-Unit: Search for Community in Prison*, pp.vii–ix. New York: Russell Sage.

Sexton, C. E.; Farrow, F. C.; and Auerbach, B. J. (1985). "The Private Sector and Prison Industries." *National Institute of Justice Research in Brief*. Washington, DC.

Shannon, Lyle. (1980). "Assessing the Relationship of Adult Criminal Careers to Juvenile Careers." In C. Abt, ed., *Problems in American Social Policy*, pp.232–46. Cambridge, Mass.: Abt Books.

———. (1985). *A More Precise Evaluation of the Effects of Sanctions*. Iowa City: Iowa Urban Community Research Center, University of Iowa.

Shover, N., and Einstadter, W. J. (1988). *Analyzing American Corrections*. Belmont, CA: Wadsworth.

Shrout, P. E., and Fleiss, J. L. (1979). "Intraclass Correlations: Uses in Assessing Rater Reliability." *Psychological Bulletin* 86:420–28.

Sigurdson, H. (1985). *The Manhattan House of Detention: A Study of Podular Direct Supervision*. Washington, DC: National Institute of Corrections.

———. (1987a). *Pima County Detention Center: A Study of Podular Direct Supervision*. Washington, DC: National Institute of Corrections.

———. (1987b). *Larimer County Detention Center: A Study of Podular Direct Supervision*. Washington, DC: National Institute of Corrections.

Sikka, K. D. (1975). "Social Work in Corrections: An Overview." *Social Defense* (April), 5–8.

Singer, R. G. (1972). "Privacy, Autonomy and Dignity in Prisons: A Preliminary Inquiry Concerning Constitutional Aspects of the Degradation Process in Our Prisons." *Buffalo Law Review* 21(3):669–716.

———. (1982). "Providing Mental Health Services to Jail Inmates: Legal Perspectives." In C. S. Dunn and J. J. Steadman, eds., *Mental Health in Local Jails*. USDHHS Publication No.(ADM) 82-1181:69–99.

Skolnick, J. and Bailey, D. (1986). *The New Blue Line: Police Innovation in Six Cities*. New York: Free Press.

Skovran, Sandra E.; Scott, Joseph E.; and Cullen, Francis T. (1988). "Prison Crowding: Public Attitudes Toward Strategies of Population Control." *Journal of Research in Crime and Delinquency* 25:150–69.

Slater, Philip. (1976). *The Pursuit of Loneliness: American Culture at the Breaking Point*. Boston, MA: Beacon Press.

Smialek, J., and Spitz, W. (1978). "Death Behind Bars." *Journal of American Medical Association* 240(23):2563–64.

Smith, Douglas A., and Gartin, Patrick R. (1989). "Specifying Specific Deterrence: The Influence of Arrest on Future Criminal Activity." *American Sociological Review* 54:94–105.

Smykla, John O. (1981). *Community-based Corrections: Principles and Practices*. New York: Macmillan.

Soler, Mark. (1988). "Litigation on Behalf of Children in Adult Jails." *Crime and Delinquency* 34(2):190–208.

Special Focus on Closed Circuit Television: Part 2 Parameters for Use (1985). *Detention Reporter*, No.24, Kents Hill, ME: CRS Inc.

Spitzer, R. L.; Endicott, J.; Fleiss, J. L.; and Cohen, J. (1970). "The Psychiatric Status Schedule: A Technique for Evaluating Psychopathology and Impairment of Role Functioning." *Archives of General Psychiatry* 23:41–55.

Spitzer, S. (1975). "Toward a Marxian Theory of Deviance." *Social Problems* 22:638–51.

———. (1979). "The Rationalization of Crime Control in Capitalist Society." *Contemporary Crisis* 3:187–206.

SPSS, Inc. (1986). *SPSSX User's Guide*. Chicago, IL.

"State Prison Overcrowding Filters Down" (1987). *El Paso Times*, Sept. 13, p.10B.

Steadman, H. J.; Cocozza, J. J.; and Melick, M. E. (1978). "Explaining the Increased Arrest Rate Among Mental Patients: The Changing Clientele of State Hospitals." *American Journal of Psychiatry* 135:816–20.

Steadman, H. J.; Monahan, J.; Duffee, B.; Hartstone, E; and Robbins, P. C. (1984). "The Impact of State Mental Hospital Deinstitutionalization on United States Prison Populations, 1968–1978." *Journal of Criminal Law and Criminology* 73(2):474–91.

Steadman, H. J.; Morrissey, J. P.; and Robbins, P. C. (1985). "Reevaluating the Custody-therapy Conflict Paradigm in Correctional Mental Health Settings." *Criminology* 23:165–179.

Steadman, H. J., and Ribner, S. A. (1980). "Changing Perceptions of the Mental Health Needs of Inmates in Local Jails." *American Journal of Psychiatry* 137:1602–5.

Steelman, D. (1984). *New York City Jail Crisis: Causes, Costs and Solutions.* New York: The Correctional Association of New York.

Steers, R. (1977). *Organizational Effectiveness: An Organizational View.* Santa Monica, CA: Goodyear.

Stelzer, M. (1983). "Health Care Services in County Jails." *Corrections Today* (Dec.), 80–81,85.

Stone, A. (1975). *Mental Health and Law: A System in Transition.* Washington, DC: U.S. Government Printing Office.

Sullivan, Ronald. (1987). "Bill of $1 Billion for Treating AIDS Seen in New York." *New York Times*, May 22.

Susskind, Lawrence, and Cruikshank, Jeffrey (1987). *Breaking the Impasse: Consensual Approaches to Resolving Public Disputes.* New York: Basic Books.

Sviridoff, M., and Thompson, J. (1983). "Links Between Employment and Crime: A Qualitative Study of Rikers Island Releases." *Crime and Delinquency* 29(2):195–212.

Swank, G., and Winer, D. (1976). "Occurrence of Psychiatric Disorder in a County Jail Population." *American Journal of Psychiatry* 133:1331–33.

Sweeney, Paul. (1982). "Texas: Have State Standards Been Properly Enforced?" *Corrections Magazine* (Apr.), 30–33.

Sykes, G.; Vito, G.; and McElrath, B. (1987). "Jail Populations and Crime Rates: An Exploratory Analysis of Incapacitation. *Journal of Police Science and Administration* 15:72–77.

Sykes, G. M. (1958). *The Society of Captives.* Princeton, NJ: Princeton University Press.

Szasz, Thomas. (1963). *Law, Liberty, and Psychiatry.* New York: Macmillan.

Taft, Philip B., Jr. (1979). "Backed Up in Jail." *Corrections Magazine* (June), 26–33.

———. (1982). "New York: A Sheriff Promotes Alternatives." *Corrections Magazine* (Apr.), 33–34.

Takagi, P. (1975). "The Walnut Street Jail: A Penal Reform to Centralize the Powers of the State." *Federal Probation* 39 (Dec.), 18–26.

Teplin, L. A. (1983). "The Criminalization of the Mentally Ill: Speculations in Search of Data." *Psychological Bulletin* 9:54–67.

"Texas County Sheriffs Are Told Prisons Closed to New Inmates." (1987). *Las Cruces (NM) Sun-News,* Feb. 6, p.2A.

"Texas Jails Packed with Prisoners as Prisons Close Doors." (1987). *Las Cruces (NM) Sun-News,* Feb. 6, p.2A.

Thomas, Jim; Aylward, Anmarie; Casey, Mary Louise; Moton, David; Oldham, Michelle; and Wheetley, George. (1985). "Rethinking Prisoner Litigation: Some Preliminary Distinctions Between Habeas Corpus and Civil Rights." *Prison Journal* 65 (Spring/Summer), 83–106.

Thomas, Jim; Keller, Devin; and Harris, Kathy. (1986). "Issues and Misconceptions in Prison Litigation: A Critical View." *Criminology* 24 (Nov.), 775–97.

Thomas, Jim. (1988). *Prison Litigation: The Paradox of the Jailhouse Lawyer.* Totowa, NJ: Rowman.

Thomas, Wayne. (1976). *Bail Reform in America.* Berkeley: University of California Press.

Thomas, W. I., and Thomas, D. S. (1928). *The Child in America.* New York: Knopf.

Thompson, Joel A. (1989). "Trouble in Mayberry: The Plight of North Carolina's Jails." *American Jails* 2(4):26, 28, 30–31.

———. (1986). "The American Jail: Problems, Politics, Prospects." *American Journal of Criminal Justice* 10 (Spring), 205–21.

Thompson, Joel A. and Mays, G. Larry. (1988a). "The Impact of State Standards and Enforcement Procedures on Local Jail Performance." *Policy Studies Review* 8(1):55–71.

———. (1988b). "State-Local Relations and the American Jail Crisis: An Assessment of State Jail Mandates." *Policy Studies Review* 7(3):567–80.

Toborg, Mary A. (1978). *Pretrial Release: An Evaluation of Defendant Outcomes and Program Impact,* Vol. I. Washington, DC: Lazar Institute.

Toby, Jackson. (1970). "Is Punishment Necessary?" In Norman Johnson, Leonard Savitz, and Marvin Wolfgang, eds., *The Sociology of Punishment and Corrections,* 2nd ed., pp. 362–69. New York: Wiley.

Toch, H. (1975). *Men in Crisis: Human Breakdown in Prison.* Chicago, IL: Aldine.

———. (1977). *Living in Prison: The Ecology of Survival.* New York: Free Press.

———. (1982). "The Role of the Expert on Prison Conditions: The Battle of Footnotes in *Rhodes v. Chapman.*" *Criminal Law Bulletin* 18:38–43.

Toch, H., and Grant, J. D. (1982). *Reforming Human Services Through Participation.* Beverly Hills, CA: Sage.

Tracey, F. (1972). "Suicide and Suicide Prevention in New York City Prisons." *Probation and Parole* 4:20–29.

Trojanowicz, Robert C. (1978). "The Logical Community Corrections Facility Is the Jail." *Corrections Magazine* (Dec.), i,73.

U.S. Code Annotated. (1988). St. Paul, MN: West.

U.S. Congress, Senate Committee on the Judiciary, Subcommittee to Investigate Juvenile Delinquency. (1973). *The Juvenile Justice and De-*

linquency Prevention Act—5.3148 and 5.831. 92nd Congress, 2nd session; 93rd Congress, 1st session.

U.S. Department of Justice. (1980). *Indexed Legislative History of the "Juvenile Justice Amendments of 1977."* Washington, DC: U.S. Government Printing Office.

———. (1981). *Indexed Legislative History of the "Juvenile Justice Amendments of 1980."* Washington, DC: U.S. Government Printing Office.

———. (1982). *Jail Removal Cost Study:* Vol. 2. Washington, DC: U.S. Government Printing Office.

———. (1982). "High Suicide Rate Found Among Inmates." *Justice Assistance News* 3(1):5.

———. (1985). *The Nature of New Small Jails: Report and Analysis.* National Institute of Corrections. Washington, DC: U.S. Government Printing Office.

———. (1988). *Report to the Nation on Crime and Justice,* 2nd ed. Washington, DC: U.S. Government Printing Office.

U.S. General Accounting Office. (1987). *Criminal Bail: How Bail Reform is Working in Selected District Courts.* Subcommittee on Courts, Civil Liberties, and the Administration of Justice, Committee on the Judiciary, U.S. House of Representatives.

U.S. Marshal's Report. (1986). *First Year Implementation of the Comprehensive Crime Control Act of 1984.* Washington, DC.

Vega, W.; Warheit, G.; Buhl-Auth, J.; and Meinhardt, K. (1984). "The Prevalence of Depressive Symptoms Among Mexican-Americans and Anglos." *American Journal of Epidemiology* 120(4):492–607.

Waldie, Larry. (1988). "The Los Angeles County Jail System." *American Jails* 2:64–68.

Walker, Samuel. (1985). *Sense and Nonsense About Crime.* Monterey, CA: Brooks/Cole.

Warren, C. (1977). *The Social Constructs of Dangerousness.* Los Angeles: University of Southern California Press.

Warren, R. L. (1977). *Social Change and Human Purpose: Toward Understanding and Action.* Chicago, IL: Rand McNally.

———. (1978). *Community in America.* Chicago, IL: Rand McNally.

Weber, Adna (1929). *Theory of the Location of Industries.* Chicago, IL: University of Chicago Press.

Weber, M. (1947). *The Theory of Social and Economic Organization.* A. M. Henderson and T. Parsons, trans. Glencoe, IL: Free Press.

Weikel, Daniel. (1988). "ACLU Alleges Inmate Abuse at OC Jail." *Orange County Register,* Aug. 13, pp.A1,23.

Weimer, David L., and Reixach, Karen (1982). "A Note on America's 'Cloacal' Jails." *Policy Studies Review* 2 (Nov.), 239–45.

Weinreb, Lloyd L. (1977). *Denial of Justice.* New York: Free Press.

Weintraub, B. (1963). "Criminal Responsibility: Psychiatry Alone Cannot Determine It." *American Bar Association Journal* 49:1075.

Wener, R., and Olsen, R. (1978). *User Based Assessment of the Federal Met-*

ropolitan Correctional Centers: Final Report. Washington, DC: United States Bureau of Prisons.

Wener, R.; Frazier, W.; and Farbstein, J. (1985). "Three Generations of Evaluation and Design of Correctional Facilities." *Environment and Behavior* 17:71–95.

———. (1987). "Building Better Jails." *Psychology Today* (June), 40–49.

Whitmer, G. E. (1980). "From Hospitals to Jails: The Fate of California's Deinstitutionalized Mentally Ill." *American Journal of Orthopsychiatry* 50(1):65–75.

Wiehn, P. J. (1982). "Mentally Ill Offenders: Prison's First Casualties." In P. J. Johnson and H. Toch, eds., *The Pains of Imprisonment*, pp.221–37. Beverly Hills, CA: Sage.

Winfree, L. T. (1987). "Toward Understanding State-level Jail Mortality: Correlates of Death by Suicide and by Natural Causes, 1977 and 1982." *Justice Quarterly* 4(1):51–71.

———. (1988). "Rethinking American Jail Death Rates: A Comparison of National Mortality and Jail Mortality, 1978, 1983." *Policy Studies Review* 7(3):641–59.

Wooten, J. (1960). "Diminished Responsibility: A Layman's View." *Law Quarterly Review* 76:224.

Yarbrough, Tinsely E. (1984). "The Alabama Prison Litigation." *Justice System Journal* 9(3):276–90.

———. (1985). "The Political World of Judges as Managers." *Public Administration Review* 45:660–66.

Yarchoan, Robert et al. (1988). "AIDS Therapies." *Scientific American* 259:110–19.

Zimring, Franklin E., and Hawkins, Gordon J. (1968). "Deterrence and Marginal Groups." *Journal of Research in Crime and Delinquency* 5:100–14.

Zoroya, Gregg. (1988). "Orange Sues to Stop County from Expanding Branch Jail." *Orange County Register*, Jan. 1, p.B1.

Zoroya, Gregg, and Serrano, Barbara A. (1988). "Judge Blocks Plan for County Jail in Anaheim." *Orange County Register*, June 7, pp.B1,12.

Zupan, L. L. (1987). *The New Generation Correctional Philosophy: An Implementation Analysis and Impact Evaluation*. Unpublished doctoral dissertation, Washington State University, Pullman, WA.

Zupan, L. L.; Menke, B. A.; and Lovrich, N. (1986). "Podular/Direct Supervision Detention Facilities: Challenges for Human Resource Development." *Proceedings of the First Annual Symposium on Direct Supervision Jails*. Boulder, CO: National Institute of Corrections.

Zupan, L. L., and Menke, B. (1988). "Implementing Organizational Change: From Traditional to New Generation Jail Operations." *Policy Studies Review* 7:615–25.

Zupan, L. L., and Stohr-Gillmore, M. (1988). "Doing Time in the New Generation Jail: Inmate Perceptions of Gains and Losses." *Policy Studies Review* 7:626–40.

Case Index

Name Index

Subject Index